danse Macabre

François Villon
*Poetry & Murder in
Medieval France*

AUBREY BURL

SUTTON PUBLISHING

First published in the United Kingdom in 2000 by
Sutton Publishing Limited · Phoenix Mill
Thrupp · Stroud · Gloucestershire · GL5 2BU

British Library Cataloguing in Publication Data
A catalogue record for this book is available from the British Library.

ISBN 0-7509-2177-3

'Je congnois tout fors que moy mesmes'
I know everything except myself

François Villon, *Poésies Diverses*, 6

Typeset in 10.5/13.5pt Sabon.
Typesetting and origination by
Sutton Publishing Limited.
Printed in Great Britain by
MPG Books, Bodmin, Cornwall.

Contents

Acknowledgements

To Sebastian d'Orsay of Leicester's New Walk for finding me my first copy of Wyndham Lewis's biography of François Villon; to M. Spenser Tachon OBE for his kindness in allowing me to explore the dungeons and oubliette of his château at Meung-sur-Loire; to Mlle S. Gautier for informing me of Meung's other poets, Jean de Meung and Gaston Couté; to Margaret Jones for her linguistic ability that lightened my problems; to Joyce Kirk for her ability to locate the most elusive of volumes; to the librarians of the Society of Antiquaries of London and of the University of Birmingham for providing me with much material; to Christopher Feeney, my editor at Sutton Publishing, and Anne Bennett for their patience and encouragement; and, above all, to Judith, my wife. All of them are part of this book.

A Note on the Poetry

By convention the poems of François Villon, little more than 3300 lines, are divided into four groups: The *Lais* or The Legacies, a light-hearted collection of comical bequests. Six years later these were followed by another group of legacies, not so farcical, the *Testament* or Great Testament. Among them are many of Villon's loveliest ballades. Other poems are placed in the *Poésies Diverses* or miscellaneous poems. Finally there are verses in an almost incomprehensible language, the *Jargon*, written in the slang of criminals known as the Coquillards.

References to these works are quoted as L, 1–40 for the forty stanzas of the *Lais*, followed by the lines, 1–320, wherever relevant, as for example, L, 40, 313, for the first line of the last stanza. The *Testament* is cited as T, 1–186 for its 2023 lines whose 186 stanzas are frequently interrupted by the interpolation of ballades, rondeaux and songs. These were unnumbered. A reference such as T, 89+ means that the ballade of his mother at prayer, 'Dame du Ciel . . .', occurs immediately after stanza 89. The *Poésies Diverses* are quoted as PD, 1–16 and the *Jargon* as J, 1–11, numbers 8 to 11 being doubtful. Long translations are cited in square brackets, e.g. [T, 86+].

There have been increasingly accurate editions. Longnon's, revised by Foulet, was for long pre-eminent but has been improved by the texts of Rychner and Henry, the *Testament*, 1974, the *Lais* and *Poésies Diverses*, 1977, and the *Index*, 1985. Because in Rychner–Henry the *Poésies Diverses* are listed in a different order from the Longnon canon the poems are quoted as PD, 1 (L, 8). The complete list is: PD, 1 (L, 8); PD, 2 (L, 7); PD, 3 (L, –); PD, 4 (L, 10); PD, 5 (L, 2); PD, 6 (L, 3); PD, 7 (L,

4); PD, 8 (L, 5); PD, 9 (L, 1); PD, 10 (L, 12); PD, 11 (L, 14); PD, 12 (L, 9); PD, 13 (L, 11); PD, 14 (L, 13); PD, 15 (L, 16); PD, 16 (L, 15); Jenin l'Avenu, PD – (L, 6).

For an English reader the most accessible edition of the entire corpus, based on Rychner–Henry but with literal line-by-line translations, is that by Sargent-Baur, 1994. Published by the University of Toronto it is available in Britain from the Marston Book Services Ltd, Unit 160, Milton Park, Abingdon, Oxfordshire OX14 4SD. The numerical sequence of poems and the quotations in French from them are taken from that text. Writers of long English translations are named at the end of the verses. Unless stated to the contrary short translations are by the writer.

Before 1940 anyone attempting to turn Villon into English was handicapped by social inhibitions that denied faithful rendering of some of the coarser verse. Since that date there have been several translations, usually with the original French placed opposite the English. In verse there have been publications by McCaskie, 1946; Bonner, 1960; Dale, 1973, and Kinnell, 1965, revised in 1977 and 1982. In 1952 Cameron produced an English text with no accompanying French. In it the *Testament*'s stanzas are misnumbered after T, 46, T, 57 becoming T, 47.

Endeavours to keep to Villon's rhyme-schemes and verse constructions sometimes resulted in distortions and misinterpretations in all these works. There have been attempts to keep closer to the original meanings by offering prose paraphrases. As well as Sargent-Baur in 1994 Chaney published an English text in 1940. A well-annotated translation was offered by Saklatvala in 1968. Fox, an authority on Villon's poetry, published a slim, very accurate rendition in 1984. His masterly explanation of the poetry's structure and imagery appeared in 1962.

Preface

This is the story of a great poet. The same poet cheated shop-keepers, stole money from the university, mixed with prosti-tutes, broke into churches. He also killed a priest, was thrashed in the streets by the public executioner, was jailed in Orléans, again in the Loire then twice more in Paris, was tortured, and at least once, perhaps three times, was condemned to be hanged.

It was many years ago in an antiquarian bookshop that I bought my first biography of Villon. It was Wyndham Lewis's *François Villon. A Documented Survey* of 1928, containing a handwritten letter from the author to an admirer. I had already heard of the poet through seeing the enjoyable although typically unfaithful to facts Hollywood film, *If I were King* but Lewis's evocative book opened the poetry to me, the whimsical *Legacies*, the darker tone of the *Testament*, the beauty of the ballades with their lingering refrains, the mockingly defiant verses in thieves' jargon. It was the contrasts that were astonishing. I was reading a man who could write about a girl called Rose, T, 93, 938–41:

Pourveu, s'il rencontre en son erre	. . . on one condition. Should he meet
Ma damoiselle au nez tortu	My bent-nosed baggage, piece of smut,
Il luy dira, sans plus enquerre,	He rudely bellows down the street,
'Orde paillarde, dont viens tu?'	'Where hast thou come from, filthy slut?'

yet also the man who could lament the passing of beautiful women, T, 41+, 336,

Mais ou sont les neiges d'anten?	But where are the snows of years gone by?

The incongruities fascinate. Had Villon been an uncomplicated master-poet like his law-abiding near-contemporary, Geoffrey

Chaucer, then it would be for his poetry but not his career that he would be known. Had he been just one more criminal of the Middle Ages then he would be as forgotten as his felonious friend, Colin de Cayeux. But Villon was both, a poetical genius of beauty and wit, and a thief whose chosen companions were swindlers, housebreakers, coiners and footpads. His family background, his education, his poverty, his sensitivity made him and his poetry. So did the times that he lived in.

Villon was born in an age of turbulence, a time of vast contrasts in wealth and poverty, in piety and villainy, in barbarity and artistry. It was a period of change during which he rejected the sterility of courtly verse in favour of sharply realistic poetry. His was a century of disruption with the Hundred Years War coming to an end, leaving France in lawless poverty. These were also the decades when the medieval western world was widening as the Portuguese began their exploration of the African coastline.

Villon was himself a contrast. 'Je ris en pleurs et attens sans espoir', PD, 2 (L, 7), 'I laugh through tears and wait without a hope', 'Je cognois tout, for que moy mesmes', PD, 6 (L, 3), 'I know everything except myself'. Many of his verses are remarkable descriptions of the decent delights and indecent depravities of the Paris that he knew so well: bishops and brothels; priests and prisons; clerics and criminals; Te Deums and taverns; ladies of the nobility and ladies of the street. This empathy with everyday life and his awareness of its brevity enabled him to write poetry so ingeniously crafted that it seems to speak without art, person to person, to his readers. There was little artless about Villon. He was a master of technique. It is the contradiction between this artistic brilliance and his weak acceptance of temptation and readiness to break the law that makes his life so complex and intriguing.

It is said, though improbable, that the recently crowned king, Louis XI, 'could not afford to hang this fellow, because although his kingdom held a hundred thousand ruffians of equal rascality it held only one poet, François Villon, so excelling in gentilz dictz & ingenieux sçavoir'. His poems were so lovely that several were later set to music by Cartan; by van Dieren; and by Claude Debussy who composed and orchestrated *Trois Ballades de François Villon* in 1910: 'Dame du Ciel . . .', T, 87+; 'Faulse Beauté . . .', T, 89+; and 'Femmes de Paris . . .', T, 144+. The bohemian painter, Modigliani, read the poems in the original.

Villon's life was dramatically picaresque. Inevitably Hollywood romanticised it. The first film, *If I were King*, of 1920 was followed in 1927 by *Beloved Rogue* with John Barrymore as Villon and Conrad Veidt as Louis XI. Three years later came an operetta in colour, *Vagabond King*, with Jeanette MacDonald. The print is lost. The second *If I were King* of 1938 featured Ronald Colman and Basil Rathbone. After eighteen years it was succeeded by a second *Vagabond King*, a musical with Kathryn Grayson. It had little to do with the real Villon.

It is strange that Villon, a legend almost in his own lifetime, was hardly known in England until the late nineteenth century. Before 1877 even his true name was unknown. But in that year there were anglicised versions of three poems by Dante Gabriel Rossetti and ten by Swinburne. The entire canon had already been daringly translated by John Payne in 1874 and published in 1878 only to be expurgated later and published as *The Poems of Master François Villon* in 1881. The Villon Society was founded 'on the occasion of the first translation of the complete works of Villon into English by John Payne, a translation which had repercussions even in France, where Baudelaire, who had a fair knowledge of English, took pleasure in reading it aloud'.

Of English biographies there is Wyndham Lewis, 1928, Cecily Mackworth's *François Villon. A Study*, 1947, and Robert Anthony Laws' *Dance of the Hanging Men*, 1993, the latter concentrating on the life at the expense of the poetry. In 1946 Edward Chaney wrote a good account of Parisian life, *François Villon in his Environment*, preceded the previous year by his *La Danse Macabré des Charniers des Saints Innocents à Paris*.

Between 1930 and 1984 although there were several English translations of his poetry they contained only brief biographies. In

1882 Robert Louis Stevenson had written a scurrilous essay, 'François Villon', in *Familiar Studies of Men and Books*. 'I am tempted to regret that I ever wrote on this subject, not merely because the paper strikes me as too picturesque by half, but because I regarded Villon as a bad fellow . . . I saw nothing but artistic evil.'

In complete contrast Joris Karl Huysmans, sensualist and novelist, in his *Drageoir aux Épices* marvelled at the delicacy, the imagination, the loveliness of the ballades in Villon's *Grand Testament*. 'What a magical stream of jewels. What a strange clustering of fires. What astonishing rending of primitive sunset-tinted fabrics. What fantastic striping of colours, vivid and gloomy.' Villon's life was a bonfire, burning, its flames swaying brightly like a graceful Arabian houri but always against the blackness of the hearth. He was never still, never constant. A thief, a man imprisoned, tortured, threatened with the gallows, this man who knew everything but himself, was yet another contradiction. He was also a genius.

Today there is a considerable advantage in writing about Villon. Censorship has relaxed. Earlier, any faithful translation was unprintable. When Swinburne made his renditions some of Villon's language was considered too crude to be turned into English. The elegiac poem, *La Vieille Regrettant le Temps de sa Jeunesse*, T, 47–56, the regret for her lost youth by the ageing but once beautiful mistress of a nobleman, contained a partly unacceptable stanza T, 53 and an unrepeatable sixth line in T, 55.

> T, 53.
>> Ces gentes espaulles menues,
>> Ces bras longus et ces mains traictisses,
>> Petit tetins, hanches charnues,
>> Eslevees, propres, faictisses,
>> A tenir amoureuses lices,
>> Ces larges reins, ce sadinet,
>> Assis sur grosses fermes cuisses
>> Dedens son petit jardinet?

And
> T, 55, 522.
>> Du sadinet, fy! Quant des cuisses

Swinburne's rendering read:

> T, 53.
> The shapely slender shoulders small,
> Long arms, hands wrought in glorious wise,
> Round little breasts, the hips withal
> High, full of flesh, not scant of size,
> Fit for all amorous masteries;

but then,

> T, 53, 506-8:
> *** ***** *** *** ****** **** ***
> ******* ***** ** **** ***** ******
> ** * ***** ****** ** **** *****?

and

> T, 55, 522.
> ** *** *** ***** ***** ** **

Before then Payne, even in his 'unexpurgated' translation of 1874, had been decorously reticent, offering the final three lines of T, 53 as:

> Wide hips and dainty quelque chose,
> Betwixt broad firm thighs situate
> Within its little garden-close.

leaving the reader to speculate on 'quelque chose'. For T, 55, 522, his

> The thighs no longer like to thighs

was little more than Victorian prudence.

Later attempts either omitted the offending 'sadinet', a word not part of polite French, or bowdlerised it. Stacpoole in 1914 suggested nothing, Lepper in 1924 offered 'the amulet', Chaney, 1940, the strangely equivocal 'queynte' which became the ambivalent 'dainty prize' of McCaskie in 1946.

Times and society became less restrictive. By 1952 Cameron could write 'twat' and eight years later Bonner was anatomically

correct with 'vulva'. In 1965 Kinnell gave 'pussy' in T, 53 and
'the hole' in T, 55, a translation that was repeated in 1992 by
the French biographer, Dufournet, with his 'ce trou mignon posé
sur de grosses cuisses fermes an milieu de son petit jardin'.

François Villon was never mealy-mouthed and he wrote as his
old woman, the former courtesan, might have spoken. A more
appropriate and honest version for T, 53 could be:

> Long arms and groping fingers sly,
> Fine shapely shoulders, and the round
> Full breasts and heaving hips that fly
> Smooth, slick and firm in thrust and pound
> Against the place where we were bound.
> Above spread loins my pulsing cunt
> Between its gripping thighs was crowned
> With gardened curls across its front.

And continued in T, 55 with

> But this is where our beauty's sent,
> Scrawny arms, hands weak and sick,
> Crooked back and shoulders bent.
> My flabby tits? Won't stir a prick.
> My arse the same. To tempt a dick,
> My cunt? No hope! As for my thighs
> Each one just skin, dry bone, a stick,
> A pock-marked sausage. Beauty dies.

Such liberation permits a more faithful range of Villon's
poetry from its most savage to its most tender. It was the same
Villon with his language of the slums who could write in *The
Ballad of the Hanged Men*:

> Freres humains qui après nous vivez,
> N'ayez les cueurs contre nous endurciz . . . , PD, 11(L, 14).

translated by Swinburne as:

> Men, brother men, that after us yet live,
> Let not your hearts too hard against us be;

The Restaurant Villon on the boulevard St Germain, one of the few indications today that Villon had lived in Paris. (*Author photo*)

> For if some pity of us poor men ye give,
> The sooner God shall take of you pity.
> Here are we five or six strung up, you see,
> And here the flesh that all too well we fed
> Bit by bit eaten and rotten, rent and shred,
> And we the bones grow dust and ash withal;
> Let no man laugh at us discomforted,
> But pray to God that he forgive us all.

which was written by the 31-year-old Villon in 1462 when he was imprisoned in the Châtelet of Paris, sentenced to death on the gallows for a crime that he did not commit.

1

Childhood Years, 1431–50

The year 1431 was one of contrasts. On 30 May Joan of Arc was burned at the stake in the market square of Rouen. In the same year the newly crowned French king, Charles VII, was hiding from his enemies, shifting from castle to penniless castle. In December the nine-year-old English king, Henry VI, in cloth of gold on a white charger, rode triumphantly into Paris with his gorgeously apparelled retinue, the boy 'staring for a long time' at three lovely, naked girls representing mermaids in the fountain of St Denis.[1] Probably in the same year, but on the other side of the city, François Villon was born in the slums and alleys near the rue St Jacques.

It was a century of flux. Old beliefs withered. The feudal system was decaying. The Church, whether abbey, nunnery or wandering friar, was soiled with corruption. But the world was widening. The Portuguese were exploring the west coast of Africa, discovering the Azores, Senegal, sending negro slaves to Lisbon in the middle of the century. By its end Vasco da Gama would round the Cape of Good Hope.

Also in the middle of the century Europe would have its first printing press with movable metal type when Gutenberg's Bible was produced at Mainz. Arts flourished with the works of Donatello, van Eyck, Fra Angelico. It was a century when universities were founded in France at Bordeaux, Poitiers, Caen and a century when great cathedrals were finished, Florence in 1434, the tallest spire in Europe erected at Strasbourg in 1439.

Yet it was a cruel time. France was in ruins. The Hundred Years War had persisted since the disastrous defeats for France at Crécy in 1346 followed by Poitiers ten years later when the

French king was captured. Frenchman fought Frenchman.
Followers of John, Duke of Burgundy, supported England.
Those of Bernard, Count of Armagnac, favoured the crown.
Even between churches there could be opposing loyalties. The
chapter of Notre-Dame in Paris was pro-Burgundian, agreeing
with the English who occupied the city that Joan of Arc was a
heretic and sorcerer, deserving death. Just across the Seine the
chapter of St Benoît-le-Bientourné, always hostile to Notre-
Dame, thought the verdict heretical itself.

The misnamed Hundred Years War from 1337 to 1453 was a
struggle for French territory. Ever since 1066 and the Battle of
Hastings when William of Normandy became King of England
large regions of France such as Aquitaine had been governed by
the English despite French protests. Claims and counterclaims
continued between the two countries until Philip VI of France
declared that England had forfeited all right to Aquitaine. Edward
III responded by claiming the throne of France through descent
from his mother, Isabella, sister of the previous French king.

Arguments deteriorated into outbreaks of warfare. There
were early successes for England at the battles of Sluys, 1340,
Crécy and Poitiers. Years later Henry V triumphed at Agincourt
in 1415. But slowly France recovered. Heartened by the success
of Joan of Arc the French finally won the decisive battle of
Castillon in 1453 leaving only Calais as an English possession
after bankrupting decades of fighting. Neither side could
celebrate. England was defeated. Whole regions of France were
in ruin.

With armies trailing across the land, with skirmishes and with
bands of robbers searching for wealth and women, the
countryside had been systematically ravaged. In 1431 it was
only sixteen years since a sprawling and impatiently over-eager
French army at Agincourt had crowded between narrow woods,
became too compressed to use their weapons, and were
slaughtered in a brief, bloody thirty minutes. The dead were in
their thousands: the Constable of France, dukes, counts, more

than a hundred barons, more than a thousand knights, many thousands of men-at-arms. Wounded common soldiers were killed. Rich men were held for ransom. One great noble, the young Charles, Duke of Orléans, unharmed but helplessly trapped under corpses, was captured and taken to England.

After that massacre there had been some successes for France. In 1429 Joan of Arc relieved the siege of Orléans and later that year Charles VII, already acclaimed king in 1422, was formally crowned in Rheims. But the war continued. There were brief truces and treaties, English attacks, civil conflicts against a background of rural despair as peasants suffered.

In the 1420s English soldiers had bought food. By the 1430s they were looting. By the 1440s looting was useless. From the Somme to the Seine and from the Seine to the Loire farms were in ruins, crops were burnt, mills, vineyards, fishponds were abandoned, horses and cattle had been stolen. Where there had been tilled fields there were brambles, thorns and shrubs, dense forests spread where there had been hedges and in them ravenous wolves prowled for food. Roads were dangerous with footpads and cut-throats watching for unprotected travellers. Villagers were warned of approaching dangers by the ringing of church bells and it was said that for years later in peacetime oxen and horses would stampede when a bell pealed.

Peasants left their threatened, impoverished homes. Within a few miles of Paris hamlets were empty: the village of Magny-les-Hameaux had none 'but three poor men from Normandy'. There was no one at Rennemoulin, eight instead of a hundred at Bièvre and fewer than thirty instead of three hundred at Chevreuse. Everywhere there was hunger. On the outskirts of Abbeville on the route taken by English army after English army a starving peasant woman had salted down the bodies of two children she had killed. Wolves dug up bodies from graveyards, even swam across the Seine to attack people in Paris.[2]

People fled for protection to the city, becoming unskilled labourers in the hovel-dense back-streets and alleyways. Among them was the family of François Villon. Born François de Montcorbier or des Loges, he was to keep the surnames until well into his twenties. Montcorbier and Loges were hamlets 35 miles south-east of Moulins in the ancient region of the Bourbonnais and from there the poet's father, mother and relatives trudged almost 200 miles to Paris in the 1420s searching for work, only for his father to die when Villon was very young. 'My father's dead. God rest his soul', T, 38. 'My father never had great riches. . . . Poverty follows and stalks all of us', T, 35. Somehow his mother eked out a desperate living.

The dangers of Paris were different from those of the countryside but just as deadly. Among the overcrowded streets with undernourished inhabitants existing in filthy conditions outbreaks of typhus and plague were commonplace. The town reeked. The streets were narrow, crooked, dirty, unpaved and thick with mud and manure lying in foul, undrained pools. The only sewer was an untended gutter down the middle of the street. Water for cooking and drinking came from a haphazard collection of pumps, troughs and fountains.

There had been improvements. In the thirteenth century the original 'drainage system' had been 'Tout à la rue', 'everything into the street'. Concerned at the recurring pestilences, especially the Black Death of 1348, city ordinances forbade the heaping of rubbish-middens outside houses and the accumulation of decomposing skins and carcases in the butchers' quarters. Nor any longer was it necessary to wait for the sporadic overflowing of the Seine for the streets to be washed down. Nevertheless, because of war and disease it has been calculated that the population of the city declined by two-thirds between 1328 and 1470.

A perpetual irritant was the presence of fleas and a Goodman of Paris advised his young wife of ways to deal with them: 'To kill fleas: smear loaves with glue or turpentine, put a lighted candle in the middle and the fleas will stick; or trap them in the weave of a rough cloth; blankets of white wool will show up black fleas for squashing; at night sleep under a mosquito net. For the nuisance of flies, coat a linen rag with honey or apples, set it at the bottom of an open-topped pot and when full of flies, shut it and shake.' There was even medieval fly-paper – a honey-coated string. If these remedies were ineffective his wife could simply swat the pests.[3]

The historian is fortunate. Details of everyday Paris life and events were recorded in the journal of a citizen, the so-called Bourgeois of Paris, from 1405 until 1449. His name, his occupation are unknown. He may have been a minor cleric at the church of Ste Merri just north of Notre-Dame and the young Villon probably saw him, living as they did only three-quarters of a mile apart. Whatever the truth he noted the tribulations, the years of famine, disease, the comings and goings of the court, the affectations of the nobility, the misery of the underclass. In 1431, he wrote, robbers came every week to the gates of the capital, 'taking men, women, children and innumerable cattle, from which they got huge ransoms, always gold or silver'.

Paris was a city of contrasts. The rich, the nobles, the merchants, the money-lenders lived in luxury. The burghers, the officials, the tradesmen lived in some comfort. The poor starved. There was poverty and degradation for the lower classes. For the penniless the only affordable entertainment was a public execution. In April 1431 thirty robbers were hanged in Paris and a few days later six more. At the end of the month thirty-two were executed and on 4 May, a further thirty at the gates of the fortified medieval city with its great inner and outer walls.

Hangings were diversions. But there were always privations. always shortages of food, always high prices. There were storms, freezing winters, epidemics like the whooping-cough of 1414 which, said the Bourgeois, afflicted many thousands of people with sharp fevers and sweatily stinking bodies. For three weeks they were tremblingly weak with a hacking cough, catarrh, hoarseness. The genitals were painfully attacked and when the sick person was recovering clotted blood oozed through the nose, mouth and anus. Urchins, as they passed the houses of the afflicted on their customary evening errands for wine or mustard, sang 'What a cough you've caught in the cunt, old girl, what a cough, what a cough in the cunt!'[4]

In 1432 when the infant Villon was one year old there was a prolonged frost, trees lost their fruit, and there was a devastating hailstorm in which one ball measured a full 16 inches round. Five people were killed when the belfry was struck and fell into Vitry church. Corn crops failed. There was a bread famine. Late that year during an epidemic Anne, Duchess of Bedford, wife of the English Regent of France, died of the plague. She was buried in the Celestins, a richly endowed church with aristocratic tombs near royal residences at the east of the city. Villon's mother would know it.

In 1433 Guillaume de Villon, a chaplain of St Benoît-le-Bientourné and professor of canon law, bought a house, the Porte Rouge, alongside the church. François de Montcorbier would come to know it well and it may have been through the devotions of his mother and her constant attendance at the church of St-Benoît that the chaplain became aware of the untutored intelligence of her growing son.

And while the child grew, shabby, malnourished, stunted, with foodless days of cold 1433 was also the year when the 29-year-old Lord Baron Gilles de Rais – Count of Brienne, Marshal of France, Lieutenant General of Brittany, a soldier who had ridden and fought with Joan of Arc, the richest man in Europe

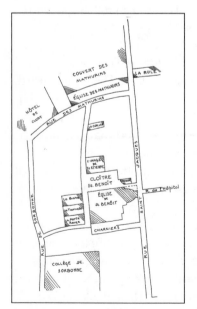

Villon's neighbourhood. The area of streets around St Benoît.

with vast estates of 18,000 square miles in Brittany, Maine, Anjou and Loire, with powerful castles at Champtocé, Machecoul, Tiffauges, Pouzauges – began the sexual abuse and murder of young children.[5]

During childhood he had been indulged to the point of insanity, deprived of nothing, unbalanced in his extravagance, in money, in display, in vice, seemingly omnipotent. Six years after Joan of Arc's success he ordered and paid for the lavish performance of *The Mystery of the Siege of Orléans* in the city, a play that celebrated his own prowess and began the irreversible process of his own ruin. Everything was paid for, the finest clothes for the one hundred and forty actors and five hundred extras, and not only paid for but renewed each day of the five months of the run. Every day food and wine were provided for the spectators. 'Each member of the cast had his own costume, according to his role and his rank . . . even beggars, valets, scoundrels . . . were no less well-dressed than kings or great folk.'

It has been calculated that he squandered as many as a hundred thousand saluts, valuable gold coins showing an angel saluting the Virgin Mary, on this prodigality, perhaps more than a million pounds of modern money. To find it he sold off estates on the outskirts of his dominions and it was only when his alarmed relatives complained to the king that on 2 July a royal edict forbade any further sales.

That was what the bemused world knew of Gilles de Rais. What was only vaguely suspected in 1435 was that his servants lured wandering refugee children to his castles with the promise of food. Sometimes they told parents in neighbouring villages that their son would become a page or asked him to go on an errand in exchange for a loaf of bread. One pathetic mother was given a meagre 100 sous for a new dress: even that was not paid in full.

Young, attractive boys were preferred, usually seven to twelve years of age. Inside the castle they were given a fine meal, with goblets of hippocras, a hot wine spiced with sugar, cinnamon, ginger and pepper, sweet to a young palate but an aphrodisiac for a sadist. Half-asleep, half-drunk the child was taken to a room high in the castle, briefly hanged by the neck to bruise the throat and prevent any scream, then cut down for de Rais to sodomise it, boy or girl. Sated, he slit the child's throat with a braquemard, a short, heavy, double-bladed sword. The body and clothes were slowly burnt and the ashes thrown into a cesspit or the moat. How many were killed was never discovered. In 1437 forty bodies were burned at Machecoul, and in 1438 up to forty-six removed from Champtocé. Forty more were reported missing between 1437 and 1440. Before 1437 there were no figures and a minimum of two hundred murders is probable.

Although safe from de Rais adults lived in fear of the bands of brigands that robbed, raped and murdered. After the ineffective Treaty of Arras in 1435 the countryside was infested with marauding bands of deserters. Known as écorcheurs or 'flayers' because they stripped captives down to their shirts, they devastated villages, violating churches, burning houses, assaulting women.

> If a decent man had a young wife that they could kidnap and if he could not pay the ransom demanded, they would torture and torment him grievously – they would put some of these men into large crates and would force their wives on to the lids of the crates and then shout, 'Peasant, I'm going to rape your wife and you can't stop me'. They would do it, too, and when their evil work was over they would let the poor man die in the crate if the ransom were not paid.[6]

Misery continued. In Paris there was a three-month long frost. Snow fell for six weeks and to worsen conditions an army of Armagnacs blockaded the city and no food came in. Then, on 17 April 1436 the unpaid English garrison quitted Paris, jeered by the delighted citizens. There were processions, bonfires and mystery plays. The price of food fell. Cherries were cheap.

With the English gone and summer coming Paris was an exciting place for a young boy. Over the centuries the population had outgrown the defensive walls built by Philip Augustus two centuries earlier. They now stood inside a taller, longer line with close-set towers and six great gates. At the east the Bastille was the strongest citadel in France. The walls enclosed two square miles of straggling streets, ten squares and eleven major crossroads in a city no more than a mile and a half across.

There was constant bustle and noise. François de Montcorbier remembered the cries of Paris: the milk seller, the farm-wives with their vegetables and cheeses. Coal-carts rumbled. There were chestnut-vendors, and the piercing shrieks of the fishwives on the Little Bridge with their colourful appeals to customers and ripostes to anyone with the effrontery to complain about their wares [T, 144]:

Brectes, Souyssez, n'y sçevent guerres,	Bretons and Swiss could never compare
Gasconnes, n'aussi Toullousïennes;	Nor Gascon girls nor from Toulouse,
De Petit Pont deux harangières	On the Petit-Pont two fishwives there
Les concluront . . .	Could shut them up . . .
Il n'est pas bon bec que de Paris.	There's no tongue like the Paris tongue.

There was noise everywhere. Church-bells clanged. Town-criers bellowed announcements at every cross-road. Twenty-six years later they would be calling the name of François Villon.

The Friday after Easter 1436 the English returned almost to the gates but did not enter. From November it froze until mid-February 1437. 'Hunger and misery', wrote the historian, Michelet, 'made of the capital a focus of revolting diseases that, as no one could distinguish one from the other, were known simply as the "Plague".'

There were always thieves at the gates. The fruit crops failed and there were no figs, walnuts or almonds, but, noted the Bourgeois, cabbages were plentiful and turnips cheap 'so that people were able to appease their own and their children's hunger with these'. Charles VII visited Paris briefly on 11 November, was horrified and left fearfully on 3 December. The English made no attempt to return.

Only wolves came. There was no food in the barren fields and every evening the ravenous animals swam across the river, packs of starving man-eaters that could smell the scent of a human being a quarter of a mile away, silently stalking their prey, man, woman or child, through the muddy streets of Paris.

The mud was everywhere and it stank. Paris was notorious for the stench, the worst of all great European cities. Droppings from horses and donkeys, snuffling pigs, urinating dogs made the stink even more pungent. 'Some places very dirty, and making it smell as if sulphur were mingled with the mud,' wrote the English diarist John Evelyn in 1643. Twenty years before him another visitor complained that Paris was 'always dirty and 'tis such a Dirt, that by perpetual Motion is beaten into such unctuous Oil, that where it sticks no Art can wash it off some Colours'.[7] Horsemen splashed by, ruining skirts and leggings. The mud stuck and it fouled. Hawkers sold stain-removers 'A la malle tache!' but the blemishes and the smell remained.

Conditions worsened and parts of Paris were like a ghost town with empty house after empty house. Armed escorts brought in hundreds of refugees but when they left they took away twice as many 'because they were dying of hunger there'.

The year 1438 was particularly bad. In April, a howling gale smashed houses and uprooted fruit trees. Caterpillars swarmed. Bread was unobtainable. Vegetables were scarce. At the beginning of May 'for lack of beet tops, people were selling cabbages, mallows, wild spinach, docks and nettles, and poor people cooked them without fat in nothing but water and salt and ate them without bread'.[8] In August there was an outbreak of smallpox and thousands died, mainly children. In September packs of wolves killed fourteen adults and ate a child in the Place aux Chats behind the charnel-houses of the Innocents. Years later Villon remembered:

Sur le Noël, morte saison,	At Christmas, cold and bitter days,
Que les loups se vivent du vent	When wolves live on the wind,
Et qu'on se tient en sa maison	Within his house a person stays
Pour le frimas, près du tyson	By warming fires, the winter logs ablaze [L, 2]

and T, 21:

| Neccessité fait gens mesprendre | Necessity drives men to sin |
| Et faim saillir le loup du boys. | And hunger drives the wolf from the woods. |

Yet it may have been in this appalling year that Guillaume de Villon adopted the seven-year-old François de Montcorbier. The church was always looking for promising youngsters and the canon had previously adopted another bright lad, Jehan le Duc, who later became a chaplain at St Benoît, and became so trusted that he acted as the executor of Guillaume de Villon when that good man died in 1468. It was a respectable career very different from that of the boy who succeeded le Duc in the house of the Red Door alongside the church of St Benoît.

On a noticeable slope up to the Porte St Jacques the church had a strange history. With cloisters built on the site of a twelfth-century Merovingian shrine the early church had its altar at the west instead of the conventional east and was known as St Benoît-le-Bestourné, 'skew-whiff'. In the early fifteenth century a new entrance was constructed, the altar taken to the east and the church renamed St Benoît-le-Bientourné, 'well-turned'. It was large, 140 × 90 feet, with a big, rectangular cloister to its north, a tiny prison built against it. There was a spacious cemetery to the south.

The Porte Rouge, named from the sign hanging from it in those unnumbered days, was one of three houses, two of them, the Doe and the Turret, in disrepair, against the west wall of the church, and it was here that Guillaume de Villon had lived since 1433. As his name implied he had come from Villon, a village in the Chablis countryside near Tonnerre a hundred miles south-east of Paris. He prospered. He owned three houses, although lax in

The façade of St Benoît, moved to the garden of the Cluny Museum, boulevard St Germain, Paris, after the destruction of the church in 1854. (*Author photo*)

collecting their rents, he had a vineyard and fifteen years earlier had been granted the benefice of a church at Gentilly on the outskirts of Paris from which he had the right to corn ground in the mill there. His comparative wealth was to become necessary.

St Benoît-le-Bientourné was not just a church. It was almost an estate in its own right, everything walled in, against the rue St Jacques. Typically litigious in an age of litigation its six canons and twelve chaplains had an unending feud with Notre-Dame about status and privileges. Cases for and against the church were heard in numerous ecclesiastical courts, one of the most sensitive issues being that St Benoît had nominated itself a Chapter, the assembly of canons of a cathedral church. The Chapter of the cathedral church of Notre-Dame who appointed the canons of St Benoît and who allowed them little power refused to accept this unilateral promotion. St Benoît ignored the ruling.

The dreaded day came on 11 July. It was the occasion of the annual visit of two canons from Notre-Dame, perhaps Guillaume Cotin and Thibault de Vitry, for the annual inspection of their rival church, ascertaining that the cloisters were clean and kempt, the accounts correct, everything and everywhere in good order.[9]

Both Cotin and de Vitry were rich and powerful, de Vitry being related to the king's commissioner, and both were noted for their truculent natures. They have been immortalised by Villon. Almost twenty years later when he was composing his flippant legacies of articles either valueless or not his to give away the canons had become ploddingly humourless octogenarians. Calling them 'jeunes et esbatans', 'little boys that just love to play', T, 132, he left them a bequest,

Deux pauvres clercs, parlans latin,	Two poor clerks, good Latin speakers,
Humbles, bien chantans au lectry,	Modest, chanting tuneful chorals,
Paisables enfans, sans estry.	Peaceful children with no quarrels. [L, 28]

laughing at their meagre grasp of Latin and worse ability to sing. Generously Villon gave them the rents of Laurent Gueuldry's house. The gift was nonsense. They had no need of the petty sum. Even if they had the whole of Paris knew that the canons of St Benoît had been trying to get the selfsame rents from the butcher, Gueuldry, for twenty years and were currently taking his heirs to court over the non-payment.

The verse, one of many in Villon's *Legacies*, would not be written for almost twenty years but it was probably composed in the poet's austere room in the Porte Rouge. In it was a webbing-strapped bed, benches, a table, candles, inkstand and books. It was so cold that ink froze, but it was a room with furniture in a proper house, easefully different from the ramshackle bits and pieces in the rundown place that had been his home for seven years. The change was to transform his life.

He would be fed although the years of deprivation had miserably affected his growth. He would be educated. As a child he may have been part of St Benoît's congregation, perhaps taught the elements of reading by churchmen, a clever and promising lad. Guillaume de Villon was to be a gentle tutor, introducing him to the Latin grammar *De Octo Partibus Orationis* of Aelius Donatus, telling him the lives of the saints, reading to him from the Bible, always in Latin, giving the boy a detailed knowledge of both Testaments. At evening meals when other chaplains and canons came to dine the conversation would be full of legal phraseology as the latest argument with Notre-Dame was debated.

A reservation must be made about the boy's good fortune. There is a wise observation that an urchin can be taken out of the slums but the slums cannot be taken out of the urchin. Years of hunger and hardship and the need for self-preservation moulded the character of François Villon, giving him a sharp awareness of the pleasures and the pains of Paris. He was a child of the city. Having known sickness and starvation he hungered for money and enjoyment. He also knew the unpredictability of life and the brevity of youth. He had elegiac eyes.

Genius comes unannounced. Sometimes through good fortune it flourishes. More often circumstances stifle it. For every Christopher Marlowe, son of a semi-literate Canterbury shoemaker, who gained a place at Cambridge University there may have been a thousand, ten thousand talented children unknown to the world in the days before education became general. Genes from a gifted but unremembered ancestor could be passed on through untutored parents. Villon's mother was illiterate.

Femme je suis, povrecte et ancïenne,	I am a poor, ignorant old woman,
Qui riens sçay, oncques lettres ne leuz	Without letters, unable to read [T, 89+]

Her only knowledge of the Bible came from the painted murals in her church. Without guidance François de Montcorbier, later self-styled Villon, could have been a medieval Jude the Obscure, as wraithlike as Gray's 'mute, inglorious Milton', buried without fame and soon forgotten. Thomas Gray mused on the wasted abilities that lay in the churchyard of Stoke Poges:

> Perhaps in this neglected spot is laid
> Some heart once pregnant with celestial fire;
> Hands, that the rod of empire might have swayed,
> Or waked to ecstasy the living lyre.

Had the young Villon not been taken in by the chaplain it is a probability that he would have been a mere droplet in the puddle that was the population of Paris, achieving no distinction, known only by his family, a few friends, one or two workmates. Maybe, frustrated by his awareness of an unfulfilled life, loathing his beggarly existence, he could have turned petty thief who died on the scaffold.

'Petty thief' is speculation; de Rais' story, alas, is fact. Miles west of Paris, near Angers, a far from petty, viciously hardened criminal knew panic for the first time in his pampered life, dreading that his murders were close to discovery.

Champtocé, a castle of Gilles de Rais, had been seized the previous November by his younger brother in the hope of preserving a little of a swiftly dissipating inheritance. Locked in that castle, but not impregnably, were the remains of tortured, slaughtered children.

De Rais had been a soldier and he acted decisively. In his brother's absence he recaptured the castle in June 1438 and ordered his servants to remove the evidence 'from a tower near the lower halls of the said castle' and take them to Machecoul almost sixty miles away beyond Nantes. The bones were desiccated almost to powder but the skulls could be counted. At his trial de Rais' servant, Etienne Corrilaut alias Poitou, said that there were either thirty-six or forty-six. He could not remember.[10]

None of this was known in Paris. In that city there were wonders and terrors for a growing boy. On 24 August 1439 a fish fully 7 feet 6 inches long was caught in the Seine. A lack-lustre English army, uninterested in the capital, plundered outside the walls. So did the écorcheurs. There was worse inside. In September wolves killed several people near Montmartre and the Bastille. 'If they found a flock of animals they would ignore the animals and go for the herdsman.' After Christmas they savagely attacked four housewives in the fields and bit and injured seventeen more adults, eleven of whom died of their wounds. A triumph in November was the slaying of the most ferocious animal. It had no tail and was nicknamed 'Courtaut'. The carcase was put in a wheelbarrow, jaws wide open, and taken all round Paris. Everyone came to look. 'They got more than ten francs in takings.'[11]

Gilles de Rais, his immense wealth almost gone, his properties sold or mortgaged, in debt, hoped to restore his fortune through magic. He sent a servant to Italy to find an alchemist who could create gold from lead. A plausible charlatan, François Prelati, lapsed priest, suave and unscrupulous, came, ordered equipment, wasted money, claimed he had raised the Devil as well as the expectations of a credulous de Rais but created nothing. Condemned to life imprisonment at the trial of de Rais he escaped but was hanged shortly afterwards.

In 1440 Charles, Duke of Orléans, was ransomed twenty-five years after Agincourt and returned to France. After a short stay in Paris he returned to his château at Blois. Villon was to go there years later. It was a better year in Paris. There was an infestation of insects, moles and night-beetles but most were killed by a cold June and although salt was expensive food was generally cheaper. Outside, the countryside was no safer. There were reports of rapacious brigands, and it was said that in the Bourbonnais, the land of Villon's forefathers, a man could travel thirteen or fourteen miles, meet no one and find nothing to eat or drink.

This same year was no better for Gilles de Rais. In May, wanting to regain a castle that he had sold, he broke into a church whose priest held the keys and the sacrilege led to his death. There was an investigation in July, rumours of his depravities were heard, and on 15 September he and his entourage were arrested. The trial in Nantes with parents mumbling of a child's disappearance lasted from 19 September to 21 October. 'With certain of his accomplices [he] had slaughtered, murdered and massacred in the most odious fashion several young boys, and that he had taken with these children pleasure against nature, and practised the vice of sodomy . . . and oftentimes had caused invocations of the devil'.[12] So abominable were the accusations that the Court had the crucifix covered.

At first defiant, then threatened with torture and excommunication, de Rais confessed to everything. He was sentenced to death and on 26 October he was hanged and his body burned in Nantes. In modern times it would be sensational national news. Two hundred miles away the Bourgeois did not even mention it.

The following year the Dauphin came to Paris for a single night when the heaviest tax for years was being levied, four times bigger than previous sums. Twelve months later in 1442 the Seine overflowed twice, four hundred scratching, screeching crows fought each other, spilling blood, and on 6 May there was heavy rain. 'It poured without ceasing [all night] and so heavily that in the widest parts of Paris's main streets the water came into the churches, into cellars, over the thresholds of high doorways, and lifted up barrels of wine to the flooring. Besides all this there was dreadful thunder and lightning which terrified the whole city'.[13]

It was also the year when the twelve-year-old Villon was admitted to the university's Faculty of Arts, a preliminary to entry into one of the major Faculties of Theology, Medicine or Canon Law. From his apparent familiarity with its layout he may have attended the college of Navarre rather than the Sorbonne. Of all the colleges the Sorbonne was the most prestigious, synonymous with the University itself. France's first printing-press was installed there in 1469.

It was one of many colleges such as the École de Médecine with its long-gowned student-surgeons, or the austere Montaigu College whose occupants slept on the floor among lice, fleas and insects. Rabelais knew it. Gargantua's tutor refused to send the boy 'to that lowsie College which they call Montague . . . for the Galley-Slaves are far better used amongst the Moores and Turks, the murtherers in criminal Dungeons, yea the very Doggs in your House, than are the wretched Students in the aforesaid Colledge'.

The oldest of the colleges was the Dix-Huits, whose eighteen students were too poor to pay the university fees and were given scholarships from Notre-Dame. It had a bad reputation as 'a den of thieves'. The college of Navarre was the largest and, significantly, the richest of all.

Among over two thousand lecturers, clerks and students, about a third being graduates, the students were assigned to one of four Nations: 'France', 'Picardy', 'Normandy' and 'Germany', the latter having replaced 'England' during the unceasing Hundred Years War. As well as the cost of graduation students had a weekly charge, the *bourse*, of one to eight sous, like a silver shilling, for books, tuition, food and clothing. Villon paid two in years when one sou bought a pint of good wine.[14] There were strict rules for the appearance and deportment of students. With thumbs in their belt they wore a heel-length black gown, its hood pulled over their eyes.

By the fifteenth century university education was no more than intellectually arid rote learning. Villon was taught the seven liberal arts: grammar, rhetoric, including poetry, the elements of law, dialectic, arithmetic, music, geometry and astronomy. Lectures, always in Latin, were dictated monotony in cold halls. After a pre-lecture that explained the chosen passage from a classical author the lecture proper consisted of tediously dictated notes on parsing, scanning, analysis of the grammar and content. For the intelligent but chilled student sitting on straw-layered flagstones the system encouraged absenteeism and it is likely that Villon and equally bored comrades frequently preferred the relaxation of taverns to the routine of taking notes.

He certainly had time in 1444 when the relic of Christ's foreskin was brought to Paris and when hundreds of letters of absolution of sins were sold in the city. Because the Rector of the university had been assaulted by officials when he protested that students should not be liable to a newly imposed levy he closed the university from September to March. It was one of many confrontations between the church and the city. There would be a more serious one in 1451.

A smallpox epidemic broke out the next year killing thousands, most of them children. Death was not selective. As the grim murals of the Danse Macabré in the Innocents proclaimed it scythed Pope, parson and peasant alike. The wife of the Dauphin, Margaret, daughter of the King of Scotland, developed a fever and died in Châlons. Despite her beauty, her gentleness, her love of poetry she was hated by her husband, Louis, because of the forced marriage arranged by his detested father, Charles VII. His neglected, humiliated wife almost welcomed death. 'Fie on the life of this world. Speak to me no more of it, for more than anything it wearies me.'

Married when eleven years old, dead by twenty-one, she was seen by the court as a fairy-tale princess, glitteringly clothed with jewel-embroidered dresses, her tall pointed hat hung with lace, her neck graced with a gold necklet with pendant pearls. In the years when the king provided his son with nothing he presented the Dauphine with two thousand livres 'for silks and furs'.[15]

Fine apparel also preoccupied women of different social status, the prostitutes of Paris. They had so brazenly flaunted their satins and sequins that the exasperated authorities finally forbade such ostentation. There were to be no insets of expensive white miniver on their gowns, their silver belts were confiscated for the royal coffers, they were not allowed to wear fashionable turned-down collars nor walk the streets in costly cloaks of squirrel fur. It was hoped to prevent them announcing their trade.

But the streets themselves were advertisement enough: rue Trousse-Puteyne, 'whore's slit street'; rue Grattecon, 'scratch-cunt street'; rue de Chapon for homosexuals with a predilection for boys. Outside the city walls was the rue du Poil au Con, 'cunt's hair street', the haunt of women who refused to obey the law that their pubic hair should be shaved. In a more prudish age the name of the Poil au Con was sanitised into the rue de Pélecan just as London's Gropecuntlane and Codpiece Alley became Grape Street and Coppice Alley.[16]

There were other associations with prostitutes. On the evening of Ascension Day 1446, the Provost of Paris, the highly placed official responsible for the police, the prisons and the gallows, died. Ambroise de Loré was despised. 'He had a wife who was one of the best and most beautiful women in all Paris . . . yet he was so lecherous that it was said for a fact that he kept three or four prostitutes as his mistresses. He always protected loose women, of whom through his laxity Paris had far too many . . . he always protected them and their bawds'.[17]

By a coincidence in the year of the Provost's death his daughter, also Ambroise de Loré, married Robert d'Estouteville who 'won' her in a tournament at Saumur arranged by René, Count of Anjou. By a further coincidence d'Estouteville became

Provost of Paris in 1447. Villon would know him and his wife well and would visit the court of René of Anjou.

The dead Provost was not the only man to have had a mistress. Charles VII made no attempt to hide lovely Agnes Sorel, friend of René of Anjou's wife, from the world. Known as the Dame de Beauté he gave her the estate of Beauté-sur-Marne as a pun on her name. The notoriety upset the queen. Devoted to his mother the Dauphin angrily rebuked, maybe even hit, the girl. He was disgraced. 'He cut the tails off all his horses, saying they might as well be cropped like their master'.[18] In 1447, a year when the Seine was so low that it could be crossed stone by stone without getting one's shoes wet, Louis, Dauphin of France, left Paris. He never saw his father again.

In 1448 Agnes Sorel visited Paris for the first time. The Bourgeois was unimpressed. 'In the last week of April a young woman came to Paris who was said to be the acknowledged mistress of the King of France. . . . It was obviously true for she lived as grandly as any countess or duchess. . . . She called herself and had herself called, "Fair Agnes". She often went about with the good Queen, not in the least ashamed of her sin; the Queen was deeply grieved in her heart, but had to put up with it for the time being'.[19] Agnes Sorel was equally unimpressed. Shown no respect by the Parisians whom she called 'low wretches' she left the city on 10 May. Less than twelve months later the eighteen-year-old François Villon, who may have gaped at her ostentatious arrival, was awarded his bachelor's degree.

In March 1449 his name was among those of the baccalauréat: Franciscus de Moultcorbier Parisius, qualifying him to read for a Master's degree. He had the crown of his head shaved in a clerical tonsure and this new status entitled him to the protection of the Church against civil law, a benefit for which he would be grateful.

One afternoon at the end of May there was a shattering thunderstorm, so fierce that it stripped the sides of the Augustinians'

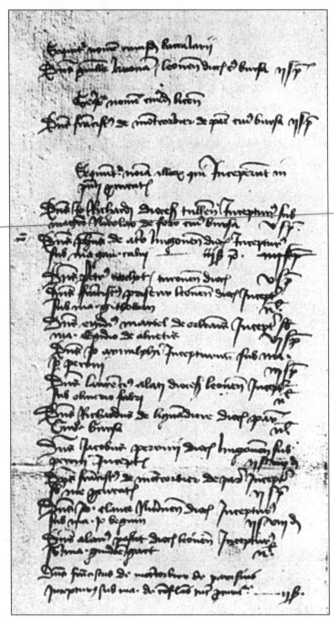

A page of the *Registre de la Nation de France* recording Villon's degree.

steeple, smashed heavy rafters and blasted half the roof away. At the first rumblings the great bell of St Germain was rung in the belief that the tolling would drive the thunder away.[20]

On 10 December Charles VII entered Rouen after thirty years of English occupation and ordered an investigation into the legality of Joan of Arc's trial. The first enquiry with seven witnesses called was held on 4 March 1450. Three weeks earlier Agnes Sorel, only twenty-eight years old, had died. There were rumours of poison, perhaps administered at the instigation of the contemptuous Dauphin. Her heart was buried in the magnificent Benedictine Abbey of Jumièges, and her body in the church of Loches in whose royal castle Charles and she had often stayed in the tower named after her, La Tour de la Belle Agnès.

Her tomb, restored after vandalism during the Revolution, is now in the castle, a life-size limestone figure whose lovely face is reputed to have been modelled on her death-mask. Two lambs, 'agni', lie at her feet. With its base of black marble the memorial must have cost hundreds of golden saluts at a time when just one was the equivalent of half a year's wages for a labourer.[21]

In the same room is an unnoticed connection with François Villon. Hanging there is a copy of her portrait and another of the Virgin Mary, both by Jean Fouquet, 'the second great realist in the history of French painting', 'the so-called Master of King René of Anjou'. The face of the Virgin is that of Agnes Sorel.

For some years Fouquet appears to have worked in the court of René, Count of Anjou, in Angers, and he may well have met Villon there is the late 1450s. The two men, a poet of genius and a painter of equal talent, had much in common. 'Fouquet's awareness of reality was so intense because he lived in a time of unrest and strife, of contrasted brilliance, and of violent change . . . Fouquet's art was courtly art. . . . It surveyed the world from a height, from the point of view of the mighty, just as François Villon, the penniless vagabond, saw it from the depths of his poverty'.[22] There was no sentimentality in either of them.

The lovely tomb of Agnes Sorel in the castle of Loches. Paintings of her by Fouquet hang on the walls. (*Author photo*)

In April 1450 the English were defeated at Formigny near Bayeux, the last set battle of the Hundred Years War. In the same year Guillaume de Villon was imprisoned by the Chapter of Notre-Dame for an unknown offence.

2

The Affair of the Pet-au-Deable, 1451–4

The year 1451 was that in which the French recaptured Gascony, leaving the English with very little in France after an entire century of ruinous warfare. It was a year in which François de Montcorbier was becoming accustomed to dishonesty. It was also the year in which the student tragi-comedy of the Pet-au-Deable began.

Through the researches of scholars such as Auguste Longnon a great deal is known of the young Villon's social life, both his acquaintance with the gentility and his choice of more reprehensible friends. Through his benefactor, Guillaume de Villon, now free from prison, he constantly mixed with Church officials, listening to learned men debating the latest affairs of Paris. He knew prosperous and powerful members of society like the Provost, Robert d'Estouteville, meeting his lovely wife, Ambroise. He chatted with well-to-do men of his own age, able to out-talk them, make them laugh, but always aware of his dowdy clothes, the money his companions had and that he lacked, always aware of his thin, unappealing physique.

The Provost, who became something of a protector of Villon, was almost all-powerful in the city. He was in charge of the police of Paris, the Royal Watch, which consisted of twenty mounted sergeants who operated outside the walls and forty foot-constables working within the city under the command of the Knight of the Watch, the Chevalier du Guet. They were assisted by the two-hundred-and-twenty sergeants of the Châtelet, municipal constabulary, many of whom were as dishonest as the pickpockets, housebreakers and cut-throats that they sometimes pursued, sometimes collaborated with.

The Provost was also responsible for the civic prisons of Paris. Of the eight municipal gaols, some were light and spacious and a bed could be rented or even brought in for payment of a fee to the jailer's wife. Elsewhere cells in other prisons might be foul and freezing subterranean dungeons to which the only access was a padlocked trapdoor in the ceiling. Of the gaols the two most important were the many-celled, many-towered Grand-Châtelet against the Pont au Change and the Petit-Châtelet by the Petit-Pont. In his *Legacies*, L, 22, Villon ironically booked himself into the *Troys Lis* (Three Lilies) cell in the Châtelet because it sounded like Trois Lits (three beds), offering pleasant but totally unrealistic luxury. As well as the city the church had prisons for its own clerks, servants and lay malefactors. Notre-Dame had one as Guillaume de Villon knew, and St Benoît had its own little gaol.

An extra function of the Provost's was to ensure the maintenance of the many civic scaffolds. Besides those outside the Porte St Denis, the Porte St Jacques and the Porte Baudet, there were others at the Place de Grève, the Place Dauphine and the Croix du Trahoir, at Montigny. In addition to these official gallows there were numerous private gibbets of the Church and of other establishments that had the right to punish and to hang.

Montfaucon, the oldest and biggest gibbet, was a hideous monstrosity half a mile outside the walls. Its name, 'Falcon Hill', came from the ghastly sight of those birds of prey plunging down on to crows and ravens as they flew away with gobbets of flesh from dead bodies. The place was like an outdoor Chamber of Horrors. It was not just for hangings. To it 'the remains of criminals previously beheaded, boiled or quartered were brought from all over France to hang in wicker baskets beside the people actually executed in situ. What was left of the body of Pierre des Essarts, beheaded in 1413, was there pecked to shreds by hordes of carrion crows before being returned, three years later, to his family for burial'.[1]

On the earthen mound of Montfaucon, 15 feet high, 30 feet wide, and 40 feet long, was a rectangular platform elevated for the benefit of spectators. Upon it was a three-sided colonnade with four rows of four square stone pillars, each about 32 feet high, linked at the top by heavy beams from which ropes and fetters dangled. Delinquents and blasphemers were often chained to the stones. In the middle of the platform was a big pit for the corpses of the hanged, normally covered by a grating to prevent the removal of bones.

From their prison condemned men, trussed in their cart, set out for Montfaucon with the Provost, superb in his furs and scarlet robes, and his bodyguard of twelve mounted sergeants in attendance. With them was the public executioner. The grim cortège stopped for a few minutes at the convent of Filles-Dieu by Porte St Denis where the prisoners were given the last comfort of bread and a cup of wine from the sisters, good, self-supporting ladies dedicated to the care of the sick.[2]

Beyond the Porte St Denis the cart lumbered half a mile north-eastwards into the country, to the rowdy crowds of expectant spectators and to the multiple gallows where as many as sixty could be disposed of at one time. Assistant hangmen tested chains, fixed the halters. The men were escorted on to the platform, tidily arranged side by side, hemp nooses around their necks. A friar recited the last prayers. The Provost's official read names and sentences from his parchment, the carts moved away, the bodies strangled into a slow and tormenting death.

With friends such as the Provost Villon had some safeguard from any minor misdemeanour. But already he had a coterie of disreputable cronies. Guy Tabarie was a university colleague and irresponsible blabbermouth who, one day, would get Villon into serious trouble. There was Robin Turgis, near neighbour, rogue and close relative of another Robin Turgis, proprietor of the Pomme de Pin (Pine Cone) tavern. Since childhood Villon had

Epitaphe dudit Villon
Freres humains qui apres nꝰ viues
Napez les cueurs contre nꝰ endurcis
Car se pitie de nꝰ pouures auez
Dieu en aura pluftoft de vous mercis
Vous nous voies cy ataches cinq six
Quāt de la char q̃ trop auōs nourrie
Elleft pieca deuouree et pourrie
et nꝰ les os deuenōs cēdres ⁊ pouldre
De noftre mal personne ne sen rie
Mais pries dieu que tous nous vueil
le absouldre   g iii.

The multiple gallows of the hanged men, 'Frères humains . . .'.

known the graduate Colin de Cayeux, son of a Parisian locksmith in the St Benoît quarter, whose skill with catches, bolts and
keys Colin quickly adapted for other purposes. Living close
together Villon and he had been friends for years. There are hints
that de Cayeux was a member of the notorious Coquillards, a
dangerous band of criminals with their own secret jargon.

Most influential of these dubious characters was Regnier de
Montigny, son of a noble family. His father, Jean, so fervent a
royalist and supporter of the Dauphin that he followed him into
exile, had returned to Paris in 1418 only to discover that the
Burgundians had pillaged his estates, leaving him ruined. His
death around 1445 left an almost impoverished widow to raise
three children.

Jean's brother, Étienne, was a canon of St Benoît. Being
Regnier's uncle the relationship probably explains how
Montigny and Villon met. Regnier, resentful of his undeserved
wretchedness, was a bad lot. On 21 August 1452 he and his
companions, Rosay and Taillemine, two reputed Coquillards,
beat up two Sergeants of the Bank, 'batirent tresgradement
lesdiz sergents', after an argument outside the tavern-cum-
brothel of Grosse Margot near the cloisters of Notre-Dame.
Because of his university degree Regnier was able to exercise his
clerical right to immunity from civil law. Rosay and he remained
confederates in crime.

It was with such associates that Villon drank. Paris was
thronged with taverns, the Boeuf Coronné (Crowned Ox); the
Cerf Volant (Leaping Deer); the Chaire (Pulpit) on the Petit-Pont
where the garrulous Tabarie would meet the priest, Marchand;
the famous Grand Godet (Big Pot) and the infamous riverside
dive of the Gros Figuier (Great Fig Tree). There were dozens,
rowdy, crowded, dingy, the Heaulme (Helmet); two Moutons
(Sheep), one by the St Jean cemetery on the Right Bank where
Montigny would kill Thévenin Pensete, the other near St Benoît;
the Mule on the rue St Jacques even closer to the Porte Rouge.
The Panier Vert (Green Basket) was a notorious drinking-den

near the Place Maubert. The Pomme de Pin (Fir-Cone) on the rue de la Juiverie was the tavern where Villon enjoyed the ill-judged credit of Robin Turgis. Rabelais, Molière, Racine, La Fontaine all knew it.

For a gourmet with money the choice of fare was extensive. There were courses of cooked apples, ripe figs, Grenache wine, pea soup, eels, herrings, perches and cuttlefish in gravy; river and sea fish, bream pasties, roast mackerel, crêpes, oysters. All one needed was cash. It is improbable that Guillaume de Villon was financially prodigal, sous rather than saluts, but his young protegé and poet would become renowned for his ability to overcome the disadvantage of an empty purse.

Almost in his own lifetime, by the end of the fifteenth century, there was a popular book of thefts and swindles attributed to him, the *Recueil des Repues Franches de Maître François Villon et de ses Compagnons*. 'The Free Feeds' went into many editions. The stories were old, derived from earlier scamps and rascals like Til Eulenspiel but their adapted association with Villon's name shows how strong his reputation became as a trickster. Suavely, slyly, he cheated shopkeepers, substituting a flagon of water for one of wine; distracting a merchant while friends stole bread, fish, cheese, meat; pretending to quarrel violently with a 'stranger' so that the alarmed tradesman rushed out to fetch the police leaving his wares unguarded. Much of it was exaggerated or simply untrue but its very existence shows what a celebrity Villon was, a laughing rogue, a scallywag.

Villon himself subscribed to the notoriety, writing that after his death:

Au moins sera de moy memoire	At least there will be a memory of me
Telle qu'elle est d'un follastre.	As one who was a merry madcap. [T, 177]

Long before Villon's birth, 'villon' had meant 'to insult' but the poet's fame modified it into a 'cunning rogue, a pleasant thief'. Words like villon, villonerie, villoner, villoniser, all carried the implication of someone who took property without payment.

The word even spread to England. The first-ever French–English dictionary, Randle Cotgrave's *A Dictionarie of the French and English Tongue*, of 1611, defined 'villon' as 'A cousener, conycatcher, cunning or wittie rogue; a nimble knave; a pleasant theefe (for such a one was François Villon)'.

Cotgrave may have learned of Villon from Rabelais' *Gargantua and Pantagruel*, 1552–3, written at a time when there were still strong memories of the poet and rapscallion. The description of Panurge is believed to be a disguised likeness to Villon.

> He was a very proper looking fellow, but for the fact that he was a bit of a lecher and naturally subject to a malady that was called at that time, 'the lack of money, pain incomparable'. However, he had sixty-three ways of finding it at a pinch, the commonest and most honest of which was by means of cunningly perpetrated larceny. He was a mischievous rogue, a cheat, a boozer, a roysterer, and a vagabond if ever there was one in Paris, but otherwise the best fellow in the world; and he was always perpetrating some trick against the sergeants and the watch.[3]

One of the tricks almost certainly involved participation in the affair of the Pet-au-Deable.[4] This prehistoric boulder whose suggestively bulbous shape, 'une diverse grosse pierre de merveilleuse façon', led to its vulgar nickname of the 'devil's fart', or more accurately 'turd', stood in the rue du Martroi Saint-Jean, in front of a grand house, the home of two respectably pious ladies, 'Mlle' Catherine de Bruyères, wife of the king's notary, and her widowed daughter, Isabelle. She was dedicated to the self-appointed mission of converting prostitutes, a task mocked by Villon in his *Testament*, T, 144, where he encouraged her reforming zeal by graciously permitting her to preach from any good work except the Gospel, advising her not to visit graveyards, the very places where prostitutes congregated, and recommending her to sermonise in the Linen

Market where the noisy chattering of the women stall-holders would drown anything she said.

Early in November 1451 jesting students uprooted the Pet-au-Deable and carted it across the Seine to the Left Bank and the Mont St Hilaire on the hill of Ste Geneviève. A few days later, on the 15th, following the complaint of the aggrieved Mlle de Bruyères, the Provost, d'Estouteville, ordered Jean Bezon, Criminal-Lieutenant of the Châtelet, and some 'robustes sergents' of the Royal Watch to bring the stone back. Having found the Pet-au-Deable Bezon and his band had it dragged to the Ile de la Cité where they put it in the courtyard of the Palais Royal. Within a week students broke into the yard, recaptured the menhir, and returned it to the Mont Ste Geneviève where, by a megalithic coincidence, there was a small stone circle. A painting of it hangs in Ste Merri church showing Ste Geneviève, patron saint of Paris, sitting in the ring guarding a flock of sheep.[5]

To the students' grateful delight the indignant Mlle de Bruyères provocatively replaced the Pet-au-Deable with a smaller stone. Calling it La Vesse, 'the silent fart', the undergraduates appropriated it as well and set it on top of the Pet. Securely fastened with plaster and iron bands both stones were garlanded with chaplets of flowers and farcically married to each other. Night after night roistering students danced around the couple against a raucous background of flutes and drums greatly to the irritation of sleepless but intimidated householders. With the assurance of invincible youth the revellers became over-confident. Physically threatened passers-by, especially the police, were forced to pay reverence to the worshipful bride and groom. The rag lasted months, became over-boisterous and ended in disorder and death.

In the middle of this long-drawn-out and worsening episode at some time between 4 May and 26 August 1452, François Villon was awarded his MA.[6] The university entries stated that his bourse had been paid and that he had been given his Licentiate to introduce him to his new equals. And then:

Dominus Franciscus Montcorbier de Parisiis, no longer simple 'Franciscus' but 'Dominus', Master, Maistre ès arts. Tutored by Jean de Conflans of the rue de Fouarre he was conversant with the works of classical authors like Ovid, Aristotle, Virgil, Cato, Macrobius, Priscian, Juvenal, Martial and Boetius.

He may have hoped for a benefice, a living somewhere in the country, idly attending to his church and congregation, dreaming of some excitement, drudging his days away, declining into a dreary lethargy. But there was no benefice. Perhaps Notre-Dame interfered. One wonders what his life might have become, a struggle between vision and virtue, perhaps a medieval Gerard Manley Hopkins, a genius in the octet of his Miltonic sonnets, a dutiful Jesuit priest in the more mechanical sestet; or an even more unconvincing John Donne, transformed from a joyful rake into the Dean of St Paul's, a meditative minister who abandoned voluptuous pleasures, preferring the great anthems of the *Anniversaries* and the *Essays in Divinity*.[7] Villon was to be as perceptive and serious but with a bitter irony that was entirely Parisian.

Those days were to come. More immediately, the students were finding new diversions. A facetious tale, *Mariage des Quatre Filz Aymon*, described how tavern-signs were used as the wedding-guests of four bridegrooms. It became the inspiration for dozens of painted house-signs to be stolen leaving their dwellings in bewildering anonymity. One young man struggled to detach the whimsically named Truie qui File (Spinning Sow) but the ladder was too short, he fell, broke his neck. Other more successful culprits arranged facetious weddings for their captures. The parson of the Stag married the Sow to the groom of the Bear and promised to give the Papegault (Popinjay) to the Sow when she was married. Not content with the signs they also filched meat-hooks from the butchers of Ste Geneviève, fowls from the poulterers of St Germain-des-Prés, and cheerfully agreed to accommodate a generous young woman in one of their houses, l'Image de St Nicolas. The continual disruption and the lawless behaviour of hundreds of near-rioters terrified householders in the neighbourhood but Bezon complained that there were too many students to cope with, and of so many nationalities that he had an almost impossible problem over language when warning them.

In exasperation d'Estouteville told the Criminal-Lieutenant to quieten things down. Ugliness followed. On 6 December 1452, the Feast of St Nicholas, the police broke into the Maison St Étienne, the home and unlikely thieves' storehouse of a priest, Henri Bresquier, who was away at mass in St Julien-le-Pauvre. His furnishings were unclerical. In the rooms the marauding constables found house- and tavern-signs, two bloodstained levers, hooks, a lot of knives, even a little cannon, 'une petite couleuvrine'. At the furious Jehan Bezon's orders: 'rompez tout, prenez tout, et se aucun rebelle, tuez tout', 'smash everything, take everything, and if they try to resist, kill them', his men wrecked the place.

The church of St-Julien-le-Pauvre, with Notre-Dame over to the left. Villon would have known it well. (*Author photo*)

Beds, sheets, books, lecture-notes, money, clothing were stolen. At the nearby house of the l'Image de St Nicolas they broke down doors, smashed windows, broached casks of wine. Then they forced their way into the College of Coquerel, interrupted a lecture, arrested thirty or forty students and marched them off to the Châtelet with one sergeant jeeringly wearing an academic gown. Almost as an afterthought following the mayhem the wine-gladdened men had the Pet-au-Deable and La Vesse heaved on to a cart and hauled away. The obliging young woman, Boisoncourt, was taken from l'Image de St Nicolas and imprisoned in a deep cell at Petit-Châtelet, left for ten hours without food or water.[8]

The outcome was inevitable. On 9 May 1453 the Rector of the university with doctors, masters and eight hundred unarmed students, went in an orderly manner to the Provost at his lovely house in the narrow rue de Jouy near the Celestins. The university spokesman, Jehan Hue, soberly requested that the unlawfully detained students should be released. Apprehensive of trouble between the Church and the civic powers the Provost agreed to the demands. It was too late.

Contentedly returning along the constricted street to reach the wider rue St Antoine the procession had just reached the Ours (Bear) when it encountered a band of police under Commissioner Henri de Fèvre. There were too many people, not enough space. After the Rector had passed there was jostling as students tried to get by. Either alarmed or more probably looking for an excuse to put down those troublemakers de Fèvre cried out, 'A l'aide, au roy, à l'arme, à la mort, tuez', 'Help, in the King's name, to arms, to the death, kill'. Swords, daggers, axes were drawn.

The defenceless students fled for shelter, tried to get into houses, hid behind fences, cowered in gardens. Out of control and looking for revenge the police put chains across the streets to prevent escape, hunted their quarry down, stabbing and beating. Some students surrounded the Rector when a bowman, maybe belonging to a volunteer militia, the One Hundred and Twenty

Early thirteenth-century tower and wall of Philippe-Augustus near the Celestins, rue de Jardins-Saint-Paul, Paris. (*Author photo*)

Archers, aimed an arrow at him. A graduate, Raymond de Mauregart, was stabbed to death by Sergeant Jean Charpentier, another man was fatally wounded. Then Charpentier tussled with the Rector, threatening him with a dagger. The police were berserk. They beat and stabbed Canon Pierre Quoque, hurled him into the gutter, leaving him so severely hurt that the first barber-surgeon he found was unable to help him, and he had to find a second competent to dress his wounds.

Three days later the university suspended all lectures and sermons and the Rector demanded drastic reparations from the Provost. He insisted that all the officers, sergeants and constables involved in the assault, excepting the Provost himself who had contracted a convenient fever, should be made to kneel, bare-footed, bare-headed, without belts, holding a lighted wax candle and clearly, without mumbling, announce publicly that they had been guilty of brutality. Several sergeants were removed from the force and banished from Paris. On 16 June Sergeant Jean Charpentier, noose around his neck, was exposed in a cart, and taken on a pilgrimage of disgrace to the bishop, to the university, to the Court and finally to the Porte-Baudoyer near St Bernard's church. In front of the crowd he admitted his sins and agreed to pay the widow of Raymond de Mauregart four hundred livres in compensation. Then his right hand was cut off at the wrist by the public executioner, a loss which, as Wyndham Lewis mordantly observed, 'taught him a proper respect for Letters'.[9]

The Royal Watch was to found four chantry chapels, pay the university six thousand livres (pounds), establish another chapel for the parents of de Mauregart and give them two thousand livres for the loss of their son. On 6 September Jean Villain of Rheims was condemned to death for his activities in the riot.

There was bargaining. In January 1454, the Provost was to be examined for his involvement in the violence on condition that the ban on lectures and sermons should be lifted. In June, Jehan Bezon, the Criminal-Lieutenant whose words had incited his sergeants into destruction, was dismissed. Finally, on 21 August, a year and a half after the assault, sermons and lectures were to be renewed.

Nowhere, from the time that the Pet-au-Deable was first stolen from Mlle de Bruyères to the attack by the police and to the restitutions that ensued, does the name Villon appear. His upbringing guided him. A street-wise child he had learned very early in life the need for self-preservation, enjoying the amusements and entertainments but at the faintest murmur of danger drifting quietly into obscurity, alibi prepared, profile as inconspicuous as he could make it. The law never touched him. But by his own words he knew of the affair of the Devil's Fart because he claimed to have written a mock-epic about the stone and the house-signs and the revelries, *Le Roumant du Pet au Deable*, which Guy Tabarie is supposed to have copied. The saga was light-heartedly bequeathed to Guillaume de Villon.

Item, et a mon plus que pere
Maistre Guillaume de Villon

Item, to Guillaume Villon, more
Than father to me, gentler far
Than mother with her child; a score
Of scrapes he's got me out of – bar
This last that gave him quite a jar –
I beg him on my knees to let
Me well alone to make or mar
This mess for all the joy I'll get.

Je luy donne ma libraire
Et le Roumant du Pet au Deable
Lequel maistre Guy Tabarye Grossa, . . .

I leave my library for a start
To him – especially that work,
The Romance of the Devil's Fart,
That Guy Tabarie, honest berk,
Copied in notebooks which now lurk
Well out of sight. A lengthy tale,
One good enough to perk
The mind if style should fail. [T, 87–88]

If ever it existed it is lost. It may have been no more than a draft, one of Villon's first exercises in verse. Champion[10] wondered whether it had included some early ballades such as *The Women of Paris*, knowing Villon's fascination with the sights and sounds of the city, the church bells, the street cries at every corner, some in rhyme like the shouting of the hot-bath keeper: 'Seigneur, qu'or vous allez baignier, Et estuver sans delaier, Le bain sont chaud: c'est sans mentir', 'Sir, come to the baths straight away. They are warm, honestly!' He was one of a crowd.

There were sellers of cheese: 'J'ai bon fromage de Champaigne, bon angelots de Brie!' 'I have good cheese, from Champagne, little cherubs from Brie!, big and small, whatever you choose, all of them delicious.' There were apples, 'fresh from the woods, and firm whites from the Auvergne', chestnuts from Lombardy; tasty figs and raisins. There were the shrilling harangues of fishwives on the Petit-Pont screeching the perfection of their herrings, eels, bream, soles, haggling, keeping shrewd eyes for the light-fingered. There were drapers with bales of cloth on their stalls, measuring a demi-toise, a yard, of linen from the tip of their nose to the end of an outstretched arm. It was hubbub from morning to evening starting with the cry of the milk seller: 'Je crie du laict pour les nourrices pour nourrir les petits enfants', 'today's milk for the children' and the women from farms with their summer salads, spinach, lettuce, sorrel, parsley, marvellous chervil, everything for sale. Even the coal-man joined in with 'Charbon du basteau, charbon de jeune bois', 'only three sous a bundle and well worth going to the quay for'. Villon loved the commotion and the backchat.

Ballade of the Women of Paris

Quoy qu'on tient belles langaigieres
Florentines, Venicïennes, . . .

Il n'est pas bon bec que de Paris.

Though women skill in speech unfold
'Neath Tuscan or Venetian sky,
Yea, even when they're waxen old
On confidential errands fly;
Let Roman dames or Lombards try,
Or Genoese, support to draw,
Bring Piedmontese, Savoyards nigh,
There's none to match a Paris jaw!

The Naples dames, like doctors, hold
Discourses, and are never shy;
The Germans cackle, we are told,
The Prussian women shrilly cry;
But search all Greece or Hungary,
Or Gypsies of no land or law,
Castile, or Spain, and squeeze them dry,
There's none to match a Paris jaw!

All tongues of Swiss or Breton mould
Or from Toulouse or Gascony,
Two wives of Petit-Pont would scold
Them dumb, and all Lorraine defy
With England, Calais hold thereby,
(Behold this list of names with awe!)
Valenciennes too and Picardy,
There's none to match a Paris jaw!

Prince, Paris ladies claim the high
Reward of speech without a flaw;
Italian lips in vain may vie
There's none to match a Paris jaw! [T, 144+]
                              John Heron Lepper

The *Roumant du Pet au Deable* has vanished. Yet it is astonishing that anything at all of Villon's poetry has survived from those days before printing, existing only on perishable paper in precarious places. Knowing his wastrel, wandering life, miles and years away from the security of a room in Paris, sometimes in bleak prisons, it is close to a miracle that any of his poems were saved. One can only guess that from time to time he sneaked back to the city from his self-imposed exiles to store precious, newly composed poems in the safety of the Porte Rouge. Thuasne thought there was a hint of this in T, 127, 1274:

Item, et j'ay sceu, ce voyaige   Item, I learned during my travels (exile)

The world is just as fortunate to have the marvellous poems of Gaius Valerius Catullus, the first-century BC Latin poet whose works have survived whereas those of his equally talented contemporaries, Calvus and Cinna, are little more than a line or two. Catullus has much in common with Villon in his directness and seeming simplicity of style. He has tenderness, delicacy, wit, but he could also be explicitly coarse, even about prestigious contemporaries, as an excerpt from Poem 57 reveals:

Pulcre conuenit improbis cinaedis	Those filthy fairies, what a pair,
Mamurrae pathicoque Caesarique	The dirty buggers, Caesar and Mamurra

It was almost by chance that we have his poems, just one collection [V] 'from a far frontier' reaching his home town of Verona in the early fourteenth century and ignorantly wedged, so legend claimed, in the bung of a wine cask but, in fact, put away in an unused measuring vessel. The bundle is lost. A copy made of it [X] is also lost. But a second copy had been made of the original [V] and is now in the Bodleian Library, Oxford [O]. The first copy [X] also was transcribed, twice, and those versions are in Paris [G] and Rome [R]. Such was the fragile survival of a genius.[11] Villon was as lucky.

Today there are four very corrupt manuscripts of his writings dating from about 1470 to 1500: [A] from the Bibliothèque de l'Arsenal containing the *Testament*, a single ballade, *Ballade de Fortune* and the *Lais*; [B] from the Bibliothèque Nationale with only the *Lais*; [C] the most reliable and most complete, from the copy belonging to Henri de Cambout, Duke of Coislin and Bishop of Metz; and [F] from the copy of Claude Fauchet of Stockholm, perhaps the earliest. In it was most of the verse and one verifiable poem in jargon by Villon with another four very doubtful members of the canon. There is also the first printed edition [I] of 1489 by Pierre Levet, with the bulk of the poems and six genuine poems in jargon.[12] The edition is full of errors, as the poet Clément Marot observed in 1533 when producing the first good, though far from perfect, edition at the request of the king, François I.

In his *Prologue* he complained that:

Of all the good works printed in the French language there is none so faulty or debased as that of Villon and I am astounded, seeing that he is the best Parisian poet, that the printers of Paris and the locals of the town have not taken greater care of it. Out of love of his understanding and as a reward for what I have learned from reading his books I have done for these works what I would like to be done to mine if they had fallen into similar abuse. I have found so many muddles in the couplets and verses, in the tempo, the rhyme, the reason that I don't know what to pity the most, the works that are spoiled or the ignorance of those that printed it. Partly by means of earlier editions, partly by the help of old people who know the work by heart and partly by guesswork Villon has been restored to his former glory.[13]

This was almost wishful thinking, given the mistranscribed nature of half-remembered, often misunderstood texts, but since Marot assiduous editors have corrected many mistakes and just as assiduous researchers have found invaluable details of Villon's life. Among the medieval archives they turned semi-legible page after page of documents written in cramped dog-Latin on yellowing parchment by the yellow light of a gas-lamp as Auguste Longnon did for twenty years before publishing his discoveries in 1892. It must have been exhausting and frustrating, nothing to be found, the Revolution had destroyed all the evidence, roll after irrelevant roll, emptily endless days, then suddenly, VILLON!

In 1458: 'quod magister Franciscus Villon iverat Andegavis' and 'ung aultre complice nommé François Villon lequel estoit allé à Angers', 'another accomplice named François Villon who has gone to Angers'. In 1463: a letter of remission to Robin Dogis that mentioned 'vint vers maistre François Villon et lui demanda. . .'.

Anyone writing about Villon today owes much to Longnon, to Pierre Champion, Louis Thuasne, Lucien Foulet and, in

English, to Wyndham Lewis, Cecily Mackworth, Edward Chaney, John Fox and Barbara Sargent-Baur.

Thanks in particular must be given to Longnon for glimpses of how 1454 finished. Like every year in late medieval Paris it ended in a bustle of litigation that benefited only lawyers financially and the 'generous' Villon poetically. In August Guillaume Colombel, rich President of the Chamber of Judicial Enquiries, hence fittingly appointed as his executor by Villon, T, 181, sued Jean Gentreu for money. On 5 September Jean Merbeuf, a wealthy merchant draper to whom Villon left a cracked egg-shell 'filled' with outdated money, L, 34, lost a dispute over a new, woollen greatcoat he had promised Lorens Leignelet. Early in December Jehan de la Garde, valet of the King's chamber and supplier of spices to the Queen, was involved in a matter of 591 missing livres. Villon bequeathed him two seedy taverns, the Golden Mortar, L, 33, and the Keg, T, 137. A week before a wintry Christmas Pierre Fournier, an attorney at the Châtelet, was left some leather caps without earmuffs and some flimsy summer shoes, L, 20. The court ordered him to pay long-overdue rents to the bishop.

In the midst of all this the pious Catherine de Bruyères reappeared. Having recovered the Pet-au-Deable and La Vesse she brought an action on 12 October against Eustache Luillier. She demanded a portion of the inheritance left by a relative, Jean de Béthisy, that Luillier, a second Châtelet attorney, had denied her. Words like 'blame' and 'infamy' were exchanged. Nicolas Gossemart, yet another attorney, said that he took personal offence at the charge levelled against his client and demanded twofold compensations for the affront.[14]

Only the tedious researches of scholars have unearthed these dusty details and enabled many of the jovial, sometimes bitter, legacies of Villon to be understood.

3

Death in Painting, in Poetry and in Practice, 1452–5

The three and a half years between the beginning of 1452 and June 1455 may have been the happiest, most secure years of Villon's life with a home to live in, free from worries and with some money in his purse. Scholars have speculated that he had been employed as a teacher or acted as a clerk and scrivener in a lawyer's office as the many legal terms in his poetry suggest. With the entertainment of the Pet-au-Deable frolic to amuse him these were carefree days with carefree companions in boisterous taverns such as the Mouton where one could dine with and enjoy the comforts of the fillettes from the nearby rue du Franc-Mûrier. There were plenty of drinking dens for a well-liked versifier. Wyndham Lewis listed some:

In the rue de la Juiverie is the Pomme de Pin, Robert Turgis's place, where there will be a blazing log-fire and company he knows. From there it is but a step across to the Trou Perrette for a throw with the dice; and thence one may comfortably go on to the Grand Godet by the Grève, or the Plat d'Estain and the Trumelières by the Halles, or the Homme Armé by the church of the Blancs-Manteaux, or the Épée de Bois by Ste Merri. Nearer home in the rue St Jacques, opposite the Mathurins is the Mule; or across two bridges . . . behind the Precinct of Notre-Dame is the house of Fat Margot.[1]

Like Chaucer's friar and like that man's numerous disreputable brothers in Paris, 'he knew the tavernes wel in every toun'. These were young days of frivolous verses and giggling girls.

It is a likelihood, even a probability, that during those convivial evenings as the wine was poured and friends talked more confidentially Colin de Cayeux and Regnier de Montigny boasted of their part-time connections with the Coquillards, the villainous bands of deserters and escaped criminals that infested the roads around Paris. Even the name was sinister, a mockery of the pilgrims who travelled those desperate highways to the shrine of St James of Compostela at the far north-west of Spain. The disciples, James and his brother John, had been fishermen and the symbol of James, worn proudly on a pilgrim's hat, was a scallop-shell, a 'coquille St Jacques'. To the Coquillards, predators of pilgrims, the parodied name was a menacingly grim joke.

From Rouen down to Moulins and from Tours across to Dijon they were everywhere, loosely drifting bands of ruffians with secret dens in every town and with receivers in every town eager to buy their dishonest goods. Prey was abundant. From the Low Countries came pilgrims, the 'Pélerins du Nord', passing through Paris, some heading towards Tours and Poitiers on their 1000-mile long journey south-westwards, the more cautious majority taking the advice of the indispensable *Guide for the Pilgrim* and choosing the longer but safer route through Orléans and Blois. From the north-east through Trèves passed the 'Pélerins de l'Est', trailing through the busy sanctuaries of Chalons, Troyes, Auxerre and Vézelay, the meeting-place for travellers from Belgium, the Ardennes, Lorraine and Champagne, all of them awed by the marvellously sculpted tympanum above the great door of the abbey.

Wise pilgrims with money bought places and safety in large groups. Less well-to-do or more ingenuous wayfarers went alone or in defenceless twos and threes and the watchful, predatory Coquillards waited for them.

They were a motley of outlaws, anything from petty bag-snatchers to casual murderers, and they were a motley of nation-alities, French, Bretons, Netherlanders, Germans, Spaniards. The mixture resulted in a secret language, a polyglot jargon of elusive words: 'mariage' for a hanging, 'spelicans' for light-fingered

The elaborate tympanum of Autun church, Saône-et-Loire, on the pilgrim route to the shrine of St James of Compostela in Spain. (*Author photo*)

thieves, 'ange' for a hangman's assistant. For Villon to know the patois would be an entrée to the fellowship. The well-known names of de Cayeux and de Montigny in themselves were passwords. And if ever Villon had to leave Paris in a hurry the nearest hiding–place was the shop of a Coquillard barber at Bourg-la-Reine only five miles south of the Porte Rouge.

But behind these private pleasures and malpractices there were more public, more important matters for the authorities. There was the question of Joan of Arc whose vital role in the coronation of the Dauphin made her rehabilitation essential if Charles VII's claim to the throne were to be legitimised. And while the Hundred Years War persisted the French crown was always under threat.

At the king's orders the Second Enquiry into the legitimacy of the trial of the Maid of Orléans was held in Rouen from 2 to 8 May 1452 under the jurisdiction of Cardinal d'Estouteville. Twenty-one witnesses were called and after long deliberations the proceedings of 1431 were declared null and void. It meant nothing. The Pope, Nicholas V, was reluctant to offend the English and refused to act upon the findings. It was not until his death in 1455 that anything further could be achieved.[2]

Death came to Pope and peasant alike. It was everywhere. In the centuries of the Late Middle Ages there was a gruesome cult in western Europe. Painters and sculptors depicted the physical decay of the body in ghoulish detail: worms feeding on corpses, bloated toads palpating on dead eyeballs. In the north chancel of Tewkesbury Abbey the tomb of the last abbot, John Wakeman, has a mouse crawling on the decaying belly of his effigy, a frog squats on the neck, a beetle on an arm. Plays and Mysteries were astonishingly factual in their details. 'The rape of virgins was enacted with startling realism; in realistic dummies the body of Christ was viciously cut and hacked by the soldiers, or a child was roasted and eaten by its mother'.[3]

Death was a familiar in Paris. It hung from the gibbets. It waited in hospitals. It lurked in the eyes of beggars as they gazed at food on stalls and in shop-windows. It was announced in the shocking sermons of itinerant friars foretelling the imminent end of the world, urging repentance. It waited in the mouldering rubbish and festering ditches, in the lice and the fleas and the rats scavenging in filthy alleyways. The gloomy fascination with death persuaded young men and prostitutes to meet for their pleasures in cemeteries. Gallows like Montfaucon with their dangling, twisting, rancid corpses were favoured venues for midnight picnics.

Death could even be inspected at leisure in the centre of Paris. A popular pastime was to visit the graveyard of the Holy Innocents, the largest in the city, where the church in its north-east corner was dedicated to the children massacred by Herod. To the west was the busy covered market of the Halles, open twice weekly when the merchants, craftsmen and traders of the city had to close their shops and carry out business under the shelter of its four roofed halls.

The Innocents was on the other side of the Seine from St Benoît, hardly half a mile from the Porte Rouge. Around three sides of the cemetery was a busy, open-air street market whose day-long traders used tombs as stalls for their wares, book-sellers, clothiers, women selling cakes, iron-mongers, pedlars with ribbons and trinkets, tinkers, card-sharps and watchful pickpockets.

Inside the walls of the Innocents were eighty vaulted arcades where the wealthy dead rested in elaborate tombs. Above, in a second storey, were charnel-houses, ossuaries stacked high with skulls and bones. Every day more were added. Each week there were fifty, sixty, seventy deaths in the neighbourhood and day after day the sextons exhumed skeletons from old graves to make room for fresh burials. In unrecorded bundles the bones were muddled with the mouldering piles in the arcades, open to the ghoulish gaze of passers-by. It was reported that during the long siege of Paris in 1590 starving people desperately ground up bones to make bread. When the cemetery was finally closed in 1786 the remains of some two million skeletons were

The cemetery of the Innocents, Paris, with its tombs and charnel-houses.

(H. Roger-Viollet, Paris)

removed nocturnally and left in the quarries of Port-Royal which became known as the Catacombs.

On high days and holidays Parisians would go to the Innocents, walk around, stare at the jumbled, anonymous remains of former citizens. Villon had been there, had wondered at the sudden, permanent loss of identity.

Quant je considere ces testes	When I consider the dry bones
Entassees en ces charniers	In charnel houses, skulls lacking name,
	Which were the poor or the wealthy ones?
	Masters of Requests, men of fame
	Or common porters? Now the same.
	King's man, merchant, soldier, baker,
	To this none-ness they all came,
	Bishop like a candle-maker. [T, 162].

The charnel-houses were intriguing but the major attraction was the Danse Macabré.[4] On the walls of the arcade along the rue la Charronnerie, now the nineteenth-century square of the Fontaine des Innocents, there was a series of painted murals and slogans of death begun in 1424 and finished the following Lent. Among them was a pulpit for preaching the mortality of man. John Lydgate, the Scottish poet, saw the frescoes some time between 1426 and 1431 and mentioned 'Machabré the Docteur', a man lost to history. There had been a similar tableau in one of the cloisters of old St Paul's before the Great Fire of London destroyed it in 1666.

The Danse Macabré was a homily in pictures. In them the half-decomposed, sometimes shrouded, skeleton of a grinning, beckoning Death holding the scythe of Time clutched a line of men, pair after pair, Pope and emperor, cardinal and king, church before state, bishop and squire, down the social scale to bailiffs and astrologers, schoolmasters, soldiers, doctors, usurers, lovers, labourers, poor men, fools.

'He! fault il que la danse mainne	'Ah! Must I lead the dance, I who am a god
Le premier que suis dieu en terre?'	On earth?', asked the Pope.[5]

LE PAPE ET L'EMPEREUR

LE MOINNE, L'USURIER, LE POVRE HOMME

Two panels from the Danse Macabré.

Seven hundred lines later the fool replied. 'Now many who were enemies in their lifetime and at variance are now good friends and dance here in complete harmony. But it was death that reconciled them; death which levels wise men with fools. When God grants it all dead men are equal.' The arcades were demolished in the seventeenth century when the street was widened. A fair copy of the Danse Macabré can still be seen in the chapel at Kermaria-an-Ansquit in Brittany twelve miles north-east of Guingamp.

It is probable that Villon, who obviously knew the Danse as well as the charnel-houses, based his greatest trio of poems on the Danse and the brevity of all life: the *Ballades des Temps Jadis*, the 'Ballades of Times Gone By': first *The Ballade of Dead Ladies* with its famous refrain of 'Ou sont les neiges d'anten?', 'where are the snows of years gone by?', followed by the equally elegaic *Ballade of Dead Lords*, and ending with the *Ballade of Dead Priests*. Dante Gabriel Rossetti translated the first [T, 41+].

> Tell me now in what hidden way is
> Lady Flora the lovely Roman?
> Where's Hipparchia, and where is Thais
> Neither of them the fairer woman?
> Where is Echo, beheld of no man,
> Only heard on river and mere,
> She whose beauty was more than human?
> But where are the snows of yesteryear?
>
> Where's Heloise, the learned nun,
> For whose sake Abelard, I ween,
> Lost manhood and put priesthood on?
> (From Love he won such dule and teen!)
> And where, I pray you, is the Queen
> Who willed that Buridan should steer
> Sewed in a sack's mouth down the Seine?
> But where are the snows of yesteryear?
>
> White Queen Blanche, like a queen of lilies,
> With a voice like any mermaiden,
> Bertha Broadfoot, Beatrice, Alice,
> And Ermengarde the lady of Maine,
> And that good Joan whom Englishmen

> At Rouen doomed and burned her there,
> Mother of God, where are they then?
> But where are the snows of yesteryear?
>
> Nay, never ask this week, fair lord,
> Where they are gone, nor yet this year,
> Save with this much for an overword,
> But where are the snows of yesteryear?

Villon's is an intensely personal poetry. It breaks sharply from the traditions of the past, shunning the charming vacuities of courtly love with its impersonal vows of eternal adoration, choosing instead to write only of what the poet himself had seen and experienced. His poems are paradoxes. They are technically intricate and structurally perfect, proving him a master of the complexities of French verse, and yet the poems are the handiwork of a man reared in poverty and, as important, reared in the sprawling city of Paris.

In the Foreword to his scholarly analysis of the metre, syntax and vocabulary of the poems Fox wrote that

> It has become the tradition to begin a work on Villon in a highly imaginative way. In the opening scene of one, the night angelus is tolling dolefully as a thin sly-looking fellow sets out to join his confederates, with whom he has planned to rob the College de Navarre. Another begins with the gates of the prison at Meung-sur-Loire clanging shut, leaving a dark-skinned little man blinking in the bright light of day he has not seen for many a month. A third – the most startling of all – makes reference to the pubs off Tottenham Court Road, in which, so we are told, Villon would have felt perfectly at home. . . . However, I have no intention of playing the game according to these rules.[6]

For his own book with its literary examination of the themes, imagery and symbolism of the stanzas, ballades and songs Fox was entirely correct. His aim was different from that of the present author which is to write a biography. In this book the city and the poet's affinity with it cannot be omitted from the story of his life and achievements. There is an intimacy between Villon's sensitivity and the evanescence of everything he saw around him, an empathy that was born of his upbringing and his constant awareness of life's brevity. He would have approved of the story of the eastern monarch who commanded his wise men to depart for a year and then come back with a single sentence that would explain the entire world and its ways. They returned with one brief statement. 'And even this shall pass away.'

It would not be correct to claim Villon as the first of the Renaissance poets, a man who ignored the past and who was a complete innovator. He had forerunners such as Jean de Meung, the first of three poets associated with Meung-sur-Loire, a town just west of Orléans, the others being Villon himself and Gaston Couté who died there in 1911, some of whose sad poems were sung by Edith Piaf.

Both Jean de Meung and Villon disassociated themselves from the long-established traditions of the now-lifeless poetry of gentility. There were exponents of chivalrous poetry in almost every court where nobles such as Charles, Duke of Orléans, and René, Count of Provence, composed delicate ballades and songs in praise of ladies, extolling the gentleness of nature and the countryside.

The archetype for these visions of a never-never world was the mid-thirteenth-century idyll, the unfinished *Roman de la Rose* by Guillaume de Lorris, full of tender allegories and escapism such as the description of men and women in days gone by:

> And when at night they sought their rest
> No beds of down their bodies pressed
> But scattered they fresh, fragrant leaves,
> Or moss in heaps, or fresh cut sheaves
> Of grass or reeds, and heaven's sweet air
> Was ever soft and gentle there,
> In one unvarying tide of spring,
> While tuneful birds made morning ring
> With the sweet singing of their lay.

The verse is attractive and neatly written but it is as artificial as silk flowers in its absence of rain, cold, discomfort and reality.

One of Villon's earliest translators, John Payne, explained the difference between Villon's directness and the artificiality of courtly verse.

> The subjects usually chosen are love and chivalry, questions of honour, gallantry and religion, treated allegorically and rhetorically after the extinct and artificial fashion of the *Roman de la Rose*. Beautiful as is often the colour and cadence of the verse, we cannot but feel that it is a beauty and a charm which belong to a past age and which have no living relation to that in which they saw the light. In perusing the poetry of the time, one seems to be gazing upon interminable stretches of antique tapestry, embroidered in splendid but somewhat faded hues, wherein armed knights and ladies, clad in quaintly-cut raiment and adorned with ornaments of archaic form, sit at the banquet, stray a-toying in gardens, ride a-hawking in fields or pass a-hunting through woods, where every flower is moulded after a conventional pattern and no leaf dares assert itself save for the purpose of decoration. Here everything is prescribed: the bow of the knight as he kneels before his lady, the sweep of the chatelaine's robe through the bannered galleries, the fall of the standard on the wind, the career of the war-horse through the lists, the flight of the birds through the air, the motions of the deer that stand at gaze in the woods, – all are ordered in obedience to a certain strictly prescribed formula, in which one feels that nature and passion have ceased to have any sufficient part.[7]

In 1939 the novelist Raymond Chandler in *The Big Sleep* had his detective, Philip Marlowe, express much the same feelings. 'Over the entrance doors . . . there was a broad, stained-glass panel showing a knight in dark armour rescuing a lady who was tied to a tree and didn't have any clothes on but some very long and convenient hair. The knight had pushed the vizor of his helmet back to be sociable, and he was fiddling with the knots of the ropes that tied the lady to the tree and not getting anywhere. . . . He didn't really seem to be trying.'[8]

Jean de Meung, also known as Clopinel, finished the incomplete *Roman de la Rose* in a far more realistic style than Lorris, rejecting the staleness and sterility, using satire to emphasise his observations.

> Femes n'ont cure de chasti,
> Ainz ont si leur engin basti

'Women do not like to be corrected, but their minds are so formed that they think they know their own business without being taught, and let no one who doesn't want to annoy them take exception to anything they do.'

De Meung's view of the weather also differed from that of Lorris. 'The winds strive together and the sky flares up and roars and wails and splits open in many a place with thunder and lightning, drumming and rattling and trumpeting until the clouds are torn by the vapours they give rise to . . .'.[9]

Villon wrote in much the same mode with a direct honesty and realism. Untrammelled by the conventions of a court or the Church he could write what he wanted but, despite this freedom, he rigorously obeyed the severely limiting rules of French verse. The ballade had to have four stanzas, the first three of eight lines, the final Envoi a quatrain that always started with 'Prince'. The lines were to be of either ten syllables or octosyllabic, the syllables meticulously scanned. Added to these restrictions the poem had to adhere to a complex but very limited rhyme scheme of a, b, a, b, b, c, b, c. Within the ballade itself each stanza had to end with the same line such as 'ou sont les neiges d'anten?', a refrain which had to be consistent with the sense of each stanza.

Acceptance of these conditions was analogous to being locked in a doorless cell with immovable furniture, where the prisoner could put things on the shelves, set the table, decorate the walls, hang tapestries but never get out, never alter the fixtures. Villon, a craftsman of genius, worked fluently in the genre. He not only observed the conventions but even added to his difficulties by occasionally including acrostics of names letter by letter in the first words of succeeding lines, as in the final stanza of the *Ballade des Contre-Verités*, the Ballad of Contradictions, which he 'signed' line by line: Voulez, Il, Letre, Lasches, Orrible, Ne [PD, 7 (L, 4)].

For rhythm he wrote in duosyllabic trochees of / . / . / . /., using the sound-lengths of the words rather than their stress. In English poetry the stressed trochee produces a dah-di, dah-di, dah-di beat as in Longfellow's *Hiawatha*:

> 'Yes, if Minnehaha wishes;
> Let your heart speak, Minnehaha!'
> And the lovely Laughing Water
> Seemed more lovely as she stood there . . .

with a clunky, clunky, clunky beat like a mountain-railway's clicking ratchet.

Villon's choice of length rather than stress in the trochees, in effect long followed by short, — . — . — . — ., provided a more languorous, long-drawn-out effect. The Elizabethan poet-musician, Thomas Campion, achieved this in what T. S. Eliot considered one of the loveliest of all poems:

> Rose-cheeked Laura come;
> Sing thou smoothly with thy beauty's
> Silent music, either other
> Sweetly gracing.
>
> Lovely forms do flow
> From consent, divinely framed;
> Heaven is music and thy beauty's
> Birth is heavenly.

These dull notes we sing,
Discords need for helps to grace them;
Only beauty purely loving
   Knows no discord.

Then still moves delight,
Like clear springs renewed by flowing,
Ever perfect, ever in them-
   selves eternal.[10]

This was the rhythm of Villon also, sometimes light, sometimes with a heavy, pounding tread, or with a chirpy lilt as he wrote one of his legacies. His output, if we have it all, was not great, a pocketful, some quips scribbled in taverns, a rondeau or two, a few songs, poems composed at his table in the Porte Rouge just a few hundred yards from Mont Ste Geneviève and the Pet-au-Deable, quill and inkstand beside him, a word erased, lines written in a black Gothic script with its flourishes and long downstrokes, in the stillness hearing the movements of the words and their cadences.

We have little more than three thousand lines of Villon's poetry, only 320 in the *Lais*, 2023 in the *Testament*, 634 in the *Poésies Diverses* and 225 from the seven accepted *Poems in Jargon*. The best is in the first thousand lines of the *Testament* with its seven Ballades and in some of the *Poésies Diverses*. Internal evidence, a slippery but not entirely unreliable guide, suggests that some of his earliest writing, rather contrived and stiff, was written in decasyllables, the stately line of ten syllables with its rigid pause of a caesura at the fourth syllable, which for centuries had been the type preferred for medieval epics. Villon's greatest poems were written in the shorter, more fluent octosyllabic line.[11]

There is something remarkable. An almost unconsidered aspect of his work is its entire absence of love poetry. There is nothing like Milton's 'With thee conversing I forget all time', or Elizabeth Barrett Browning's,

If thou must love me, let it be for naught,
   Except for love's sake only

or John Donne's,

> I wonder by my troth, what thou, and I,
> Did till we lov'd?

or the anonymous,

> Western Wind, when wilt thou blow,
> The small rain down can rain?
> Would that my love were in my arms,
> And I in my bed again!

There is just one apparent but deceptive exception: 'Mort, j'appelle de ta rigueur . . .'

> Death, I plead against your cruelty
> Who took my only love away,
> And still, unsatisfied, you stay
> To keep me in this misery.
>
> No strength have I, no energy.
> How did she ever hurt you, pray?
> Death, I plead against your cruelty
> Who took my only love away.
>
> Two we were but heart just one.
> If it is dead then I must die
> Or if alive no life have I,
> Like a statue carved in stone.
>
> Death, I plead against your cruelty
> Who took my only love away,
> And still, unsatisfied, you stay
> To keep me in this misery. [T, 94+]

The metaphor of two people with one heart, 'Deux estions, et n'avions q'un cueur', has become a cliché but when Villon created it it was an astonishment. Yet poignant though the poem was Villon was not writing of a personal loss. He emphasised that he had composed it, a *De Profundis* for Ythier Marchand, in memory of his former mistresses whose names Villon would not mention as Marchand would hate him for ever if he did.

The legatee was to compose a tune for the orison and play it mournfully on a lute with its long neck and pear-shaped body.

The story of Marchand, who may himself have been pear-shaped as some verses hint, is enlightening. It reveals how the seeming simplicity of Villon's gaiety was often a veneer that covered laminates of darker jibes, frequently with obscene meanings. Little is known of Marchand.[12] Supposedly an old friend and university colleague of Villon's there is no proof of this. The man came from a wealthy family of dignitaries and financiers but the answer to why Villon should have given him a bequest is not straightforward.

In the eleventh stanza of the *Lais* the poet left Marchand a razor-sharp steel sword, 'un branc d'acier', the double joke known to all who heard it being that Villon never had anything as valuable as a sword. Even that was an irrelevance. He had already pawned the mythical weapon. On the surface this is a flippancy but there were hidden insults. 'Branc' could be a pun on 'bran', excrement, as though Marchand were 'a shit'. Worse, 'branc d'acier' was Parisian slang for 'un sexe érigé', an erect penis, a bequest from Villon that Marchand presumably had need of. The implication is that behind his generous 'gift' Villon, learning from some woman of the man's sexual inadequacy, was jeering at the impotence of a rich rival.[13]

Several years later in the *Testament*, T, 99, the sword was taken away from Marchand with an even more insulting refusal to describe its sheath. Then in T, 94, the names of Marchand's girl-friends were not revealed,

> pour ses ancïennes amours
> Desquelles le nom je ne diz

probably because there were none. Even worse,

> Au fort, quelqu'un s'en recompence
> Qui est remply sur les chantiers!
> Car la danse vient de la pance. [T, 25]

Which Bonner translated as:

> And so, let someone else take over
> who has tucked away more food –
> dancing is for men of nobler birth.

In this address to an apparently anonymous successor Villon is cryptically referring to Marchand, often spelled Marchant, and it is of interest to read how other translators have rendered the final two lines, T, 25, 199–200.

Line 199:   *Chaney*, Someone with a well-lined belly;
            Dale, Who has the stomach for the tarts;
            Saklatvala, Whose belly is filled and stuffed amain;
            Sargent-Baur, Whose tun's well-filled upon its frame;

and line 200:   *Cameron*, He dances best whose belly's lined;
            Chaney, The state of the paunch settles the dance;
            Dale, The dance is one for larger grafters;
            Kinnell, For the dance starts in the belly;
            Sargent-Baur, For from the belly comes the dance.

Constraints upon the translators to find apt rhymes inevitably caused discrepancies but there are impressions of a fat, overfed body clumsily engaged in sexual intercourse, the 'dance'. To understand this, a 'chantier' could be either a heavy beam in a cellar to support bulky wine-barrels or a stick used as a bung for the barrel, once again, slang for 'an inserted penis'.

In that stanza Villon cryptically identified his victim in an anagram. Qui esT RAMplY sur les CHANTIERs. The letters in capitals, TRAMYCHANTIER being rearranged as 'Ytier Marchant', someone derisively physically incompetent to take Villon's place in the 'dance'.[14] What is not stated is how Marchand had caused offence. As will be seen, an affair with a woman was likely.

Described as a 'slippery adventurer' by Kendall, he later entered the service of Charles, Duke of Guinenne, the younger brother of Louis XI. It is said that Marchand became the man the king most hated, 'dont il demeurera l'adversaire implacable'. In 1474 he was implicated in a plot to poison the king, was imprisoned and died mysteriously, probably assassinated, some time after March.[15]

What Villon's intentionally ambiguous references to Marchand do reveal are the poet's associations with women, many of them of variable social graces and activities. As Mackworth stated, 'There can be no doubt that an important clue to the real Villon is to be found in his relations with women. He frequented, in general, only the lowest type and avoided the fine ladies who would be less easily impressed with bravado. Yet he wrote some of the loveliest poems to women in the French language, heartbreaking in their sadness and longing, and which have kept their freshness and poignancy through the passage of five centuries'.[16]

In Villon there are chucklingly fond reminiscence of trulls and harlots he had consorted with, Guillemette the tapestry-maker, Jeanneton the bonnet-maker, Denise, Marion the Idol, Big Jeanne from Brittany, many others including two lovely young things from St Généroux in Deux-Sèvres,

Ice m'ont deux dames apris
....
Illes sont très belles et gentes
Demourant a Saint Generou [T,103, 1061–3]

who taught him the dialect of Poitou 'but ah'm not goin' to say jus' weah they pass the tahm, day in day out. Good Lawd! Ah'm not as dumb as that; ah keep mah romance to mahself.'[17]

However affectionate such memories were they were matters of physical enjoyment, not of love. The only woman believed to have impassioned Villon was Catherine de Vausselles. Little is known of her. She is considered to have been of a different social class from the others and, from Villon's writings, like a wanton she attracted him, encouraged him and finally spurned and humiliated him.

Item, a celle qui j'ay dit,
Qui si durement m'a chassé
Que je suis de joye interdit
Et de tout plaisir dechassé
Je lesse mon cueur enchassé.

Item, to her of whom I write,
Who so cruelly set me free,
Who forbade me all delight
And from pleasure banished me
I leave my heart enshrined to thee. [L,10]

And

Qui me fist macher ces groselles
Fors Katherine de Vauselles?

Who made me chew this bitter fruit
But Catherine de Vausselles? [T, 64+, 660–1]

With such emotion and with his early regard for the woman it is hard to believe that he had not written a single poem of love to her. One wonders if they had existed and had been destroyed when Villon was raging against her.

But all that was to come. The year 1453 was a good one – of good companions and good news for France. On 17 July John Talbot, Earl of Shrewsbury, 'the English Achilles', reluctantly attempted to relieve the siege of Castillon, a town in the Dordogne thirty miles east of Bordeaux. Facing him was a French army guarded by a dauntingly entrenched artillery park of three hundred cannon, a host of men-at-arms with batons-au-feu handguns, and detachments of archers. Talbot was the only mounted man. Riding his sturdy, short-legged cob, the silver-haired veteran was conspicuous in his crimson cloak of satin. He wore no armour, having given his word not to do so when released by the French some years before.

The attack was fierce but unsuccessful. Driven back by the un-ceasing cannonade and threatened on their right by a newly arrived Breton army the English retreated towards the Dordogne river. Talbot's horse was wounded and fell, trapping his rider who was killed by the battle-axe of an archer, Michel Perunin.[18] The manner of his death was military irony. The war had begun with victories for the archers of England at Crécy and Poitiers. They routed the French at Agincourt. But cannons defeated them at Castillon. Yet it was a French archer that killed England's most successful warrior while gunfire was driving his men from the field.

On 19 October the French recaptured the last stronghold, Bordeaux, and only Calais was left to England. It was the end of the Hundred Years War although no one realised it. There was no formal acceptance of defeat and England retained the empty title of King of France until 1801 during the reign of George III.

It may have been such news that caused Villon to write his 'Ballade against the Enemies of France', a poem in the ten-syllable heroic line. It is stiff, academically stilted in its conceits like an early experiment, PD, 8 (L, 5).

Rancontré soit des bestes feu gectans,	Let him meet beasts that breathe out fiery rain,
	Even as Jason did by Colchis town,
	Or seven years into a beast remain,
	Nebuchadnezzar like to earth bowed down.
	....
Qui mal voudrait au royaume de France.	Who would wish ill unto the realm of France.

John Payne

These were years of a poetical apprenticeship that produced delicate lyrics such as the rondeau, PD, – (L, 6 or 7), that tinkles like a five-finger exercise. The verse may not be his. It was not included in any of the authenticated manuscripts and was printed only in a slim volume, *Le Jardin Plaisance*, published by Antoine Véraud around 1501.[19] Eight of its nine pieces were repeated in other collections of Villon and can be accepted as genuine. The sixth, the rondeau, is unique and is frequently omitted from the *Poésies Diverses*. Yet it is a charming 'balon de joie'.

Jenin l'Avenu	Jenin l'Avenu
Va-t-en aux estuves	Go to the tub
Et toy la venu	And when you're there
Jenin l'Avenu	Jenin l'Avenu
Si te lave nud	Get in bare
et te baigne es cuves	And have a scrub.
Jenin l'Avenu	Jenin l'Avenu
Va-t-en aux estuves.	Go to the tub.

It lilts almost frivolously with three ingenious puns, 'la venu', 'l'Avenu', and 'lave nud', just the kind of word-play that Villon loved but, like Ythier Marchand's stanza, it may not be what it seems. 'Jenin' was not a common name. Rather, as Dufournet pointed out, it was a term applied to a henpecked husband, a meek man under the thumb of his wife.[20] 'L'Avenu' meant 'nothing', 'nobody'. As for the étuves, these were public baths of which there were over a score in Paris, usually to be found in back-alleys and culs-de-sac because many of them were no more than aquatic brothels.[21]

En petiz baings des filles amoureuses	In little tubs with women that give screws.
(Qui ne m'entant n'a suivy les bordeaux)	(You wet! You've not been to the stews!) [T,141+, 1449-50]

One infamous establishment, l'Image de St Martin, was owned by Jacques James, a legatee in the *Testament*.

In this light the rondeau can be reinterpreted as, 'Hey, down-trodden good-for-nothing, go to the baths, you know, nudge in the ribs, the "baths", strip off, and get yourself an accommo-dating "scrubber".' It reflects Villon's own sardonic humour.

These hidden meanings, entertaining though they are when decoded, are only one of the problems that make Villon difficult for the modern reader. In France today his vocabulary and spelling are often as archaic as lines in Chaucer's *Canterbury Tales*, a mixture of the plain and the perplexing:

> Thanne longen folk to goon pilgrimages
> And palmeres for to seken straunge strondes,
> To fernë halwës, couthe in sondry londes

or Langland's *Vision of Piers Plowman*:

> Ac on a May mornyng on Maluerne Hulles
> Me byfel a ferly of fairy me thou3t

Yet his sentiments and imagery can be brilliantly modern in translation. He made pictures of Paris like a camera, seeing everything, the bishop walking through the streets making the sign of the cross, friars gorging at tables of rich food and wine. He saw workmen, knew their language, quarrymen with pick-axes and shovels, 'fouÿr en carrière'; the barber with his basins and kettle, 'deux bacins et un coquemart'; mountebanks with performing monkeys, 'bateleurs, traynans marmotes'; mummers, magicians and flute-players, 'farce, broulle, joue des fleutes'. He saw old women squatting around a fire, reminiscing about good old days; younger women gossiping:

Regarde m'en deux, trois, assises
Sur le bas du ply de leurs robes

See them, two, three, carefully seated
On the hems of neatly folded skirts [T, 145]

This was his outstanding quality, the ability to encapsulate a scene in a few words, express the transience of life, the pain of a dying man:

> Death makes him shudder, swoon, wax pale,
> Nose bend, veins stretch, and breath surrender,
> Neck swell, flesh soften, joints that fail
> Crack their strained nerves and arteries slender.
> O woman's body found so tender,
> Smooth, sweet, so precious in men's eyes,
> Must thou too bear such count to render?
> Yes; or pass quick into the skies. [T,41]

Algernon Charles Swinburne

Writing for a small audience, men of his age, education and interests who would understand and guffaw at the insults and the double-entendres, he had the talent to be both concise and explicit, the gift to connect things that seemed to be opposites, linking them, fashioning them into new, brilliant images. Weavers removed loose threads from their woven cloth by brushing burning straw across the fabric, 'tient ardente paille', T, 28, and Villon likened it to the passing of a man's life. He quoted Job, VII, 6, 'My days are swifter than a weaver's shuttle'.

The Biblical simile was good. Villon's was better. The hand-thrown shuttle was fast but the extinction of the thread was instantaneous, a flash and gone. 'Mes jours s'en sont alez errant', 'my days go running away'. In 1455 the words were to be prophetic for the poet.

It was a critical year for him, one that transformed his life. It is sometimes claimed that 5 June 1455 was the turning-point of his career but knowing the company he kept, the women he consorted with, it is likely that what happened on that day could have happened on any day in any part of Paris. The facts are plain. On one of the holiest days of the year he killed a man. Worse still, the man was a priest. Quite typically, Villon wrote not one line about the incident.

The facts are plain but they may not be adequate. It must be remembered that we lack unbiased intimacies of Villon's life. There is no independent evidence from friends. Rabelais provided some anecdotes but that was seventy years later. Many details have been extracted from legal documents but they are bleak, impersonal reports. And to rely upon Villon to tell us the truth is akin to trying to make out the epitaph on a tombstone lying deep in the waters of a swirling river. Nothing is clear. There is no objectivity.

The fifth of June 1455 was the Festival of Corpus-Christi, Fête-Dieu, a day of city-wide celebration when green branches and bright tapestries and cloths decorated the houses, when masses were chanted, when children scattered flowers in the streets, when bells pealed and rang from every church, when processions with lighted candles and smoking censers, long parades of monks and friars, moved through Paris with the Sacred Host carried by the priest under the solemn, sacred canopy, this was one of the great days of the religious year. It was a joyously devout day with people standing at their windows, women with their heads covered, spectators crossing themselves as the Host passed by.

Late that evening, in the twilight, Villon in a short cloak was sitting on a stone bench in the rue St Jacques below the belfry of St Benoît-le-Bientourné. With him was a priest, Gilles, and a girl, Ysabeau, maybe the one with the irritating habit of ending sentence after sentence with 'Enné?', 'reelly?', T, 149. It was about 9 o'clock. Along the street came a priest and a clerk, perhaps drunk after the long day, and it may have been the clerk, Jehan le Mardi, who recognised Villon and pointed him out to his companion, Philippe Sermoise. A year later the embittered Villon had not forgotten the interference:

Et celluy qui fist avangarde	And the man who began it all
Pour faire moy griefz emploix	To bring down trouble on my head [L, 33]

and in his resentment at the outcome wished le Mardi to be infected with St Anthony's Fire, a painful form of erysipelas with its burning inflammation and discoloration of the skin.[22]

Le Mardi may have started the trouble but it was Sermoise who turned it into a fatality. 'By God, I have found you and will heat your ears', he shouted at Villon who rose in alarm only to be pushed down roughly. Three witnesses disappeared. With the streetwise discretion of Parisians Gilles, Ysabeau and even le Mardi instantly chose the safety of darkness.

What had enraged Sermoise has never been explained, a woman, a demeaning quatrain, an affair of the church, whatever it was he slashed Villon's upper lip with a dagger, gashing it into a stream of blood, disfiguring the poet for life. In panic and self-defence the seated Villon reached for his own dagger hanging from a belt beneath his cloak, stabbed Sermoise in the groin and ran for the shelter of the Porte Rouge.

One report said that le Mardi returned and tried to intervene. Another does not mention this. What is certain is that the wounded Sermoise chased Villon into the cloisters of St Benoît, staggering after him, dagger waving, that Villon picked up a heavy cobble and smashed it into the face of the priest, stunning him. Then realising that his unstaunched lip needed treatment, he rushed from the cloisters, across the gated rue de Sorbonne and into the rue de la Harpe where he went to a barber-surgeon,

Fouquet, purposely selecting a man who did not know him. The barber stitched the stranger's deep cut and then, as the law demanded, enquired his name and asked what had happened because the affair had to be reported to the Watch. Villon told him that Sermoise had been the assailant. All he had done was defend himself.

This is entirely Villon's version. He told Fouquet he had risen courteously, asking Sermoise, 'Good brother, why are you so angry?', offering him a seat. What followed was not his fault. It may be the truth. But when asked his name he did not answer, 'Villon' or 'des Loges' or 'de Montcorbier' but 'Michel Mouton', perhaps unconsciously because he had just rushed by the Mouton tavern in the rue de la Harpe. The pseudonym reappeared in the *Lais*, L, 18, 142, where Mouton is described as a 'changeling', maybe a reference to the alias.

Sermoise had been carried into St Benoît's prison where he was interrogated by an examiner from the Châtelet who, as the official report stated, asked if 'il alaste de vie à trespassement, il voulut que poursuite . . .', 'whether if he died of his wound, he wanted a hue and cry raised against Villon by his friends and others?' 'No', the priest pardoned and forgave Villon for his death, 'pour certaines causes qui à ce le mouvaient', 'because of certain reasons that moved him to do so'. After this rather equivocal exoneration he was taken to the Hôtel-Dieu hospital, where he died the following Saturday.[23]

Villon was summoned to the king's tribunal but distrusting the impartiality of medieval justice he had already fled to the Coquillard sanctuary in Bourg-la-Reine.

In his absence he was banished from France.

4

The First Exile,
June 1455 to January 1456

The year 1455 continued eventful. The rehabilitation of Joan of Arc proceeded. The Portuguese explorer, Alvise de Cadamosto, discovered the Cape Verde islands. Less than a fortnight before the killing of Sermoise the Wars of the Roses had begun in England with the first Battle of St Albans. In October a gang of Coquillards was captured at Dijon. In Mainz Johannes Gutenberg printed a Bible in movable metal type. And except for an occasional surreptitious return to the city for more of his guardian's money François Villon stayed away from Paris for seven months.

He wrote that he hid for a week with Perrot Girart, a licensed barber, 'barbier juré', of Bourg-la-Reine, T, 115, a man believed to be a fence for the Coquillards. It was said that his 'barber's shop' was a façade for something more disreputable and profitable, a brothel whose rooms were let out promiscuously, the only question asked being a request for payment. Girart's skill as a professed barber is dubious.

Even among the crude practitioners of medicine in the Middle Ages standards were demanded. There were justified fears that unskilled claimants could as easily maim as cure their patients. An accredited barber-surgeon could set fractures, stitch wounds and perform minor operations. He knew how to examine urine for its tell-tale colour, could bleed a client by making an incision above the elbow and letting the blood flow into a palette, a small brass bowl in which, Villon noticed, the blood would change colour to black or green when the moon shone on it, T,

141+, 1446. The fact that he termed Girart 'licensed' almost certainly meant the opposite, that the man was a quack and not an admitted member of the Guild.[1]

It was probably either Colin de Cayeux, the locksmith's son, or Regnier de Montigny, degraded nobleman, who had informed Villon of the hideout. The former was already notorious for his misdemeanours and more serious crimes which included his skill as a pipeur, a dishonest gambler using loaded dice. By 1455 he had been imprisoned twice in the Châtelet, was there again in 1456 and was finally hanged in 1460 as 'an incorrigible thief, picklock, marauder and sacrilegious scoundrel'. Surprisingly it was never officially proved that he had been a Coquillard. But Villon knew and said so in jargon.

Coquillars enaruans a ruel	Coquillards, on your way to Rueil
....	....
uon fist de collin lescailler	Colin, nicknamed 'scallop-shell',
Devant le roe babiller	A court made tell all he could tell,
Il babigna pour son salut	He babbled on to dodge the noose,
Pas ne scavoit oignons peller	With onion-tears he pleaded well
Dont lamboureux luy rompt le suc.	But still the hangman sucked his juice. [J, 2]

Regnier de Montigny, by contrast, was unequivocally denounced as a Coquillard. On a list of scores of ruffians captured in Dijon in 1455 a notary added some years later, 'Regnier de Montigny (mort et pendu)'.

Villon did not linger for more than a few days in the open death-trap of a hamlet as small as Bourg-la-Reine so close to Paris. He needed the anonymity of a city like Orléans eighty miles to the south, a tediously long trudge across the emptiness of the plain of Beauce. Other places were farther, Bourges nearly a hundred and sixty miles south of Paris, Tours about the same to the south-west, Angers about seventy miles more to the west. Villon must have hated the travelling. He had no liking for life in the open air. His attitude towards countryside was hostile, quite unlike English poets before and after him.

Over sixty years earlier Chaucer wrote of his pilgrims on their way to Canterbury, delighting in April showers that enriched the earth, soft breezes waving through the young crops, birds singing, the pious group riding through villages of half-timbered houses, trotting through rich oak forests and then out among cultivated fields where cattle and sheep grazed. Over a hundred years after 1455 the Elizabethan poet, George Peele, enthused about an idyllic sunlit southern England:

> When as the rye reach to the chin,
> And chopcherry, chopcherry ripe within,
> Strawberries swimming in the cream,
> And schoolboys swimming in the stream . . .

No birds sang for Villon. No strawberries grew. Instead, he tramped past burnt farmsteads, collapsing barns, abandoned hamlets, overgrown fields, miles of wilderness. The land was a lifeless waste of dead villages and desecrated churches like the convent of Vaux-de-Cerny where the last inhabitant was reduced to eating grass, 'grazing like an animal through poverty. He seemed more like a savage than anything else.'[2] This was the land that Villon saw. He longed for Paris. 'The countryside to Villon is a place where idle scholars may steal ducks out of ponds, where brambles grow that tear the clothes, where there are frozen rivers in winter and a hot sun in summer. He prefers to be a poet of the town.'[3]

But finally he reached the security and comradeship of Orléans and the meeting-places of the Coquillards. They were the unscrupulous remnants of bands of merciless écorcheurs, themselves deserters from Armagnac, Burgundian and English armies. In 1444 they had been employed by the Dauphin to fight against the Swiss whom they defeated in a bloody battle, 'the victory of St Jacques', at Basle. Four thousand of the ruffians were slain. Some survivors stayed in the army. The rest, unpaid, disinclined to work but intent upon a life of pleasure, returned to France where they coagulated into bodies of middle-aged veterans who preyed on anybody travelling the most dangerous roads in Europe.

In Switzerland they had been vicious. 'I have seen and heard about cruelties and atrocities such as no one has ever heard of before', wrote an eye-witness. 'It would be impossible to imagine the kinds of torture to which the écorcheurs submit the poor folk they hold in their hands.' Villages were burnt or ransacked. Peasants were held over smoking fires until they shrieked out where money was hidden.[4] The blackguards stole, raped and murdered. In France, secure in their numbers and their experience of weapons and warfare, unafraid of opposition from helpless villagers and ineffectual police, they were worse.

They were of many nationalities, mainly French but also Spaniards, an Italian, even a Scotsman, Jehan d'Ecosse, who had deserted from a Scottish detachment in the English army. Operating in loosely knit bands of hundreds, speaking their private jargon, scarred from skirmishes and warfare, two were described as earless, a punishment for having committed a minor offence. So great was the stigma of this disfigurement that a law-abiding thirteenth-century Englishman, John de Roghton, having lost an ear when his horse reared and kicked him, obtained a certificate to prove his good character.[5]

In the archives of the Justiciary of Dijon, a city 160 miles south-east of Paris, is a document of 1455 describing the Coquillard way of life. It was discovered in 1842 by the town's archivist and published by Marcel Schwob in 1890. 'Depuis deux ans en ça ont repairié . . .'.

For two years past there has infested, and still infests, this town of Dijon, a number of idle and vagabond companions who, on their entry and during their stay in the said town, do nothing except eat, drink and squander money at dice, at cards, at *marelle* [a challengingly agile form of hopscotch], and at other games. Most usually, and especially at night, they hold their assembly in a brothel, where they lead the filthy, vile and dissolute lives of ruffians and scoundrels, often losing and squandering all their money until they have not left a single denier. And then, when they have taken all they can from the poor, common prostitutes they frequent in the said brothel, some of them disappear, in directions unknown, and are absent, some for fifteen days, some for a month, and some for six weeks. And then they return, some on horseback and some afoot, well clothed and harnessed, with plenty of gold and silver, and once more begin, with those who await them or with new arrivals, their habitual games and debauchery. . . .

'Et en vrai, comme l'en dit . . .'

It is also a fact, as is affirmed, that some of the said Coquillards are picklocks of coffers, chests and treasuries. Others work with their fingers in cheating over the changing of gold to small money and back again, or in the buying of goods. Others make, carry and sell false ingots of gold and chains resembling gold; others carry and sell false jewels in place of diamonds, rubies and other precious stones. Others lie at an inn with some merchant and rob themselves and him alike, passing the booty to a member of the band; and then they lodge a complaint in the company of the said merchant. Others play with loaded dice and win all the money of those who play with them. Others practise such skilful tricks at cards and *marelle* that none can win money of them. And, what is worse, most of them are footpads and bandits in the woods and on the highways, robbers and assassins, 'some were even highwaymen and murderers', and it is presumed that it is thus that they are able to lead such a dissolute life.[6]

These were the desperadoes that Villon joined. Probably not reluctantly. The prospect of easy money while he waited for Guillaume de Villon to obtain the king's pardon for him was enticing. Two pleas had been sent in the separate names of François des Loges and François de Montcorbier. Until exonerated he could enjoy the good fellowship and ready cash of his new acquaintances.

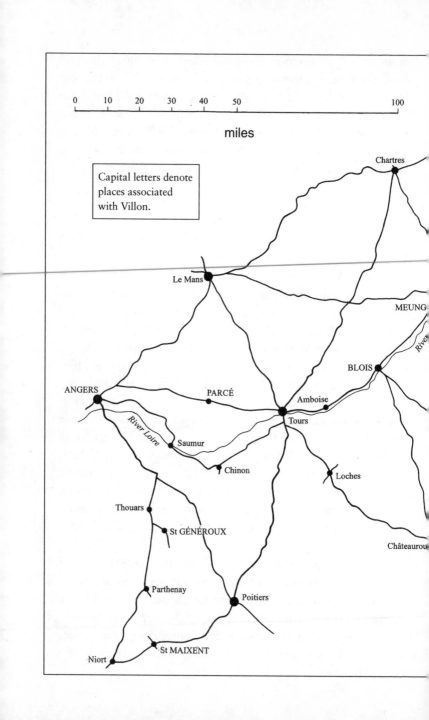

0   10   20   30   40   50   100

miles

Capital letters denote
places associated
with Villon.

Chartres

Le Mans

MEUNG

River

BLOIS

ANGERS   PARCÉ   Amboise

River Loire   Saumur   Tours

Chinon   Loches

Thouars

St GÉNÉROUX

Châteaurou

Parthenay   Poitiers

Niort   St MAIXENT

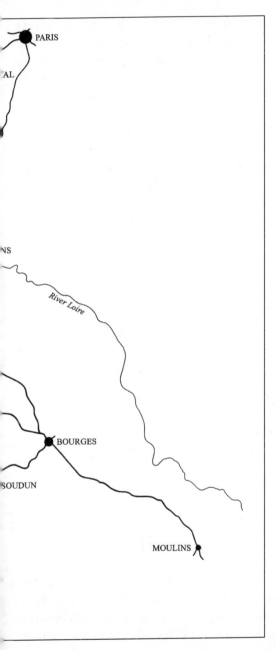

Map of Villon's travels.
(*Mike Komarnyckyj*)

The Dijon statement included a reference to the secret language of the Coquillards. 'Lesdiz compaignons ont entr'eux certain langaige de jargon . . .' and it fascinated Villon. The polylingual patois of a dozen tongues produced a virtually unintelligible vocabulary that even today remains such an almost unbroken code that many collections of Villon's work, French or in translation, omit the poems in jargon altogether. Some words have been deciphered by researchers such as Burger and Lanly. Most remain obscure. It is the mixture of devices that baffles. Some terms were onomatopoeic, 'babiller' for chattering being an example. Some were comparative. Ears became 'handles'. Some were descriptive, 'sur les joncs', 'on the straw', meaning being in prison where the floors were straw-covered. Others were sarcastic, 'montjoy' or hill of joy describing the gallows, 'banc', bench, also the gibbet.

It is a trackless marsh with few signposts for travellers to follow. 'Parouart' for Paris, 'gaigneur' for thief, 'beffleur' for a cheat are a few of the words that have been recognised but 'gours passans', 'la paillardie', 'l'evagi', 'eschiques', 'piarde', 'point à la turturie', all in Villon's ballades in jargon, remain anyone's guess rather than judgement.[7] But it is instructive to read what he could do with the language.

Maint coquillart escorné de sa sauve	Many a Coquillard deprived of his liberty
Et desboué de son ence ou poue . . .	and his ear and hand cut off . . .

Vive David! Saint archquin la baboue!
Jehan, mon amy, qui les feuilles desnoue!
Le vendengeur, beffleur comme une choue
Loing de son plain des sa flos curieulx.
Noe beaucop, dont il reçoit fressoue,
Jonc verdoient, havre du marieux. [J, 10. (Stockholm 4)]

Interpretation is elusive. David is thought to have been the saint of picklocks, 'baboue' was gambling, Jehan may refer to Petit-Jean who was to be an accomplice in a robbery, 'vendengeur' is accepted as meaning a cutter of purses, 'flos curieulx', simpletons easily duped, but then, 'if you're caught enjoy the fresh green reeds on the prison floor and the caresses of the hangman'. Curious enough but dangerous to have the verse widely known because the first words of the lines were: Vive, Jehan, Le, Loing, Noe, V, J, L, LO, N. It was almost a defiant signing of one's death warrant. Yet he actually bragged about his knowledge of the jargon. 'Je cognois quant pipeur jargonne', 'I know when gamblers speak the jargon', PD, 6 (L, 3), and even referred to himself as a 'jeune coquart', T, 72, 736, seemingly a 'young sillybilly' but just as probably a 'greenhorn Coquillard'.

In reality there was no danger. The only copies were his in manuscript. There would be no printing-press in France until 1469 when one was installed in the Sorbonne. The Coquillards might guffaw at his jests, witty rhymes and sly allusions but few of them could read or write. As long as the poems were taken to the secrecy of the Porte Rouge he could write in jargon, insert his name, insult the powerful, mock the law just as he wished.

The minor English poet, William Ernest Henley, so much enjoyed the challenge of the language that he composed a parody, 'Villon's Straight Tip to all Cross Coves' or 'Tout aux tavernes et aux filles':

> Suppose you screeve? or go cheapjack?
> Or fake the broads? or fig a nag?
> Or thimble-rig? or knap a yack?
> Or pitch a snide? or smash a rag?
> Suppose you duff? or nose and lag?
> Or get the straight, and land your pot?
> How do you melt the multy swag?
> Booze and the blowens cop the lot.
>
> Fiddle, or fence, or mace, or mack,
> Or moskeneer, or flash the drag;
> Dead-lurk a crib, or do a crack,
> Pad with a slang, or chuck a fag;
> Bonnet, or tout, or mump and gag;
> Rattle the tats, or mark the spot:
> You cannot bag a single stag –
> Booze and the blowens cop the lot.

Suppose you try a different tack,
And on the square you flash your flag?
At penny-a-lining make your whack,
Or with the mummers mump and gag?
For nix, for nix the dibs you bag!
At any graft, no matter what,
Your merry goblins soon stravag –
Booze and the blowens cop the lot.

ENVOY

It's up the spout and Charley Wag
With wipes and tickers and what not;
Until the squeezer nips your scrag,
Booze and the blowens cop the lot.

Villon might have enjoyed the humour. It is equally probable that his felonious comrades enjoyed the ballads he wrote about them and their exploits.

Like them he also had to leave from time to time in search of money. Where he went is unrecorded. He could gone on to Bourges seventy-six miles beyond Orléans, even to Angers a hundred and thirty-three miles to the west where it was said that he had an uncle. In 1456 he wrote that he intended to go there, 'Adieu! Je m'en vois à Angiers', L, 6, 43, although this may have been intended to mislead.[8] Yet, as will be seen, there is persuasive evidence that he did go to the city in 1455.

Where he went is questionable. How he travelled is known from his own statement that he disguised as himself as a pedlar, one of a wandering population of minstrels, clowns, rogues and ne'er-do-wells, a 'povre mercerot de Renes', T, 42, 417, 'a poor pedlar from Rennes', a place he never saw but which was the headquarters of the Mercers Guild. 'Pedlar' was a euphemism. The men were notorious for deceit, theft and general wrongdoing. That Villon chose to become one strongly suggests that the poet who had left Paris with an affectionate reputation for dubious pranks and minor felonies had turned into a serious criminal. Consorting with malefactors, learning how to snatch purses, cheat at cards, pick the locks of doors and chests, heartless in the acquisition of money, over the months he changed from a petty, opportunistic rogue into a wrongdoer prepared to swindle, rob and burgle to keep himself in comfort.

One can imagine him along the rutted tracks and lanes, bale on his back filled with tawdry knick-knacks for gullible village girls: laces, bright ribbons, strings for lutes and harps and viols, lengths of cheap cloth, garish jewellery, writing materials, rosary-beads, coloured pictures of saints, toys, a package of rubbish as a passport against suspicion. The roads were invitations to suicide. There was a saying, 'Qui porte l'argent porte la mort', 'carry money, carry death'. Villon did not carry money. He carried the petty trivialities of an honest hawker to satisfy officers of the law and he carried the jargon that proved him a confirmed Coquillard if he should be accosted by other members of the underworld. As long as the weather was good he could go where and as he fancied, even to Angers.

It has been claimed that he could not have gone as far as that, nearly two hundred miles from Paris, but simple arithmetic shows this to be incorrect. He was away for over seven months. Even passing half that time carousing with congenial, equally indolent comrades and even loitering from village to village over the remaining days at an idle eight miles a day he could have covered nearly eight hundred miles, a distance that would have taken him on an ambitious and quite improbable grand tour from Paris to Orléans, eighty-one miles, to Tours, seventy-two, to Angers, sixty-eight, return to Tours, sixty-eight, on to Bourges, ninety-six, down to Moulins, sixty-three, the region of his family, and then the long return to Paris, two hundred and fifteen, a total of six hundred and sixty-three miles. Allowing a more probable rate of ten miles a day, still quite slow, he could have covered a further two hundred miles. These calculations introduce a curious mystery.

It was not only the archives of Paris that scholars investigated. Those at Orléans, Bourges, Angers, even Chartres were rummaged through for Villonesque snippets and it was from Treasury documents at Chartres that in 1873 Auguste Vitu came upon an account of two robberies. Except for Thuasne the affair has inexplicably been disregarded by nearly all writers about Villon. They were probably mistaken.[9]

In October 1455 a young man of nineteen was arrested in Angers for having stolen twenty-six gold écus from Guillaume des Pres in Parcé, now Parçay-les-Pins, in Poitou, a small town twenty miles north of Chinon and halfway between Tours and Angers. He then went thirty miles to Angers where he broke into Jehan le Gay's dwelling, taking goods valued at two hundred écus, many thousands of pounds in modern currency.

Trying to sell some of the articles he was arrested. At the civil court he claimed to be a clerk and was transferred to the custody of the Bishop of Angers from whose inadequate prison he promptly escaped. Re-arrested in a tavern late at night he was locked in the temporary lodging of the Seigneur de Champagne. He got away. Once again he was caught. This was 'le cas d'un certain Jehan des Loges, mercier, et natif du pays d'Anjou', the man Jehan des Loges, pedlar and native of Anjou as he claimed in his petition, 'umble supplicacion', to the king, pleading, quite unconvincingly, that only extreme poverty, 'par povreté', had led him to these desperate measures and larcenies, 'furs et larrecins'.

A considerable disadvantage for the accused of these 'humble supplications' was that they had to be both full and true. One omission, one mistake, one falsity and the whole statement was invalidated leaving the appellant guilty. Knowing this, just as the accused would have done, it is worth considering whether the suspected thief could have been François Villon.

The testimony claimed that Jehan des Loges was a pedlar. Villon himself said that he was. The suspect stated that he was a clerk. Villon was. Des Loges was nineteen. Villon must have been about twenty-four but in the absence of birth-certificates and, presumably, with a youthful appearance, an apparent age in the teens might elicit more sympathy. Des Loges had committed a crime in Poitou. Villon had been to Poitou, T, 103,

104. The accused averred that he came from Anjou. Villon's mother was an Angevine. Both men were named 'des Loges'.

Six such comparisons are too many to be dismissed as coincidence. There have been only two objections to identifying Jehan des Loges as François Villon. The first, that he could not have reached Angers, has been disproved. The second was that the housebreaker called himself 'Jehan' rather than 'François'. This is not an obstacle. It was a desperate attempt at evasion. Only a month or two before October the king had received a request for pardon from François des Loges for the killing of Sermoise. To have the same man appealing for mercy in the same year for having broken into two houses was almost a guarantee of the gallows. The slight change of name to confuse the king's attorneys is explicable.

From this it is likely that Jehan des Loges and François Villon, competent burglar but incompetent fugitive, were one and the same. It becomes almost a certainty when the legal records reveal that the accused was released on the offer of immediate repayment of some of the stolen money and a promise that the balance would be given back within two years. No medieval court would accept the worthless word of a worthless pedlar for the return of a small fortune. There must have been a reliable surety. In 1458 Villon's friend, Guy Tabarie, testified that the poet had gone to see his wealthy uncle in the abbey of Angers and it may have been he, with the assistance of Guillaume de Villon, who obtained the freedom of 'Jehan des Loges'. In 1456 Villon wrote that he was going to Angers, 55 L, 6. He may have had to return there to appear before the court as a condition of his release. The remainder of the money had been paid by December 1457.[10] The affair plausibly was the first of Villon's fortunate escapes from the severity of fifteenth-century justice.

But the protective Coquillard world was crumbling around him. With the ending of the war civic authorities could concentrate upon the elimination of the scoundrels that had taken advantage of the lawless conditions. In the same month that 'Jehan des

Loges' was being tried another Jehan, Rabustel, the public prosecutor of Dijon, arrested several Coquillards. Among them were Regnault Daubourg; Dimanche le Loup or Sunday the Wolf; and a barber, Perrenet le Fournier. Even under torture Daubourg said nothing but the Wolf and le Fournier were rapidly persuaded to inform against their fellows. In his almost incomprehensible jargon le Fournier gave the names of sixty-four local Coquillards, adding that there were probably hundreds of others around Dijon. One of the names was that of Regnier de Montigny.

Acting upon the information Rabustel raided the brothel of Jacquot de la Mer, the Dijon headquarters of the Coquillards, arrested nine or ten, had them tried and hanged. Le Fournier and the Wolf had their sentences commuted. Their revelations were passed on to the Prosecutors of other regions and more ruffians were taken into custody over the months as far away as Orléans and Saumur near Angers. Others went into hiding. Villon departed for safer places.

Two years later Jacquot de la Mer was found guilty of counterfeiting money. Such forgery was an offence against one of the king's most fundamental rights, that of issuing currency, and the punishment was one of the cruellest inflicted upon malefactors, 'pour boulli dans une cave d'huile bouillante comme faulx monnoyer', 'to be boiled in oil for the crime of forging money'.

In Paris the public executions were held in the Marché des Porceaux, the Pig Market near the Porte St Honoré. The heavy vat of oil was suspended above a large stone slab on which kindling had been laid. The convicted man, trussed hand and foot, was lowered into the cool oil and the fire was lit. To spectators the special attraction was that death was not instant but could take a long time, the screams intensifying, the long hooks of the executioners preventing the dying man from writhing out of the boiling, bubbling liquid. Villon knew.

Pour eschever de la soe	Miss the risk of the Sow's hot graces
Danger de grup en arderie	Where the grip of the claw and the rising heat
Fait aux sires faire la moe.	Make frying men pull doleful faces. [J, 6]

There was better, less distressing news. The reputation of Joan of Arc, La Pucelle, 'the virgin', was gradually being restored. On 21 July the new Pope, Calixtus III, had allowed the petition of Isabel Romée, Joan's elderly mother and her two sons and on 7 November they were heard in Notre-Dame by four judges. Political and ecclesiastical expediency demanded that the verdict should condemn neither the 1431 court nor offend the English. To the contrary, it was proposed that Joan had been too ignorant and unlearned to have understood the serious charges brought against her. Because of this a formal request for her rehabilitation could be allowed. After ten days' deliberation the request was approved and 12 December was fixed for the beginning of the appeal.[11]

It was probably around that November that Villon decided to get closer to Paris to learn whether his request for a pardon had been granted. If he was in or near Angers the most direct route would have been through the war-worn towns of Le Mans, Chartres and Rambouillet about twenty-five miles south-west of the capital. Once there he may have remembered what the barber, Perrot Girart, had told him about the infamous abbey of Port-Royal only a few miles away. A hundred and fifty years later it was to be transformed into a model of piety under the guidance of its new abbess, Angélique Arnaud, only eleven years old but from an influential family of lawyers who averred that she was seventeen. What they said about her sister, Abbess of St Cyr, five years of age, is unrecorded. But that was in 1602. In 1455 the abbey had a very different fame as the corruption of its name, 'Pourras', 'rotten-ness', implies.

It was degenerate. On the death of the abbess, Michelle de Langres, around 1454, her place was taken by Huguette de Hamel, lascivious daughter of Hugues Cuilleret, the irreligiously debauched abbot of St Riquier. She was in her early forties and although a nun for some years had a lover, Baude le Maître, whom she appointed attorney to the abbey. It was a poor place, dilapidated, the countryside around it in the Chevreuse valley derelict and without money. It has already been noted that the village of Chevreuse just three miles south of the abbey contained only a tenth of its peacetime population. In the abbey itself there was just one novice but Huguette had energy and enthusiasm for many things in life. She soon recruited four or five more although, as Dale dryly observed, 'she was more likely to initiate her novices into sex than religion'.[12] Villon may have rushed there.

Rumours soon rippled, spread, became louder, that the abbess went to masked balls and revels at night, more like orgies than seemly parties, she disguised but so openly promiscuous that knowledgeable soldiery composed bawdy verses about her. It was dangerous. Whatever her morals de Hamel held high rank in the church and the penalty for being proved guilty of defaming a lady could be fierce. Villon would learn this. The author of the insulting couplets learned it sooner but briefly. He was thrashed at the stake so severely that he died.

Some years later two more than dubious and unquestionably foul-mouthed acquaintances of Villon, Casin Cholet and Jehan le Loup, Sergeants of the Verge ostensibly safeguarding the quay-sides of Paris but actually plundering them, swore at another abbess, Driete, calling her 'ribaud mariée, putain et paillarde', 'married slut, whore and tart'. They were both imprisoned.[13]

In the *Testament*, T, 115, there is a cryptic allusion to Huguette de Hamel claiming that she could confirm Villon's delight at the 'good, plump porkers' supplied by the barber at Bourg-la-Reine.

. . . de cochons gras	. . . of good, fat pigs,
Tesmoing l'abesse de Pourras.	Witness the Abbess of Port-Royal.

Rather than the succulence of roast pork this has been interpreted as the enjoyment of women at Port-Royal on the barber's recommendation. From what is known of the abbess she would not have discouraged such amorous explorations.

One of the most widespread stories about her concerned an adolescent novice, Alison, newly arrived and uninitiated. The initiation was to come. Huguette de Hamel and Baude le Maître, both naked, were indulging themselves in a communal bath. In a tub alongside them was Baude's cousin, a young man of Villon's age. The abbess instructed the young girl to take off her clothes and join the cousin. Alison refused. Baude grabbed her and dropped her, robes, shoes and all, into the water in which, shocked, drenched, the novice 'fait bien obligée lui fut bien de se dépouiller', was forced to undress, and in her enforced nudity in the warm water alongside the enthusiastic cousin 'la journée comme bien l'on pense', 'the day's work ended as might be expected'. There was a report that the no-longer-maiden was later sold to Huguette's father.[14]

News of the dissolute activities in the abbey were widespread and even in the ecclesiastical laxity of postwar medieval France the church could not ignore the increasing scandals. In 1463 de Hamel's superior, the abbot of St Chaalis, had her incarcerated on the far side of Paris in the prison of the abbey of Pont-aux-Dames in Meaux, a place of internment for important but abandoned women. Released in 1469 the abbess returned to Port-Royal, found Baude, took all the abbey's money, four hundred and eighteen livres, and faded into luxurious obscurity.

For Villon there was good news. In January 1456 his pardon arrived. He had used both his surnames, de Montcorbier and des Loges, applying to separate Chancelleries in the hope of receiving at least one Letter of Remission. In the event he received two, one from the Grande Chancellerie, addressed to "'Maistre François des Loges, autrement dit de Villon', and the other from the Petite Chancellerie, to 'Maistre François de Montcorbier', in which it was stated that he had been summoned earlier, had failed to present himself and had been banished.[15] The first Letter stressed that he had until then been of good character. The royal warrant therefore pardoned and acquitted François des Loges of all punishments and enjoined the Provost of Paris and his officers not to deprive him of any rights. 'Given at Saint Pourcain, in the month of January in the year of grace 1456'.

The second Letter awarded to François de Montcorbier differed slightly. Jehan le Mardi, who in the first Letter had run away with Gilles and Ysabeau, in the second had returned, had seen Villon with a dagger and a stone, tried to disarm him but failed to prevent the stone being flung into Sermoise's face. Only in the Remission to François des Loges was there a mention of 'Michel Mouton'.

Such Letters were usually presented after the person concerned had given himself up but if he had run away relatives, parents and close friends could apply on his behalf, explaining clearly the circumstances for which a pardon was asked. Normally the accused had to appear in person before the Court with his Letter of Remission. In Villon's case this formality must have been waived, probably because of Guillaume de Villon's impeccable reputation. There is no evidence of Villon's having appeared personally. Whatever had happened in Angers he was home and at liberty in Paris.

The First 'Testament', Villon's Legacies, 1456

It was a critical but abbreviated year for Villon. He returned to Paris after 1456 had begun. He left it before the year ended. He started as a free man. If he committed any felonies during the spring, summer and autumn they are unrecorded and, presumably, undetected. It was the year of a miserable affair with a woman. It was the year when he dashed off amusingly spurious bequests to friends and associates, and to those officials and pompously important people that he despised. And if the greater part of the year had been a unlikely time of honesty or, more probably, a lucky period of police inefficiency it concluded in a burst of larcenies and a burglary after which he went into his second, self-imposed, exile.

It was the year for another exile. Louis, Dauphin and estranged son of Charles VII, had retired to the Dauphiné in the far south-east of France. From there he pleaded with his father to allow him back to court. The weak-willed and resentful king not only refused but despatched a force to arrest him. In August the Dauphin, always more intelligent and resourceful than his parent, fled to Brussels and the Burgundian court of Philip the Good, a man loathed and dreaded by Charles VII.[1]

It was also the year of three women. Joan of Arc's reputation was finally vindicated. The behaviour of the coquette and wantonly flirtatious Catherine de Vausselles led to humiliation and deep bitterness for the poet. And 1456 was the year when La Belle Heaulmière died, she whose beauty had been the envy of every woman in Paris, who had power over 'merchants, clerks and churchmen', but who died old, ugly and penniless. Her lament for the decay of her body was quoted in the Preface. Villon saw her in her great old age, a hag. Today even her proper name is unknown. Born around 1375 she became the mistress of a rich and well-connected canon of Notre-Dame, the physically powerful Nicolas d'Orgement, known as 'the Lame' because an accident had left him with only one foot. Defying church law he installed the young woman in a house, le Queue de Renard (the Fox's Tail), in the precincts of the cathedral. The affronted Chapter evicted her. D'Orgement kept her in luxury elsewhere.[2]

Over twenty years later, in 1416, the king imposed an exorbitant tax on the citizens of Paris. There was a plot against him. D'Orgement and two others were arrested. On 24 April they were paraded through the streets in a filthy rubbish-cart, 'une charrette infamante', and taken to the Halles where his companions were beheaded. His goods were sequestered and he was sentenced to perpetual confinement in the underground prison of the Bishop of Orléans in Meung-sur-Loire, condemned to endure 'the bread of pain and the water of anguish'. Conditions were so bad that despite his strength he went mad and died within six months aged forty-six. Villon would know the horrors of the place almost fifty years later.[3]

Without support and in her forties la Belle Heaulmière went to a man who maltreated her despite her favours. 'I refused it to many a man, which was not very clever', she regretted, 'for no other reason than that I loved that untrustworthy fellow', T, 49, 469. The liaison did not last. He died around 1426 leaving her with only the mean streets for a livelihood at a time when both the Church and the civil law were determined to clear prostitutes off the streets. By Parisian irony, one of the congenial duties of Perrinet Marchand, lustful sergeant of the Châtelet, was the surveillance of harlots, especially in the rue de la Pute-y-Musse, Whore Street. Villon twice bequeathed him bales of straw and sacking for the hard floors of 'his' brothels, L, 23; T, 73; T, 108. In 1456 Pierre Lomer d'Airaines, a clerk of Notre-

Dame, was given the task of expelling the women from 'certain houses in the Ile de la Cité'.

To mislead the authorities and avoid harassment many prostitutes attached themselves to a respectable occupation by day. Villon knew many of them: Jeanneton the bonnet-maker; Guillemette of the tapestries; Blanche the cobbler; Catherine the seller of purses, T, 56+. The real names of the glover, the sausage-girl, even the widely famed Belle Heaulmière of the helmet and armour trade have been lost. But she was immortalised. One of Villon's greatest poems was about her, T, 47–56.

Advis m'est que j'oy regreter	Methought I heard in great distress
La Belle qui fut Hëaulmiere	That ancient woman thus complain
Soy jeune fille subzhaicter	Who was the beauteous armouress
Et parlez en telle maniere	And wish herself a girl again:
'A' vieilliesse felonne et fiere	'Ah age, so fell, whom all disdain,
Pourquoy m'as si tost abatuer?	Why hast thou conquered me so soon?
Qui me tient, qui, que ne me fiere	What hinders me to strike amain
Et qu'a ce coup je ne me tue?'	And find the stroke of death a boon?' [T, 47]

J.H. Lepper

To translate a great poet into great poetry in another language is an impossibility whatever the talent of the translator. A few lines at the end of this elegaic poem are sufficient to show this. Villon has the aged armouress talking about herself and some friends:

> . . . povres vieilles sotes . . .
> Tout en ung tas comme pelotes
> A petit feu de chenevotes
> Tout allumées, toute estaintes
> Et jadis fusnes si mignote [T, 56, 529–31]

to be literally translated as, 'poor, stupid old women squatting . . . all in a heap like balls of wool, around our tiny fire of bare hemp-sticks, quickly lit, quickly put out, and once we were so lovely . . . '. Five short lines, little more than twenty brief words. But it is the work of a genius.

Poetic shorthand was one of Villon's strengths. Where contemporaries were sincere but long-winded he was sincere but succinct, stripping a thought to its essence. A typical example of this was how contemporaries expressed the idea of laughing through one's tears. Charles, Duke of Orléans, wrote:

Je ris des yeulx, et mon coeur pleure	I laugh with eyes and my heart cries

Alain Chartier wrote:

Ie pleure ens, et me ry par dehors	crying within, and laughing outside

Jean Molinet wrote:

Ma bouche rie et mon povre cueur pleure	My mouth laughs and my poor heart cries

Villon wrote:

je rie en pleurs	I laugh in tears.[4]

It is short, sharp, direct. The same is true of his words about the old women. The images are brilliant in their simplicity, the women slumping there like lumps. Everything is precise, even the physical description which had a subtle metaphysical undertone. The hemp fire blazed brightly but did not last. Like life itself. It is a perfection of economy in its delicate choice of words. Villon did not write of 'des tiges du chanvre', stalks of hemp, as most translators have read 'chenevotes'. That word means not just hemp-stalks but hemp-stalks from which the tow-coloured fibres had been stripped.[5] Villon knew that it flared even more quickly but did not last. The metaphor is exact.

It is, of course, not what the old woman said but what Villon saw. In that sense it is a man's poem. What Villon gives is an impression of the appearance and the despair of lost beauty.

It is the pathos underlying the misery of the 'povres vieilles sotes'; more than that it is the feeling that Villon himself has for the old women, a feeling so strong that he almost identifies himself with them. It is owed to the fact that his own experiences provide the starting point for his soundings of human misery. . . . When he writes in the third person it is in the spirit of the first person, and when he writes in the first person the spirit of the third is never far away. . . . With Villon nothing stands between the writer and the reader. Could this, after all, be the explanation of the mysterious life and the magic of the poetry that Siciliano finds in Villon's verse and not in that of his contemporaries?[6]

Villon often is known only for one beautiful line, 'où sont les neiges d'anten?', 'where are the snows of one year past?', but he was much more than a genuine one-line poet like John William Burgon, later Dean of Chichester. Burgon's early nineteenth-century poem 'Petra' described the lovely site in southern Jordan as 'A rose-red city – half as old as Time!' Burgon should more aptly be termed as a semi-line poet as he stole 'half as old as Time' from Samuel Rogers' *Italy. A Farewell*. Sadly, when he eventually visited Petra he was disillusioned with the colour. 'There is nothing rosy about Petra', he wrote. He should have seen it sunlit at dawn.[7]

In contrast to Burgon Villon wrote many memorable lines. 'Qui n'estoit a moy grante sagesse', complained the old woman at her lack of wisdom, T, 49, 470. 'Deux estions, et n'avions q'un cueur', 'two we were but with one heart', T, 94+, 985. 'Frères humains qui après nous vivez', 'brothers among men who live after we are dead', PD, 11, 1 (L,14). 'Les loups se vivent du vent', 'wolves that live on the wind', L, 2, 11. And the poignant, 'Et pain ne voient qu'aux fenêtres', beggars that 'saw bread only through the hard panes of shops', T, 30, 236.

Poetry was not an afterthought to him. It was his life. But he also happened to be poor, weak-willed, longing to be liked, with an irresistible need for pleasure. His reaction to the certainty of life's shortness was not one of pessimism but of realistic opportunism. To him the nearness of death meant that life should be enjoyed at every instant. His philosophy was that of the late classical poem 'Copa Surisca', 'Dancing Girl of Syria'.

Per morsum tenerae decerpens ora puellae
....
Pone merum et talos. Pereat qui crastina curat.
Mors aurem vellens, 'vivite', ait, 'venio'.

And delight in the scarlet lips of a pretty girl.
....
Bring out the wine and the dice and to Hell who thinks of tomorrow.
Here's Death twitching my ear. 'Live', he says, 'for I'm coming'.[8]

It was Villon's attitude, enjoyable evenings with friends, women, good food and wine, the raucous laughter of the tavern as he recited his latest nonsensical gift of a horse-trough to the celebrated drunkard, Jacques Raguier, son of the king's master-cook, L, 19, together with a tavern although the 'trou', 'hole' in the Pomme de Pin may have been a chuckle at the man's uncontrollable lechery. Villon ended the stanza with 'Et qui voudra planter si plante' best interpreted as 'whom he feels like shagging he's to shag', just the sort of dirty joke and insult that the company relished.

There was no shortage of taverns or of food, wine and wenches. Only money was the problem. There was wine from Alsace, Anjou, Burgundy, Gascony, there was Côtes-de-Beaune and Chablis, there was the expensive but grandly intoxicating, aromatic hippocras made from half a pound of good cinnamon, a pound of sugar, an ounce of white ginger, one part each of cloves, mace, black pepper and nutmeg, all finely ground together and stirred into hot red wine, preferably the strong, deep red Gascony that some vintners imitated by adding red dye to cheaper wines. A Parisian, Jubert, did, swearing that it did no harm.

There was food. Cattle and poultry were driven into the city to the markets. There were piggeries and pigs snuffling in the street. There were herb-gardens with parsley, marjoram, borage, sage, mint, fennel, sorrel and basil. There was fish, cod, turbot, bass, mullet, eel-like lampreys of which it is reputed a surfeit killed Henry I of England. There was good quality pale-cream wholemeal bread, white bread, cheap dark rye bread. There was unhopped beer, usually brewed by the women of the ale-houses. When they could afford it people could be discriminating about the food they ate. There is a late fifteenth century recipe book, *De Honesta Voluptate*, advising cooks how to prepare healthy and nourishing dishes. One is for meat sausage.

> Take the meat from a haunch of veal and cut it up finely with the soft fat or with lard. Grind marjoram and parsley together. Beat the yolks of eggs together with grated cheese. Sprinkle with spices and work this into one mass and mix it with all the meat. Then cut pieces of sausage casing from pork or veal and roll up the meat mixture inside them in lumps the size of an egg. Cook them on a spit in the hearth over a slow fire. The common folk call this *exicium*. Indeed, when they are a little underdone they are more flavourful than when cooked too much.

In the taverns there was choice: beef pasties and rissoles, lampreys with cold sage, German meat broth, herbolace, a cake stuffed with herbs, there was beef and mutton, young rabbits with hot sauce. A delicacy was a tart devised in Pisa with little birds in the stuffing. There was boar's tail, bream and salmon pasties, and darioles, small pasties filled with meat, herbs and spices. All one needed was money.[9] It is all in Villon in unromantic language. There was no manna, no nectar or ambrosia in his mind. Instead there were onions, turnips, sausages, bread, cheese soup, sauces, fish, fried eggs.

No authentic portrait of him exists. There is a conventional picture in the 1489 edition of his works but as the identical figure was used for other poets like Virgil it is no more than a generality, a slight person in a broad-brimmed hat, cloaked, gowned, dagger in his belt, the reality probably being of an undersized man with a deeply scarred upper lip. Around 1832 the poet and novelist, Théophile Gautier, suggested that Rabelais had based his description of Panurge on Villon: 'thin as a red herring, and walked gingerly like a lean cat. . . . He was of middling stature, neither too big nor too small, and his nose was somewhat aquiline, the shape of a razor handle. At that time he was about thirty-five or thereabouts, and about as fit for gilding as a lead dagger.'

Centuries after Rabelais, decades after Gautier, the French novelist, Joris Karl Huysmans elaborated in his *Le Drageoir aux Epices*: 'I see before me, O venerable master, your bloodless visage, crowned with its mangy *bicoquet*; I see your hollow stomach, your long bony arms, your heron-like legs, encased in hose of a dirty pink, starred with rents, covered, as with scales, by mud-splashes'.[10]

It was this unprepossessing figure who wrote some of the finest of all French poetry, the introductory lines of the *Testament* and the ballades contained within them. Earlier the *Legacies* of 1456 were more run of the mill, a few witty legacies to friends, many more sarcastic donations for privileged but unprincipled members of Parisian society. These eight-line, octosyllabic verses are preliminary sketches for what was to come, amusing, sardonic but not great art.

Mock testaments were a favourite medieval entertainment and their format followed that of a genuine will: an introduction, a statement of the testator's health, life and faith. Then came advice to friends, a commitment of his soul to God and his body to the earth. Only after such a lengthy preamble were there any bequests before the final arrangements for funeral and burial. In his *Testament* of 1462 Villon followed this traditional layout religiously but in the forty stanzas of the *Legacies* the farcical bequests occupy almost nine-tenths of the work.

Internal evidence suggests that stanzas L, 3–9 and L, 35–40 were composed late in the year long after the bequests which were probably scribbled over a few months and declaimed in taverns to audiences of happy-go-lucky girls, off-duty trollops, tipsy cronies and drunkards, a new stanza heard in cheerful approval, old ones bellowed by all, tankards banging to the beat, the company chanting the words as one victim after another was remembered and derided.

The *Legacies* started simply enough:

L'an quatre cens cinquante six	In the year fourteen fifty-six
Je Françoys Villon escollier	I the scholar François Villon [L, 1]

but from the third verse to the seventh the poem is interrupted by a complaint about an unnamed woman. The poet may have left her anonymous for fear of the law but whoever she was her heartless treatment was to drive him from Paris. She had encouraged then spurned him, suddenly and callously turning to another.

> La tres amoureuses prison
> Qui faisoit mon cueur debriser [L, 2, 15–16]

'love's imprisonment which had my heart at breaking-point'. 'She gave my ruin her consent', L, 3, 19, 'I took as favourable her sweet looks, her charming airs', L. 4, 26. I was 'caught by one cruel and hard', L, 5, 34. 'Farewell! I'm going to Angers, since she does not see fit to grant nor give me any of her grace', L, 6, 43–5.[11]

Then, abruptly, from regret the mood changed to one of resentment. 'Bien ilz ont vers moy les piés blans', she was as untrustworthy and vicious as a horse with four white hooves. The lines became sexually explicit. He would find another. 'Planter me fault autres complans', L, 4, 31, 'I have to go and "plant" somewhere else', 'et frapper en ung aultre coing', L, 4, 32, 'and plough in other fields'.[12]

The mood altered for a third time. 'Je lesse mon cueur enchassée. . . . Mais Dieu luy en face mercy', L, 10, 77, 80, 'I leave her my enshrined heart . . . but may God forgive her for what she has done'. Then the humorous legacies, L, 11–34, began.

A page of the manuscript of the *Legacies*, 'In the year 1456 I, François Villon, scholar . . .'.

He had already bequeathed his lordly but non-existent tents and pavilions to his adopted father, Guillaume de Villon. Now he gave other things away, things he did not possess, things that were worthless or legacies that were quite unwanted by their recipients. To the knowledgeable Paris was a village. The rich, the aristocrat, the churchman, usurer, social climber, hypocrite, all were known. It was a city of rumour and gossip. That man's debt, another's ambition, a law-suit, a straying wife, everything was talked about whether a peccadillo or an outright crime. Villon's satirical pen converted the soon-forgotten into enduring vignettes. It is unlikely that the ghosts of Pierre de St-Amant and his wife, Jacques Cardon, wealthy merchant, Jean de Harlay and other eminent citizens, or the gluttonous friars and nuns rejoice in their unwanted everlastingness.

He was liberal with his favours. Items that no one believed were owned by an impoverished clerk included 'his' sword and armour, silk cape, hunting dogs and a couple of castles, all of them the exclusive property of the nobility. Prodigally he gave away no fewer than eight taverns. He dispensed with a litter of geese, capons, huge hogsheads of wine, a horse-trough, a fig tree, two rubies, a bishop's crozier and a shiny mirror.

Other legacies were useless. For the windows of a poor hospital he donated spiders' webs for curtains. Chapter 1 has already explained how two canons of Notre-Dame were to receive Gueuldry's unpaid rents. To others deserving of his benefits Villon generously parted with a pot of Seine river water, the goodwill of the jailer's wife, three bales of straw and an acorn. He left 'possessions' that were either too petty for anyone to want, an egg-shell with obsolete money, four small coins, a fly swat to a butcher who already had a dozen, hair-clippings to his barber, old shoes to a cobbler, torn trousers and clothes to a ragman. There were private jokes.

Item, je lesse a noble homme	Item, I leave to nobleman
Regnier de Montigny trois chiens . . .	Regnier de Montigny three dogs [L, 17]

The law permitted hunting-dogs only to the nobility. Montigny, a law-breaking friend of Villon, did come from noble stock but with his current dishonest career he had no need of expensive hounds. In the next stanza, L, 18, even more dogs were left to a completely undeserving case.

Item, au seigneur de Grigny . . . [L, 18]   Item, to the lord of Grigny

> I leave him Nigeon's mighty tower
> And six more dogs than Montigny
> And Bicêtre's fort and cells as a dower.
> As for that bastard Mouton, sour
> As anybody called a debtor,
> I'll have him whipped, make him cower
> In prison, leg-locked in a fetter.

The jest was that Philippe Brunel, minor Lord of Grigny, and therefore entitled to the dogs if he had money for their upkeep, was irascible, and in later years was so short of funds that he robbed his own church at St Antoine-de-Grigny, was arrested, became over-truculent in court and was imprisoned for fourteen months. He may have offended Villon in some way, perhaps threatening to take him to court over something owed as the unexplained jeering reference to 'Mouton' suggests. Villon was too discreet to be more revealing. As for the castles of Nijon and Bicêtre, both were in a state of complete ruin. Brunel must have upset Villon. He was one of the few legatees to receive a bequest in the *Testament* six years later. Villon was still not finished with the vexatious knight. He appointed him one of his three executors, T, 184:

trois hommes bien et d'honneur   three good men of honour

the others being Jacques Raguier the drunkard and Jacques James, the owner of the bath-house brothel. It is not a flattering portrait of that ignoble nobleman.

Socially the *Legacies* are informative about Villon's background. He derided the unpopular, the usurers, the greedy friars, the acquisitive litigants, he laughed at drunkards, teased his friends but no unpleasant words were ever written against well-born people like the Provost and his wife, Ambroise. Although some critics have doubted it Villon probably did mix with the upper classes and tried to keep in their favour.

But to others he lacked mercy. Like the pseudo-gift to Grigny some of Villon's presents were simply jokes. Others had a hard edge to them. By a small coincidence in L,12, Pierre de St Amant, an important official in the Treasury, also appeared twice, briefly in the *Legacies* and then with his wife in the *Testament*, T, 97. In the *Legacies* he was bequeathed the Cheval Blanc, a heavy, motionless sign. On the surface this was because in Paris wealthy commoners often aped the nobility by riding white horses and the gift hints at some snobbishness in St Amant. There was an underlying sarcasm. The docile horse symbolised an impotent husband. He was given a frigid wife. St Amant was granted not only the white horse but also 'une mulle', 'a female mule'. Mules were the sterile offspring of a horse and a donkey and Villon's combination of a motionless horse and an infertile mule implies that St Amant's was a sexless marriage.

That was in the light-hearted days of 1456. By 1462 the poet's mood was blacker. St Amant is thought to have been a contemporary of Villon's at university and had perhaps lent the poet money until his wife, Jehanette Cochereau, stopped him, calling Villon a 'truand', a beggar, a sponger. In revenge, he reversed the presents. Now the feeble white horse was coupled with a mare, a lubricious female. And the she-mule was partnered with an 'âne rouge', 'a red-hot ass', an animal renowned for its sexual enthusiasm.

Others were just as nastily lampooned. Jacques Cardon, a prosperous and presumably overweight cloth merchant [L, 16], was bestowed with unnecessary gloves and a silk cape as well as an unbotanical acorn from a willow tree. To keep him in good shape he was provided with daily presents of a plump goose, a fat capon and 'dix muys de vin blanc comme croye', ten

hogsheads, each of 268 litres, of white wine to wash the birds
down. There was also the unexpected right to graze pigs in an
oak forest, probably an apt reflection of Cardon's piggish
eating-habits.

None of the largesse was acceptable. The 2680 litres was of a
thin, sharp wine that had to be clarified with plaster-of-Paris to
make it drinkable. Perhaps sorry for being so unpleasant Villon
ended with 'deux procès que trop n'engresse', 'two law-suits to
stop the worried merchant growing fat'.

It was necessary for Jean de Harlay, the Chevalier du Guet or
Knight of the Watch to be of noble birth or he would not be
entitled to wear the helmet that was his badge of office, L, 22.
As his social status was questioned by his predecessor, Philippe
de la Tour, Villon imaginatively handed him the Helmet tavern
to prove his legitimacy. His men, pietons or foot-soldiers,
groping around the markets in the dark were enlightened by the
receipt of the Lantern, a disreputable house/den in the rue de la
Pierre-au-Lait near Châtelet. They also got two lovely rubies,
fairy jewellery from a ruby-less poet, because they were believed
to glow and provide illumination.

Not only the well-off were included in the *Legacies*. Perrinet
Marchand, the debauched Sergeant of the Twelve, was one of
the Provost's bodyguard. Also rudely known as the 'Bâtarde de
la Barre' he had the reputation of being a procurer and a whore-
monger, 'un très bon marchand', 'a good tradesman' Villon
called him in a pun on his name. The man's unwholesome
sideline led the poet to provide him with bundles of straw that
his prostitutes could spread on their floors to make their work
less depressing. Many of them spoke affectedly, like Ysabeau's
'Reelly!', and Villon smilingly lampooned the foible, rhyming L,
23 in the same artificial manner, Barre, fuerre, terre, querre, like
the 'refained' speech of Morningside ladies.[13]

He chuckled at the anomaly of police corruption. Two of his
'friends', Sergeants Casin Cholet and Jean le Loup, were River
Police with responsibilities for measuring salt, preventing filth

from being thrown into the Seine or into the ditches. In their floppy cloth caps and grubby cloaks they also drove cattle out of the ditches and moats which they were supposed to clean. They were crooks. They had a dredging-boat which provided convenient transport for the goods along the quays that they theoretically guarded but systematically looted to sell cheaply with no questions asked. Villon may have profitably accompanied them on some of their nocturnal depredations. In L, 24 he considerately gave them a stolen duck, a long Franciscan cloak down to their feet in which they could conceal his other 'gifts' of their filched firewood, coal and delicious peas with pork fat. To all this he lavishly added two pairs of fatuous boots without tops to help them wade from one tempting barge to the next.

It would be tedious to translate all the *Legacies*. Much of the humour is as anachronistic as many jokes in Shakespeare. Even more frustratingly, lots of the allusions have been lost. Guffawed over by friends, the picklock Colin de Cayeux and the more sinister Regnier de Montigny, by Robin Turgis and Villon's unreliable companion, Guy Tabarie, applauded by a crowd of dissolutes and disreputables, the wit has become meaningless today because it has no background.

Little more has been learned about Jean Raguier, pronounced 'rag-wire', than what Villon tells us in L, 17. As for 'celluy qui fist avangarde', 'that man who began it all', L, 33, 261, and caused all kinds of trouble for Villon, the line is a complete puzzle. It has already been suggested that it may have been the vaguest of references to Jean le Mardi who tried to intervene in the fight between Villon and Sermoise. We simply do not know.

Clement Marot writing in 1533, less than eighty years after the *Legacies*, regretted that even though he had met Parisians who could recite whole passages from the poems so much had been forgotten. 'For a man rightly to understand all the meaning of the legacies of Villon he should have lived in Paris and in his day, and should have known the places, the things and the men of whom he speaks; for the more the memory of these fades away, the less shall a man apprehend the meaning of the aforesaid legacies'.[14]

Little could more clearly demonstrate this confusing biographical ignorance than two seemingly straightforward stanzas, L, 25–26, 'Item, je lesse, en pitié . . .'

> Item. I leave from my deep pity [L, 25–6]
> To three penurious little boys,
> Known to all in this sad city
> As hungry orphans without toys,
> Who suffer pain but make no noise,
> Barefoot in the mud and grime,
> Here's emerald and rich turquoise
> To get them through the wintertime.

> First Colin, Gerard and then John,
> As Laurens, Gossouyn, Marceau known.
> They have no goods, their parents gone,
> Not a bucket-handle, so to each one
> I give my lands and all I own,
> Four shiny farthings, and then lots
> Of healthy food, not skin and bone,
> For these weak and homeless tots.

Before the researches of Schwob and Longnon such kindness convinced Victorians and Edwardians that Villon had been a sincerely compassionate man who cared deeply for those parentless children. Théophile Gautier wrote, 'Assuredly, Villon was not born to be a thief, he had a kind heart, easily touched by fine feelings. . . . He provided for three orphans. He exhorted them to be diligent in school.'

The truth was different. The 'orphans' were aged, affluent and avaricious moneylenders. Gossouyn, speculator in salt and a tight-fisted usurer, was convicted for fraud in 1456. Laurens, a spice merchant, was hated by the Parisians for his imposition of a salt tax. Marceau was a rich and unscrupulous pawnbroker who had sold arms to the English. Mean and grasping he had Jean de Maréchal arrested for the minor debt of three écus. All three were loathed by the Parisians.

So were the friars and the nuns. Perhaps the most sarcastic and bitter of all the twenty-five stanzas of bequests is L, 32 with its attack on the mendicants, the four Orders of begging friars that infested the streets of Paris with their whining pleas for money because of their vows of abstinence and poverty. There were the Dominican Jacobins on the rue St Jacques, the Franciscan 'Cordeliers' with their knotted cord belts; the sandalled and hypothetically ascetic Carmelites; and the Augustinians, all of them 'committed' to celibacy and perpetual deprivation. They were despised for their hypocrisy. A group of Carmelites had been discovered with girls disguised as men, were taken to the Châtelet and found to be carrying clubs and weapons.

Eighty years before Villon William Langland in *Piers Plowman* had observed similar sanctimonious self-seeking in England. In 'a faire felde ful of folke':

> I fonde ther freris * alle the fore ordres,
> Preched the peple * for profit of hem-selven,
> Glosed the gospel * as hem good lyked,
> For covietise of copis * construed it as their wolde. *Prologue*, 58–61

This has been translated as 'all four Orders preaching for what they could get. In their greed for fine clothes they interpret the Scriptures to suit themselves and their patrons. Many of these Doctors of Divinity dress as handsomely as they please, for as their trade advances, so their profits increase.'[15] The same was true in Paris.

Corruption was the norm. Desire for power increased. Forbidden to hear confessions friars arrogated this lucrative benefit to themselves, ignoring the angry protests of churchmen. They triumphed. A papal bull of 1449 not only granted that right but allowed other privileges, to preach and to attend deathbeds, previously prerogatives permitted only to priests of the Church. By 1456 the conflict culminated in the University and Church arguing against the four Orders in front of Parliament. There were semi-comical, entirely venomous reprisals with defamatory notices nailed to doors of convents and put up in front of pulpits where the entire congregation would see them.[16]

The self-indulgence of the 'austere' friars had disgusted Jean de Meung and it disgusted Villon. He knew the friars and he knew their sisters, the Béguines, nuns without permanent vows, living in small communes. Over two centuries they had become morally decadent, as had their counterparts of the Filles-Dieu, once repentant women choosing to live a hard life. By 1456 they had become impenitent women living in hypocritical self-satisfying pleasure.[17]

To alleviate such abstinent hardship Villon gave them custard pies as compensation, patés, succulently plump hens, roosters, savouries such as flaöns, puddings of spiced and sugared minced fish or meat with eggs or cream added and baked in a crust. They could enjoy Jacobin soup made from the best cheese on toast, steeped in a good beef bouillon, the thin broth to be poured over a tender roast plover or a capon. Then, replete, they could go out sanctimoniously to preach the Fifteen Signs of the Last Judgement 'et abatre pain a deux mains', and beg for 'bread' in the colloquial sense of 'money' with greedy hands. What the hell! 'Carmes chevauchent nos voisines, mais cela, ce n'est que du mains', 'Carmelites ride our neighbours' wives. It's not important', L, 32, 255–60. Five hundred years later the words have lost none of their bitterness.

In July the truly pious Joan of Arc was rehabilitated. On 16 February the Court reassembled in Rouen, the Archbishop of Rheims presiding. Between 2 April and 10 May eighty-one witnesses, from thirty-six to seventy years old, testified in Orléans, in Paris; others in Rouen, one in Lyons. On 7 July the Archbishop read the court's findings:

We, the newly appointed Tribunal, first declare that the articles on which Joan of Arc's condemnation was based were slanderous, fraudulent, vicious and evil; and secondly decree that the entire proceedings of her trial in this city, and

Portrait of Joan of Arc from the mid-
to late fifteenth century. (*Archives
Nationales, Paris/Giraudon/Bridgeman
Art Library, London*)

particularly and most especially the judgement of condemnation pronounced against her were, are and shall ever be
known to be unfounded, invalid, null and void; and therefore
that Joan herself, her family and relations and all those who
supported her are free of all faults, stains and blemishes and
accusations cruelly and wickedly preferred against her in this
town twenty five years, two months and eight days previous.

Commemorative crosses were erected in Rouen, on the triumphal
bridge at Orléans and elsewhere. Only one survives in the Forest
of Saint-Germain. It was badly damaged during the Revolution
but still bears the inscription, CROIX PUCELLE, 1456. The
heroine of Orléans was finally canonised on 16 May 1920.[18]

The *Legacies* finished strangely with Villon waking up late on
a cold night to find his ink frozen and his candle blown out. He
went to sleep wearing mittens, L, 39.[19] Although late in the year
much was to happen before 1456 ended.

Lust, Love and Larceny, December 1456

By this time Villon was probably leading a saint-and-devil, gallery-of-mirrors existence, a respectable if unemployed cleric by day and a bacchanalian roisterer by night. As long as there was money. And little imagination is needed to realise how he contrived to pay for his convivial evenings. A meagre allowance from Guillaume de Villon would never have been sufficient. If that once-benevolent churchman had been required to repay part, perhaps all, of the riches stolen in Angers his generosity would have been reduced to grudging levels. Villon's solution was crime. He remained a gamin of the Paris slums using every advantage he could find, encouraged by similarly nefarious allies like Colin de Cayeux.

Because of the vainglorious braggings of another associate, Guy Tabarie, Villon's felonies are recorded. In May 1457 Tabarie boasted to a stranger, a priest from Paray near Chartres, of various robberies that his gang had committed. The priest informed the authorities who checked, verified, consulted and when convenient arrested Tabarie on 25 June 1458. He was questioned. Painfully stretched on the little rack with a two-foot high trestle wedged under the middle of his back he admitted nothing, probably on the principle that agony might be endured. Execution would not. Transferred to the unendurable torture of the great rack with the assurance of unlimited returns he confessed on 22 July.

One morning, he muttered, late in 1456 one of his companions approached Father Guillaume Coiffier of the Augustinians, asking him to offer a mass on his behalf at the church of St Mathurin on the rue St Jacques. While the two of them went away three thieves picked the lock of the priest's room, discovered a small chest and took its contents of five or six hundred gold écus. They also stole silver plate. Tabarie had not been with them. After a brawl with Casin Cholet, that quarrelsome Sergeant of the Verge, he had been locked in a cell of an ecclesiastical prison because of his clerical status. The same night the four robbers, all of them named by Tabarie, lucratively broke into the abbey of the Augustinians. They would also have burgled the church of St Mathurin, 'que les chiens les avoient accuser', but were deterred by barking dogs.

It was all taken down. The document has survived in its quaint Latin and medieval French and among the ominously methodical phrases occur: 'die ipse obviavat magistro Francisco Villon', 'he met François Villon that day'; 'magister Franciscus Villon iverat Andevagis', 'Villon was going to Angers'; 'ung complice nommé Françoys Villon', 'an accomplice named François Villon'. It was a death-sentence if Villon were to be apprehended but July 1458 was not December 1456 and there was money to be spent.[1] Abundantly and quickly. As Henley perceptively wrote, 'Booze and the blowens cop the lot'.

One of the dives where booze and blowens coincided was the tavern-cum-brothel of La Grosse Margot with its gaudy sign in a 'coy, darkish court' off the rue Cloche-Percé near Notre-Dame. It was the subject of one of Villon's best-known ballades and is of interest for several reasons. It may be one of his first successful ventures into true poetry. It is also a matter of vigorous argument as to whether La Grosse Margot was a disreputable hostelry or a disreputable woman, whether the poem is an exercise in ingenuity or a genuine piece of autobiography. To some translators the contents were so foul and degrading that they bowdlerised the poem or omitted it. Others shrugged. 'It is just Villon.' The English version quoted is by John Heron Lepper but alternative lines have been cited:

Se j'ayme et sers la belle de bon het . . .

If I do serve my love, nor ask for hire,   [T, 150+]
Must that be termed a vile or foolish trade?
For she possesses all that men desire.
I don for her the buckler and the blade.
When folks come in, with pot in hand displayed
I fetch the wine as silent as the dead,
Fruit, water, cheese, loaf, on the table spread,
And, if they pay well, show politeness great:
'Revisit us, when looking for a bed,   'En ce bordeau ou tenons nostre
Within this brothel where we keep our state!'   estat.'

But other times the fat is in the fire,
Margot comes home without a penny made;
I hate her sight; my heart is filled with ire;
And swear her finery shall be conveyed
To pawn, since giving credit I forbade.
At that in scorn she tosses high her head
And, arms akimbo, swears in language dread,   . . . So then I snatch some club
By Christ, I shan't! To finish the debate   and with it write a message on
A sudden slap upon her visage red   her nose.
Within this brothel where we keep our state.   *Anthony Bonner*, 107

Then fully charged my rearguard gun I fire   Then peace descends and she blows
Of dunghill stench; when peace at last is   me a mighty fart, more bloated than
    made.   a poisonous dung-beetle. Laughing,
She pats my head all smiles, and coming   she slaps her fist on top of my head.
    nigher   'Get on with it', she says and
We bill and coo like turtles in the shade.   whacks my thigh. Both drunk, we
As drunk as owls in bed together laid;   sleep like logs. Waking up with a
When we awake by longing she is led   rumbling belly, she climbs on me so
To save love's fruit and cover me instead.   I don't spoil her fruit. I groan
I groan below no burden light of weight;   beneath her weight, she squashes
Caressing her my strength and health are shed   me flatter than a plank. Her obscene
Within this brothel where we keep our state.   ways kill my desire.
                                                       John Fox, 1984, 89

Come wind, come hail, come frost, I've
    baked my bread!
A brawling bully to a baggage wed.   I am debauched, so's she who shares my life.
Each worthy of the other be it said.   *Barbara Nelson, Sargent-Baur*, 165

Like follows like; the beast must find its mate.   Like unto like. 'Bad cat for a bad
We sought the mire, and mire befouls our   rat.'
    tread.   *Norman Cameron*, 97

We fled from honour, honour now is fled,
Within this brothel where we keep our state.

J.H. Lepper

Kinnell devised an ingenious version of the final stanza:

> Wind, hail, frost, my bread's all baked.
> I'm a lecher, she's a lecher to match.
> Like one of us better? We're a pair
> Like unto like, bad rat bad cat
> On filth we dote, filth is our lot.
> Now we run from honor and honor runs from us
> In this whorehouse where we hold our state.

Galway Kinnell, 129

He has very nearly repeated Villon's initial letters of: Vente, Ie, Lequel, L'ung, Ordure, Nous, possibly one of the first examples of the poet's acrostic signatures which he was to repeat in several ballades, maybe as tokens of his satisfaction with a poem.[2]

The 'Ballade of Grosse Margot' is controversial. Some critics believe that Villon was describing a corrupt episode in his life. Others thought the stanzas literary fiction. The latest editors, Rychner and Henry, concluded that Margot was a real person. Favier said that the fetching and carrying, the arguing, hitting, the sexual intercourse had happened whatever the prostitute's name. Bonner wrote that the ballade was 'an extraordinary confession of the degradation into which Villon had fallen'. McCaskie agreed. There was 'no justification for . . . regarding this grim ballade as a flight of fancy' and 'the moralist may well rejoice on the sick, self-disgust of Villon's envoi'. To the unsympathetic Stevenson 'out of all Villon's work that ballad stands forth in flaring reality, gross and ghastly, as a thing written in a contraction of disgust'.[3]

A contrary view would be that these beliefs are vigorous testimonies to Villon's growing ability to write realistically about something that was entirely imaginary. What he had composed was a competent sotte chanson, a 'stupid song', a form of grossly vulgar verse that was very popular in the fifteenth century, in which two loathsome lovers squabbled, fought, belched, farted, fornicated, performed debased actions with nothing wholesome or redeeming about their relationship. There were many examples of the vogue. 'Tout l'art de ce genre grotesque consiste dans la recherche du maximum de l'horreur', 'the most disgusting images, the most absurd things, the most ignoble scenes'.[4]

To the present writer there is a false note in the ballade betraying its artificiality. In it Villon, through inexperience, appears to have tried too hard and overdid the repulsive picture. Line T,150+, 1617, reads, 'monte sur moy, que ne gaste son fruyte', which Lepper translated as 'to save love's fruit and cover me instead'. McCaskie was clearer, 'and for her brat's sake mounts me', the description of a heavily pregnant but lustful woman protecting her unborn child by copulating on top of the man. It seems exaggerated, an unpleasantness too many. Rather than a nauseating recollection it gives the impression of a studied effort, one that in Plutarch's phrase 'smells of the lamp'. It remains a good poem.

La Grosse Margot may have been a sign outside a tavern rather than a woman. Another woman, Catherine de Vausselles, already mentioned, certainly existed. It is a disappointment yet a challenge that the women in Villon's life are so ill-defined, La Belle Heaulmière shuffling into death, La Grosse Margot a board or a bawd, Catherine de Vausselles little more than a name and not even a name in the *Legacies*, just an anonymous breaker of Villon's heart late in 1456.

En ce temps que j'ay dit devant,
Sur le Noel, morte saison . . .

At the time I said before
Near Christmas, the dead of the year,
. . . .
The need came to me to depart
From the gaol of love sincere
That was like to break my heart. [L, 2]

Her looks ensnared me,
She who was false and cruel . . . [L, 5, 33–4]

She had perhaps led him on, smiling, promising, but like the conditional mistress of Ben Jonson granting him every favour save the last. He 'lay divers tymes with a woman, who shew him all that he wished, except the last act which she would never agree to'.[5] For an ardent man, fervently in love, the frustration must have been agonising, particularly when he suspected that bountiful suitors had been granted what he had been denied through lack of money despite his charming, flattering poems. In the *Legacies* he complained that others had made love to her:

> . . . . mon povre sens conçoit
> Autre que moy est en quelongne [L, 7]

'Quelongne' is old French for 'quenouille', a distaff for spinning, and the lines have been variously translated as 'I sense that someone else has thrust his shuttle in and out a bit', or 'someone else winds on her spindle'. It is reminiscent of Sir Toby Belch's crude retort in *Twelfth Night*, 'and I hope to see a housewife take thee between her legs, and spin it off'.[6] Six years later in the *Testament* her name and her treatment of him were explicit.

De moy, povre, je vueil parler:	I was, poor me, I must reveal,
J'en fuz battu comme a ru telles,	Battered like some laundry at a well,
Tout nu, ja ne le quiers celler.	Quite naked too. Naught to conceal.
Qui me fist macher ces groselles	Who made me drink this calomel
Fors Katherine de Vauselles.	But Catherine de Vausselles?
Noël, le tiers . . .	Noel was the third one there. [T, 64+, 657–62]

A rival had taken his place, taking unfair advantage of a larger purse. 'Qui plus billon et plus or songne. .', 'whose money makes more noise', L, 7, 52–3.

Hardly anything has been proved about Catherine de Vausselles, his greatest love, even her address. Longnon associated her with a Pierre de Vaucel, canon of St Benoît, emphasising the coincidence of a second canon, Étienne de Montigny, and a Nicolas de Cayeux, all of them living in the vicinity of St Benoît. Such 'facts' were, as Villon might have pointed out, 'harengs saurs', red herrings. Canon Étienne de Montigny was a probable

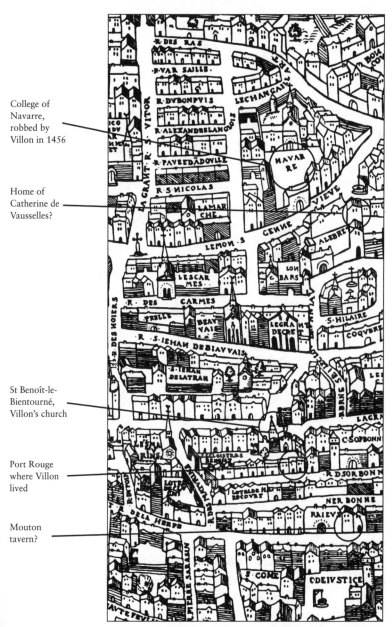

College of
Navarre,
robbed by
Villon in 1456

Home of
Catherine de
Vausselles?

St Benoît-le-
Bientourné,
Villon's church

Port Rouge
where Villon
lived

Mouton
tavern?

A section of a fifteenth-century map of Paris.

uncle of the un-canonlike Regnier, the name of Vaucel was not
Vausselles, and Nicolas de Cayeux lived in the rue de Poirées,
White Beetroot Street, an unlikely residence for Colin de Cayeux's
father, a locksmith.

A more persuasive location for Catherine de Vausselles' home
was near the College of Navarre less than a quarter of a mile
from the Porte Rouge. It is recorded in dusty documents that
between 1440 and 1450 rents were paid to the chaplain of Ste-
Geneviève for a dwelling that had been divided into a house and
a hostelry, the Rose, one of them occupied by Gilles de
Vaucelles. 'Rose' may be significant. No street-name was listed
but the hostelry was a neighbour to another situated in an alley
that led to the college where it joined the rue du Puits de la
Boucherie, Butchers' Wells street near Brothel Street. It proves
that at least in Villon's youth there was a family of Vausselles
living close to St Benoît in an area well-known to him.[7]

Following her shocking rejection of him Villon would have
been delighted to toy insultingly with her name, 'Vausselles'. It
has an equivocal meaning. 'Vaucel' or 'vaucele' meant 'valley'
but it was also slang for the little crevices of the female body,
'les desirables vallées de tendre corps feminin'.[8] In his rancour
the poet would have enjoyed stressing this, stigmatising his
former coquette in the harshest, most revealingly obscene satires
that his biting mind could devise.

Who the successful rival was has never been resolved. The
most convincing was Ythier Marchand whose overweight body
was mentioned in Chapter 3.[9] In the *Legacies* he is referred to
ironically. Villon wrote that he was obliged to him for some
unspecified favour, perhaps a failure to lure Catherine de
Vausselles away from him, L, 11. For this misfortune he was
bequeathed the poet's non-existent sword, the symbol of an
erect male organ, as though Villon were teasing him for lacking
virility. Yet even in the *Legacies* there was a change of mood
with Marchand being termed a 'piece of shit' as though
something had enraged Villon.

The comments in the *Testament* are even sourer. The sword was taken back, leaving Marchand impotent, surely wishful thinking on Villon's part, T, 99. In its place the beneficiary was given a *De Profundis* for his dead lover whom Villon would not name, T, 94. Marchand, the son of an opulent family, may have ousted Villon through the enticement of his money, leaving the poet helplessly revengeful, wishing the unnamed woman dead. The emotion is venomously sincere but the reason for it was not made clear. The key to the riddle is contained in eighty acidic, revealing lines of the *Testament*, T, 90, 910 to T, 93+, 989. They begin with an attack on a woman called Rose. Following is a ballade about 'a false beauty' who has cost Villon dearly, and the section ends with a stanza about Ythier Marchand and the lovely but cryptic rondeau that Villon composed for him. Only three names are given: Rose, Marthe and Marchand. Rose and Marthe appear nowhere else in Villon's work.

'Rose' is the subject of stanzas T, 90 to T, 93, from 'Item, m'amour, ma chière rose' to T, 93, a verse in which every line rhymes with 'erre', 'R', a letter signifying 'treason' in the Middle Ages, and in which the woman is termed a 'bent-nosed slut'. Villon bequeathed her neither his heart nor his liver, she being too expensive for him, but he understood that she would like money and something else, perhaps a large, coin-stuffed silk purse and a 'targe', a euphemism for a male organ. In the succeeding lines he repeated his references to money: 'cash', 'écus', 'But hang the man . . . who leaves her either coin or shield', the 'shield' being obscene slang for sex with the insinuation that she was little better than a professional harlot.

The defamation continued in T, 91 in which his backside was no longer hot, an allusion to a beating he had been given. She was indiscriminate in her choice of men, so insatiable of appetite that appropriately she herself was donated to the heirs of 'Michaud, Bon Fouterre', 'the accomplished fucker' buried in St Satur church near Sancerre, 'the finest workman in that merry trade that's done without a light'. Finally, when Perrinet de la

Barre, Châtelet tipstaff and disgusting fornicator, met her in the street he was to shout at her, 'Where hast thou come from, filthy slut?'

Various attempts have been made to identify 'Rose', that she was another of Villon's sexual disappointments, that she was a friend of Marthe's, that she was a prostitute, but the truth is that in the fifteenth century 'rose' was not a Christian name.[10] Given Villon's allusive mind it is quite credible that 'ma chière rose' was the expensive Catherine de Vausselles who lived in a house, the 'Sign of the Rose'. This would explain the ballade that comes after, T, 93+, 942–69.

> Faulse beauté qui tant me couste chier,
> Rude en effet, ypocrite doulceur,
> Amour dure plus que fer à macher,
> Nommer que puis, (de ma deffaçon seur)
> Cherme felon, la mort d'ung povre cueur,
> Orgueil mussé qui gens met au mourir,
> Yeulx sans pitié, ne veult Droit de Rigueur.
> Sans empirer, ung povre secourir?

Its following stanzas were ingeniously though contrivingly translated by Lepper as:

> False beauty, costing me so very dear,
> Right harsh in deeds and yet dissembling far;
> Ah love, more sharp of wound than sword or spear.
> No deadlier these, whose name I could declare;
> Charm stained with crime, my heart in twain to tear,
> Indocile pride, whence many wounded are;
> Spare, eyes so pitiless, your rigour spare,
> A poor man's fortune mend, and never mar.
>
> My better hap had been to seek, I fear,
> Another's grace, and so escape this care;
> Reflection warned me from her danger sphere;
> Thus I must fly and be of honour bare.
> Help, one and all, help, help in my despair!
> Ah what? To die without one blow in war,
> Since pity will not (hard the lot to bear)
> A poor man's fortune mend, and never mar.

A time will come that shall turn dry and ere
Vainglorious beauty's blossoms now so rare:
If still alive, 'twill give me cause to jeer,
Laugh? Ah but no; 'twould have too mad an air!
Lo, I grow old, while ugliness you wear!
On! Drink apace, while streams do flow afar,
Nor let us all alike this hardship share;
A poor man's fortune mend, and never mar.

Prince lover, of all loves beyond compare,
May naught from your good will me e'er debar;
But every true heart should, by *God* I swear,
A poor man's fortune mend, and never mar. [T, 93+]

Even in the original French it is not great poetry, little more than a young man's attempt to be clever: Francoys, Marthe are neat enough but there was a failure, probably intentional, to demonstrate how disturbed the poet had become, with the final disrupted Villon of the French: Ung, Jaunyr, Je, Lors, Viel, Or, Ne. The ballade seems an early piece of versification, probably of 1456 itself, but there are hints of what was to come, the withering of lovely blossoms, beauty declining into ugliness, life to be enjoyed while there was time. The experience with Catherine de Vausselles was to transform Villon into a master of the elegiac line. It is not credible that the poet had not written verses to her, lilting songs, passionate love-poems. They have gone. He may have destroyed them in his anger. She may have thrown them away as frivolities of no importance.

'Marthe' is an enigma, mentioned only once and set between 'Francoys' and a disconnected UJJLVON. One theory is that Villon regretted not having been faithful to her. McCaskie wondered if Catherine de Vausselles' second name had been Marthe. Most critics dismissed the question. Nothing was known about her. It was even speculated that the ballade was an exercise written to order, maybe at the court of Charles d'Orléans in Blois that Villon was to visit.[11]

A more credible explanation, quite cohesive in its context, is that 'she' was a 'he', a contraction of Mar-The, an ingenious anagram of Y*thi*er *Mar*chand who had come between 'Françoys' and the broken 'Villon' by seducing the poet's faithless paramour. Devising such an anagram of a girl's name the poet could derisively if optimistically feminise his hated rival, emasculating him, just as he would metaphorically castrate a bullying magistrate near Moulins a few years later, transmuting Macé d'Orléans into Macée, a nagging scold. Knowing the poet's tortuously elliptical thinking it is not unlikely.

Reading between lines that no longer exist and which he dared not preserve for fear of further legal reprisals by the law it has been surmised that in the autumn of 1456 he composed far worse defamatory verses, unwritten but remembered and loudly, untunefully declaimed by drunken friends outside her house. Puns on 'vaucelles', 'les petites vallées du corps de la femme', would have been obligatory linked with unambiguous aspersions against her morality.

It was unwise. It could only have been written and encouraged by a man in a state of emotional unreason. Cholet and le Loup had been imprisoned for insulting an abbess. A soldier was beaten to death for his coarse poem about Huguette de Hamel. Villon also suffered. Catherine de Vausselles or her family reported the matter and the poet was condemned, 'luy frappa au cul la pelle', to be tied to the back of a cart and thrashed on his bare backside at every crossroads with a 'pelle', a flat-bladed paddle like the implement used by washerwomen.[12] It was humiliation. Like the stocks and the pillory this was a public shaming with his name bellowed for all the onlookers to hear and for them to laugh derisively, ridiculing the prisoner as the blows fell. To some lumpish oaf it was an embarrassment. To a sensitive poet it was an unforgettable mortification. That he had become a laughing-stock was made worse by his fame. All Paris knew of the witty François Villon. Now they watched and sniggered at his disgrace. Worse still, Catherine de Vausselles was present, smirking at his indignity.

Of the three central participants Villon stated that Noel Jolis was the third person there implying that while Catherine de Vausselles watched the punishment Jolis was the man who administered it. He is another shadow. Five years later on 29 April 1461 Colette la Charette was fined by the corporation 'for committing adultery with him on many occasions' over the past two years.[13] He may have been one of the Onze-Vingts, the Two Hundred and Twenty foot sergeants, which would explain why Villon sarcastically awarded him eleven times twenty lashes of freshly cut willow branches from the poet's garden, the beating to be given by the strong arms of Henry Cousin, the public executioner, T, 152.

By 1462 the occasion may have dwindled into a comical half-memory but in 1456 everyone knew of Villon's abasement. For once it was he who was derided. Maybe to escape the continual giggles he decided to leave Paris once more. As always, he would need money. He had some. He wanted more.

In his writings what he did late in the year is no more than an obliquity, a reference never to be deciphered by the most expert of code-breakers. What he actually did is contained only in official records. He was not writing a diary. His work contains obscurities, evasions, omissions but very rarely a direct lie. It is incorrect that 'we know nearly nothing of the life of this poet'. It is misleading to claim that he had become a legend and 'like most legends this one has been built of conjecture, along lines laid down by a cliché'. Years later Kinnell modified this pessimistic overstatement.[14] Villon wrote his own history of December 1456.

> At last, composing these bequests
> Tonight, at ease and feeling well,
> Writing as each legacy attests,
> I heard the pealing of the Sorbonne bell,
> Always at nine its solemn knell
> Rings out the Angelus in the city.
> I stopped my work, quill down, and fell
> To praying in deep piety. [L, 35]

An innocent statement. The bell was only a few score yards from his room in the Porte Rouge as it clanged its message of the angels across Paris, announcing the time of curfew, 'couvre-feu'. Called 'Maria', *EGO VOCOR MARIA*, it was not the largest of the bells. That was 'Jacqueline' at Notre-Dame, so big that it was fragile and had been recast only five years earlier. But 'Maria' was privileged. All other bells rang at eight in the evening. The beadles tolled her an hour later at nine.[15]

Suddenly Villon tumbled into a confusion of academic gibberish, L, 36–8, losing track of time, dozing off with Dame Memory in his mind brooding on true and false judgements, abstractions, the poet referring vaguely to Aristotle, and then lapsing into fantasies, almost into a coma where forgetfulness was dominant, twenty-four lines of obscurantism. In reality, so far from being in a suspension of near-death, he was in the Mule tavern with a quartet of thieves. The clerk, Guy Tabarie, was there. That day he had chanced upon Villon, a university friend, in the company of Colin de Cayeux, a man he had met only once before. They asked Tabarie to arrange supper for five of them at the Mule opposite the church of the Mathurins on the rue St Jacques only a hundred yards from St Benoît. They would meet at 9 o'clock that night when 'Maria' rang.

At the trestled table with its veal pasties, puddings, sausages and nuts, flagons of white Sancerre and robust red Beaune, all chosen by Tabarie, there was Colin de Cayeux with two others. One was Dom Nicolas, a lapsed Picardy monk, probably the Nicolas de Launay who later broke into the church of St Jean-en-Grève with Regnier de Montigny. Sitting beside him was Petit-Jean, stocky, black-bearded, an excellent picker of locks with his set of rossignols. They were planning to burgle the nearby College of Navarre that night. There was nothing hasty or ill-conceived about the plot. These were not spur-of-the-moment amateurs but professionals who had debated every aspect of the crime: the way to the college decided, on a night when there was no moon, a necessary ladder already hidden in an empty house, everything considered and agreed. All that was required was a gullible acquaintance to act as a cheap look-out. They took Guy Tabarie with them to the College of Navarre.

It was the biggest and richest of the colleges in Paris, founded in 1304 by Jeanne de Navarre, wife of Philip the Fair. During the war its allegiance had been suspect to the majority of Parisians, untypically Armagnac and loyalist whereas all the other colleges were Burgundian and pro-English. During an anti-royalist uprising in 1418 it had been ransacked and its splendid library ravaged. Only a quarter of a mile from St Benoît it seems that Villon knew its layout in detail, including the location of a chest of coins, most of whose contents belonged to the Faculty of Theology. It may have been his university college or perhaps churchmen had talked too freely over food and wine at the Porte Rouge.

After their satisfying meal the five went a short distance up the rue St Jacques, into the rue des Noyers, low-lying and often flooded, another few minutes down the rue des Carmes, keeping careful eyes for Sergeants of the Watch, then a twisting of short-cuts to the unoccupied house of Master Robert de St-Simon against the college. They climbed over a low wall into the house. Except for Tabarie they took off the hindrance of their cloaks. He was left to look after them.

In his intriguingly titled book, *A Walk to an Anthill*, Bengtsson thought the arrangement bizarre and worth a comment:

The planning of a burglary by a great poet together with a band of thieves is strange enough in itself – probably no exactly parallel case can be found in literary history – but it is an even more curious fact that when as in this case five people, among them a poet, set to work on an undertaking which must certainly have appeared to be both arduous and risky, it is by no means the poet who is detached from the company as being unequal to any responsibility greater than that of mounting guard over the discarded clothing

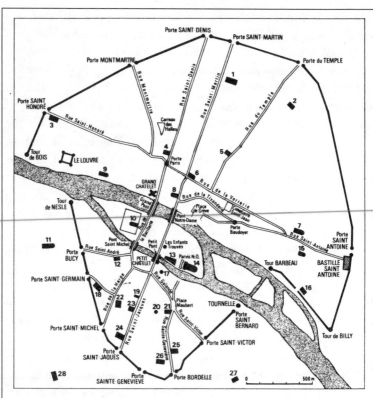

1. Abbaye de Saint-Martin-des-Champs. 2. Le Temple. 3. Hôpital des Quinze-Vingts. 4. Cimetière des Saints-Innocents. 5. Sainte-Avoie. 6. Sainte-Merri. 7. Sainte-Catherine-du-Val-des-Écoliers. 8. Saint-Jacques-de-la-Boucherie. 9. St-Germain-l'Auxerrois. 10. Le Palais et la Sainte-Chapelle. 11. Saint-Germain-des-Prés. 12. Saint-André-des-Arts. 13. Hôtel-Dieu. 14. Notre-Dame. 15. Saint-Paul. 16. Couvent des Célestins. 17. École des Arts. 18. Couvent des Cordeliers. 19. Couvent des Mathurins. 20. Clos Bruneau. 21. Couvent des Carmes. 22. La Sorbonne. 23. Saint-Benoît. 24. Couvent des Jacobins. 25. Collège de Navarre. 26. Sainte-Geneviève. 27. Abbaye Saint-Victor. 28. Chartreuse de Vauvert.

Sketch-map of Villon's Paris with major buildings shown.

while the central organisation is taken over by the more practical element in the group . . . the poet was obviously deemed by experts such as Colin de Cayeux and Petit-Jean, a valuable and active assistant, in all respects their equal, and one in whom they had complete confidence.[16]

This is an over-simplified assessment of the psychology of great poets, the majority of whom came from law-respecting middle-class homes. Villon did not. He grew up in the alleyways and dead-ends of deprivation in a starving Paris. From early child-hood he learned to seize every lucky chance, an apple from a stall, a piece of coal from the back of a cart. As a student he acquired an ever-increasing reputation as a prankster whose activities were not so humorous to his victims, the baker staring at an empty pannier once full of rolls, the butcher whose leg of lamb had disappeared, the vintner finding that his keg of wine had been transformed into a keg of river water.

Tricks became misdemeanours. Stealing sous and deniers from a distracted shopkeeper, and then a progression into serious crimes, breaking into houses, taking silverware, gold, valuables that could be sold. For a year and a half he had associated with criminals, committed undetected offences, met Coquillards, knew their jargon.

> A parouart la grant mathegaudie
> On accollez sont duppez et noirciz,
> Et par les anges suivans la paillardie
> Sont greffiz et print cinq ou six,
> ....
> Eschec eschec pour le fardis [J, 1]

which can be translated as, 'The conspicuous landmark of Paris where fools hang, blackening, five or six of them, put there by the cops, criminals themselves. The con-men are highest, exposed to rain and cold winds. Keep well away from the thick walls of prisons because a cut-purse with his ears lopped off is no good to anyone. . . . And watch out, watch out for the noose!'

It is a truism that Villon became an accomplished thief before he became an accomplished poet. Experience and privation would mould his words. But at the end of 1456 as the felons crept towards the College of Navarre the only greenhorn among them was Guy Tabarie. The college was imposing. It was guarded on two sides by steep walls and on the other two by buildings, one of them St-Simon's. The entrance to the college was a great Gothic archway flanked by canopied stalls long closed for the night. From the garden of the house four of the gang scaled a high wall into the college with the ladder taken to the house days before, climbing down to a spacious quadrangle. It was 10 o'clock. Tabarie was left to shiver in the dark house while the others forced a window of the college, bypassing its stout oak door.

It was probably Villon who led them to the Sacristy, the robing-room where not only the vestments were kept but also the sought-for chest. The door was skilfully forced. The massive chest was iron-banded with four locks, all for different keys that were held by three canons. Patiently, over long, silent minutes, Petit-Jean worked, probed, twisted, undid the locks one by one. Under the lid was a smaller coffer of walnut with three locks. They too were picked. Inside were over five hundred gold écus, a fortune. Carefully, the locks were refastened. It was late, almost midnight. One of the four dissuaded the others from opening the aumbries, the small recessed cupboards in the walls. They were believed to contain up to four thousand écus, a king's ransom – but a death-warrant if the thieves delayed.

They relocked the door, closed the window behind them, clambered down the ladder, went over the wall, lifted the ladder back, and triumphantly showed Tabarie their loot in a small canvas bag which, they laughed, held almost a hundred coins, a considerable sum. They gave Tabarie ten, threatening to kill him if he gave them away. They put two coins aside, about two hundred pounds in modern money, for a supper in celebration the following evening.

Then they sidled, not a muffled coin clinking, to their lodgings, five separate and dangerous journeys along wary alleys, alert for foot-patrols. If one of them were caught they were all dead. What medieval interrogation lacked in psychology it compensated for with its directness and persistence. Possession of ten gold coins, let alone a hundred, or a collection of well-used rossignols, would doom them. But they all arrived safely, four of them each with over a hundred gold crowns.

It was not until 9 March 1457, almost three months later, that the theft was discovered. When the plundered chests were opened and the money found to be missing the rooms of the three masters with keys were searched. Futilely. Only a few coins were found.[17] Nine locksmiths were paid to examine the felonious handiwork. They deduced that the larger chest had been 'crocheté', expertly pick-locked with rossignols. It cost sixteen deniers to repair. More tellingly still, the door of the robing-room had been opened by people who must have been very familiar with the layout of the college. Who they were was a mystery.

Villon left Paris. He stated his intention, gave reasons for it.

> To overcome these loveless dangers
> I think it wise that I should go.
> Farewell! In exile towards Angers
> Since she thinks fit to grant me no
> Affection, leaving me in woe.
> Through her I die, my life in vain,
> Another of love's martyrs. So
> One more saint that love has slain. [L, 6]

It is always assumed that this was only a pretence to conceal the real cause of his departure, the robbery. This makes little sense. The crime had not been detected, there was no incriminating clue. Nothing would be discovered about the perpetrators until Tabarie confessed a year and a half later. Nor had Tabarie himself seen any reason to hide. He remained in Paris. As long as the stolen cash was not too openly broadcast everyone was secure.

It was sensible for notorious crooks and suspected Coquillards such as de Cayeux, Petit-Jean and Dom Nicolas to quit the city as inconspicuously and quickly as possible. But for a madcap poet there was no threat. Indeed the absence of the others, if noticed, would divert suspicion from him. The likelihood is that, characteristically, Villon was being at least half truthful. He was going away because of Catherine de Vausselles but not because she had found a man more rewarding of her pleasures. It was her condemnation, the punishment, the public beating, the widespread news, the ignominy that drove him out.

Except for an occasional and brief nocturnal return he was to be away for five years. He would know the courts of two minor poets: Jean, Duke of Bourbon at Moulins, the land of his forefathers, and René, Duke of Anjou and Lorraine at Angers. He would become the temporary beneficiary of a very good poet, Charles, Duke of Orléans, at Blois. He would know the privations of at least two prisons. He was to write some of the loveliest, self-revealing and most enduring of all French ballades.

On 17 December 1456, in the Pig Market of Paris, Christopher Turgis, taverner, and Coquillard, a man related to Robin Turgis, inn-keeper of the Pomme de Pin and optimistic creditor of François Villon, was boiled in oil for counterfeiting.[18]

The Second Exile, 1457–60

'Adieu! Je m'en vois a Angiers.' 'Farewell! I'm setting off for Angers', L, 6, 3. The words are like snowflakes, insubstantial, melting into nothingness. They are the bewildering prelude to five years of confusion for the biographer, four of them with Villon drifting from city to city in the Loire valley and from aristocratic court to court, the fifth, in 1461, imprisoned at Meung-sur-Loire near Orléans.

Where he went is conjectural. His wanderings are unrecorded and his journeyings from here to there are like gusting autumn leaves that blow unsettled across the centuries. Some places, Blois, Bourges, Orléans, are documented. Angers, Moulins are suspected. Rennes and Roussillon are improbable. But when he went to this town or that, in what order, whether he returned, how long he stayed, these questions cannot be answered. Marc Bloch was right. 'There are times when the sternest duty of the savant, who has tried every means, is to resign himself to his ignorance, and to admit it honestly.'[1] An itinerary based on a sparsity of facts is given in this chapter. It is not history. The only history is his reason for leaving Paris:

Rigeur le tranmist en exil	Exiled by the injustice of a court
Et lui frappa au cul la pelle	His backside walloped with a blade,
Non obstant qu'il dit, 'J'en appelle'	Despite protesting at being flayed,
Qui n'est pas terme trop subtil	A protest of unsubtle sort.
	[T, 178+, 1899–1902]

Yet these were also the brief, broken years of his genius, a few years of restless trudging through the countryside alone, nothing to disturb his thoughts, a sudden memory of an old woman or a strutting money-lender, a clatter of skulls in a charnel-house. The images melded into rhythms and rhymes in his private world in which the eyes saw nothing and the only awareness was the blending of words into a perfection of lines, shape and sound. He knew everything. Only his own self remained a mystery to him, a seemingly jovial extrovert, in reality an intro-spective melancholic, an agony of talent and weakness, his sharp mind recalling the obvious, that flies feed on milk,* recognising the man by his clothes, the monk by his gown, the nun by her veil, being fluent in the jargon of the Coquillards, adding Beatrice and Belet because a rhyme was needed for 'mulet', understanding the Bohemian heresy of the Hussites, knowing so much but never understanding himself.

Je congnois bien mouches en let,*
Je congnois a la robe l'omme,*
Je congnois le beau temps du let,
Je congnois au pommier la pomme,
Je congnois l'arbre a veoir la gomme,
Je congnois quant tout est de mesmes,
Je congnois qui besongne ou chomme,
Je congnois tout, fors que moy mesmes.

Je congnois pourpoint au colet,
Je congnois le moyne a la gonne,*
Je congnois le maistre au varlet.
Je congnois au voille la nonne,*
Je congnois quant pipeur jargonne,*
Je cognois fols nourris de cresmes
Je congnois la vin a la tonne,
Je congnois tout fors que moy mesmes.

Je congnois cheval et mulet,
Je congnois leur charge et leur somme,
Je congnois Bietris et Belet,*
Je congnois gect qui nombre assomme,
Je congnois vision et somme,
Je congnois la faulte des Boesmes,*
Je congnois la povoir de Romme,
Je congnois tout fors que moy mesmes.
Je congnois tout fors que moy mesmes.

Prince, je congnois tout en somme,	Prince, everything is known to me,
Je congnois coulorez et blesmes,	I know the coloured and the bland,
Je congnois Mort qui tout consomme,	I know that Death takes all that be.
Je congnois tout fors que moy	Only me I do not understand.
mesmes.	[PD, 6 (L, 3)]

The years were broken by the artificiality of ducal courts, interrupted by the dread of attracting the law, evenings relaxing in the company of scoundrels, broken by periods in jail. It is yet another contradiction in the life of Villon. At the time when his condition was worsening his poetry was becoming great.

Leaving Paris as he did in the early winter of 1457 it is likely that he hurried once more to the quick haven of Bourg-la-Reine where his wealth made him welcome. Then, shifting from unsavoury inn to flea-infested inn, he tramped unhurriedly towards Orléans and the safety of a Coquillard hideout, staying there until spring. Then, before the speculative journey to Angers to see his questionable uncle, he intended to go to Blois and the court of Charles, Duke of Orléans, hoping to obtain a patron. Unknown to him the Navarre robbery had been discovered in March. It was of little consequence. No one was suspected. He was miles from Paris. He had thousands of pounds and his prospects were good. It was a green spring, full of optimism. He was hoping to obtain the sponsorship of a great nobleman and good poet.

The road to Blois meandered alongside the Loire, through Meung-sur-Loire and Beaugency to the brown city of steeply winding streets around the château on its hill. Much changed today it was still a medieval castle in 1457 with towers, narrow corridors and a clutter of small rooms. It was the favourite residence of the royal-blooded Charles, Duke of Orléans.

Sixty-three, grey, partly deaf, wearing his familiar long furred gown of black velvet he was courteous, learned, patient after a quarter of a century of imprisonment in England, resigned to the dislike of his cousin, the king, Louis XI, who preferred commercial entrepreneurs to an anachronism of chivalry like

Charles. To the monarch the duke was a self-indulgent hedonist, a lover of the arts, a devotee of chess. It was from such a man that Villon hoped to obtain an allowance.

Blois was a world of privilege and social stratification.[2] Nearly ninety people served the duke, over thirty Mary his third wife. Charles ruled everything. Below him were his counsellors, his chamberlain, his treasury officials. They in turn commanded scores of young men of good birth, esquires that oversaw the minions of the château, the valets, minstrels, cooks, huntsmen. Even among that class there were distinctions down to the scullions of the kitchens and the peasants on the duke's wide estates. Lodging for months, sometimes years, among this court were the artists, musicians, craftsmen and, above all for Charles, the poets.

It was an existence of dank chambers, straw bedding for everyone except the duke and his wife, but it was also a magical world of tapestries, large allegorical paintings, and of a lavish table with sumptuous food, excellent wines and brilliant conversation between the duke and his companions whether a nobleman such as René, Duke of Anjou, who was there in 1457, perhaps meeting Villon, or the anxious, clever supplicants for the duke's favours. There were long evenings of joking, exchanging witticisms at which Villon excelled, hours when Catherine de Vausselles and the humiliation were forgotten.

It was luxury. It was also tedium for a genius. The meals were good but had to be eaten with decorum. Behaviour, clothes, deportment, everything was affected by ceremony. To someone liking the bawdy, drunken jests of the Coquillards, the grubby, uninhibited requirements of Blanche the cobbler, Jeanneton, or Guillemette the hours must have seemed days of frustration.

Charles of Orléans was a poet although a very different one from Villon. His poetry was good whether in native French or acquired English but it was courtly verse, mannered to the modern ear, delicate and with gentle emotion, but it was detached from the savagery of the fifteenth century, the work of a nobleman with little experience of poverty and disease.

Le temps a laissé son manteau
De vent, de froidure et de pluye,
Et s'est vestu de brouderie,
De soleil luyant, cler et beau.

The time hath laid his mantle by
Of wind and rain and icy chill,
And dons a rich embroidery
Of sunlight pour'd on lake and hill.[3]

Rondeau XXXI

Extracts from two poems on a similar theme, people and sex, one his, one Villon's, will point the difference between the men. The first by Charles is the fifth stanza of his own English version of his *Chant Royal*, 'Priez, galans joyeux en compaignie . . .'.

> Pray, gallants, that enjoy good company,
> Who long to spend money freely;
> War keeps your purses ill-supplied.
> Pray, lovers who wish to serve Love
> In happiness, for war by its harshness
> Hinders you from attending to your ladies,
> Which often makes them change their minds;
> And when you have got hold of the cord
> A stranger comes and takes it from your hand.
> Pray for peace, the true treasure of joy!

Villon in his 'Ballade of Pardon', regretting his misdeeds, wrote of lower life and city people with his distinctive eye.

> To fat Chartreux and Celestines,
> To lustful friars, nuns with chores,
> To loafers, dandies, little queens
> Of serving-girls and preening whores
> In flesh-thin dresses, and the scores
> Of love-sick fops like harlequins,
> Buckskin-booted paramours,
> I beg all pardon for my sins.
>
> To prostitutes that flaunt their tits
> To stimulate their clientele,
> To drunkards swinging drunken hits,
> And showmen with their apes that smell,
> To idiot men – and girls as well –
> Whistling with their gawping grins,
> Each with toy and bagatelle,
> I beg all pardon for my sins. [T, 186+]

To make any comparison between the two poets is an empty exercise. As the German critic, Georg Bullrich, observed, 'the difference between the two is so great that the best course is to abstain from playing off one against the other'.[4]

How long Villon remained welcome at Blois he did not say. Something happened. As always, he only hinted. He may have disgraced himself much as Robert Burns did in 1794 at Friars Carse near Dumfries, the home of his friend, Captain Robert Riddell and his pretty young wife, Maria. One evening 'when wine flowed much too freely Burns . . . grievously offended his hostess', maybe oafishly sneering at her chocolate-box odes. Sober next day he apologised to her in verse and prose but Riddell never forgave him.[5]

Something similar may have happened to Villon. At the beginning of his *Testament*, T, 1, 2, he wrote, 'Que toutes mes hontes j'eus beues', 'When I had drunk down all my shame and disgrace'. An almost identical line was written by Charles d'Orléans. It is a 'sufficiently rare expression for the suggestion to have been made more than once that, in using it in a rondeau giving a condescending and unsympathetic portrait of a down-and-out, the aristocratic prince-poet was referring to his contemporary, Villon'.[6] Nothing is clear, just vague words. When drunk, a cynical Villon may have derided the duke's genteel verses. Or was just nastily drunk.

One of the many entertainments in the château and one highly esteemed by the duke was a poetical tournament in which Charles devised the first line of a rondeau or a ballade on themes such as 'The gown does not make the monk'. On it the contestants had to extemporise. To avoid sycophancy the duke always wrote his version last. The best of the resulting poems were copied into a parchment-covered book in his own elegant handwriting. Three of Villon's poems were included but in a different hand, just possibly that of Villon himself PD, 1–3 (L, 8, 7, –).

The most famous of these challenging lines was, 'Je meurs de soif auprès de la fontaine', 'I die of thirst at the fountain's side', PD, 2 (L, 7). At least eight competitors entered the contest including the duke's doctor, his butler, Villon and Charles. None of the results was excellent, stilted, made heavier by the ponderous ten-syllable line. Good poets do not write well to order. Poet Laureates seldom create splendid poems about state occasions, producing verses that are adequate but uninspired because they were not born of inspiration. Villon's ballade was no exception, dutiful rather than lyrical. But its Envoi provides a clue that somehow the poet had misbehaved and been deprived of the duke's allowance.

Prince clement, or vous plaise sçavoir
Que j'entens moult et n'ay sens ne
  sçavoir
Parcïal suis, a toutes loys commun
Que said je plus? Quoy! Les gaiges
  ravoir.
Bien recueully, debouté de chascun.

O clement prince, pray hear me when I say
All things I know but sense has gone away.
Felon am I yet still to law a thrall!
What want I more? What! Again to have
  your pay.
Welcomed at first and now dismissed by
  all.

It suggests that he had been banished from the château for rudeness, sottishness or theft but there is controversy over the translation of 'gaiges ravoir' for which there is an alternative rendering, 'retrieving what I have pawned', a very different interpretation and typical of the kaleidoscopic Villon. To add to the ambiguity it is not clear whether the mishap, whatever it was, occurred during the poet's first or second visit to Blois. As it is equally unclear whether he ever did return it is best to leave the matter at its most economical.

He departed from Blois and began the drudging, hundred-mile journey to Angers deprived of a pension, stolen coins dwindling, his reputation in ruins. Worse followed. Just after Easter in Paris a wine-sodden Guy Tabarie had met an attentive and far from drunken stranger at the Chaire tavern on the Petit-Pont and bragged about the Navarre burglary.[7]

His new acquaintance was a country priest, Pierre Marchand, from Paray-le-Moniau not far from Chartres. His testimony was later documented by the Bishop's official, Truisy, copied from the criminal records – significantly at the request of the university's Faculty of Theology. By midday when Tabarie and a companion met Marchand they had enjoyed sufficient

hippocras to boast indiscreetly of their lucrative exploits a few
months earlier, the robberies at the Augustinians, at St
Mathurin, of the friar Guillaume Coiffier and of the College of
Navarre. It was easy, claimed Tabarie, for an expert picklock
like himself, particularly with the fine tools, *crochets*, that the
jeweller, Petit Thibault, made for him. Unfortunately he could
not show them to Marchand because he had thrown the
incriminating rossignols into the Seine. Thibault was doubly
useful because he would also melt down the stolen gold and
silver. Most of the thieves were still in Paris but one of them,
François Villon, had gone to Angers to work out a method of
robbing a rich uncle.

Having heard of the notorious Navarre affair the curious Pierre
Marchand, servant of God turned amateur sleuth, arranged to
meet his bibulous friends next day at the Pomme de Pin. Naively
trusting him when he said he would like to join the band and
make some money they offered to introduce him to some
members. The three strolled to the cloisters of Notre-Dame. Four
or five of the gang were there in sanctuary after breaking out of
the Bishop's prison, just waiting to get away. One was a man of
about twenty-eight to thirty years of age, short, well-dressed with
a black beard, Petit-Jean. Another was 'ung . . . petit homme &
jeune de xxvi ans . . .', 'one who was a small young man, of about
twenty-six years old or thereabouts with long hair behind. . . . the
most skilful of all the company, and the cleverest at picking locks,
and that nothing was ever impossible to him', quite probably
Colin de Cayeux.[8]

The next scheme, confided the suicidal Tabarie, was to pick the
locks of the money-chest belonging to a monk, Robert de la Porte,
while he was absent from Paris. A cousin of Thibault was to
supply them with clerical gowns so that they could pass through
the abbey inconspicuously with their concealed jemmies and
rossignols that Thibault had crafted. The raid had been planned
for some time but postponed when all the fuss about Navarre had
erupted. Saying that he was eager to take part in the venture

Marchand promised to meet Tabarie the following Monday. Instead, on 17 May he went to the Châtelet with his story.

Early that March two of the king's Examiners, Jehan Mautaint and Jean du Four, had taken notes of what was missing from the college, a hundred gold coins of Rogier de Gaillon's, sixty of Laurens Poutrel's, the balance belonging to the community. Nothing more could be done. The perpetrators were unknown. There were no suspects. That ignorance disappeared with the testimony of Marchand. Instantly the Provost sent parties to arrest the bunch but hearing rumours everyone, Tabarie included, had fled.

The damage was done. Dompnus Nicolaus de partibus Picardie, Petit Jehan, Colinus des Cahyeux, all their names were known but they were aware of it and hid. But magistro Francisco Villon, magistrum Franciscum Villon, magister Franciscus Villon iverat Andegavis, un aultre complice nommé Françoys Villon . . . estoit allé à Angers, time after time the name appeared, he had broken into the college, had taken his share of the pickings, had cheated Tabarie. It was a death sentence.[9]

Unaware of the betrayal Villon plodded westwards, miles towards Amboise on the far side of the river, the land almost deserted, an occasional farmstead being repaired, scattered fields of crops. Fifteen more miles to Tours, another twenty-nine to Chinon. Perhaps he drank there in the hillside Painted Cellar, the Caves Peintes on the rue des Caves, a drinking-place made famous by Rabelais. 'I know where Chinon is', said Pantagruel, 'and I know the painted cellar. I've drunk many a glass of fresh wine there, and I don't doubt that Chinon is an ancient city. Its motto proves the fact, for it reads:

Chinon, Chinon
Petit ville, grand renom,
Assise sur pierre ancienne,
Au haut le bois, au pied la Vienne.

Chinon, Chinon,
Little city, great renown,
Perched upon its rocky brow,
The woods above, the Vienne below.[10]

A few more coins gone, some lost through carelessness, some stolen but enough left as Villon reached the lovely old town of Saumur with its slogan:

High towers and low town

to which was added the words of a civic assessment

Rich for a trollop, poor for a gown.

Villon happily approved of the first four. There were alcoholic days with ruffians, another coin gone as the wine was ordered, lubricious nights with girls, more haggled coins gone but sufficient remaining for good times to come. It was a summer of hard, ankle-rutted roads alongside the river. At last he came to the walled city of Angers almost 200 meandering miles from Paris, dominated by its stupendous castle, a Jordanian Krak of the Crusaders transferred to western Europe, its pepperpot-roofed towers banded in alternating courses of light and dark stone. The stronghold was the court of another poet-nobleman, René, Duke of Anjou and Lorraine, titular king of Naples, a man who had also hoped for the crowns of Hungary, Jerusalem and Sicily but received none.

As a poet he was a minor figure of less merit than the Duke of Orléans. His long and intricate saga, the *Livre du Cuer d'Amour*, with its adventures of the knight 'Heart', who eternally courted 'Sweet Pity', with almost endless journeys through the 'Forest of Long Waiting' and across the 'River of Tears' is as unworldly as moondust and just as far from humanity. Yet this plump, beardless amateur was a polymath, fluent in five languages, conversant with mathematics, geology and the law, writing sweet verses, playing and composing music, painting in oils, putting on Mystery Plays at Angers, Saumur and Aix-en-Provence. He was less formal, more relaxed than Orléans. Loving flowers he caused a garden to be laid out on the castle ramparts with beds of lavender, marguerites, hollyhocks and vines. Its descendant survives. The castle was a wonderland of oak panelling, carpets, carvings, tapestries, it was thronged with musicians, painters, Fouquet was there, and poets. There was shelter, warmth, food, drink and money. Villon must have longed to be admitted.

Again it is not known what happened except that Villon was disappointed. It is believed that he had been given a letter of introduction to René by Andry Couraud who lived near St Benoît and who was a Treasury counsellor to the king, an advocate in Parliament and René's representative in Paris.[11] The letter did not gain Villon's admittance. Stewards may have reported his shabby, mud-stained appearance. Disapproval from Blois may have preceded him. A horseman could cover the distance in days. Villon may have loitered weeks, even months. He was refused. A pleading quatrain achieved nothing.

Prince amoreux, des amans le
    greigneur . . .

Prince of lovers, greatest of all who wooed,
I could not welcome your grim frown,
But, by our Lord, the mighty should
Help the poor, not beat them down.
[T,93+, 966–9]

There was no reprieve. Villon took predictable but cautious revenge. Embittered, he attacked René's over-idyllic pastoral, *Regnault et Jehanneton, les Amours de Berger et de la Bergeronne*, which the infatuated duke had written to his second wife, Jeanne de Laval, the 'fair shepherdess'. It was a romance extolling the delights of rural life, the idealised simplicity of sunlit meadows, moon-reflected streams, the joyful hands of country lovers. It was the dream-world, as Bonner neatly put it, of the 'Ah got plenty of nuttin' school of thought'.[12]

To Villon, for whom the only countryside pleasure was the sight of an approaching inn, it was an irresistible temptation. He did not dare mock the courtly pastoral directly. Dukes could imprison, assassinate. Instead he ridiculed its fifteenth-century prototype, *Les Dits de Franc Gontier* by Philippe de Vitry, a poet much admired by René. Villon may also have resented Couraud's ineffectual letter of credentials. He bequeathed him a *Contradiction of Franc Gontier*, making reference to an unnamed but obvious 'tyrant on his throne'.

Item a maistre Andry Courault
'Les Contreditz Franc Gontier' mande

To Andry Couraud I donate
Franc Gontier Denied.
As for the tyrant on his throne
I'm sensible and stay tongue-tied.
The Wise Man warns the poor to hide
From might and wealth, and take all care
To dodge the pitfalls spread out wide
To trap poor wretches in their snare.

[T, 142]

To Villon city comforts were preferable to the discomforts of the countryside. He imagined himself a voyeur, spying on two urban lovers at their naked pleasures:

A jolly canon on down cushions laid
Beside a stove in room both neat and gay,
Dame Lovesome lying at his side displayed,
Fair, tender, smooth and tricked in rare array:
A-drinking wine from dawn to eve were they,
Rejoicing, kissing, toying, full of glee,
And both all bared the easier to be,
I saw them through the keyhole on my knees:
Then knew, that if from care we would be free
No treasure is like living at our ease.

If Franc-Gontier and Helen his sweet maid
Had ever made of such delight assay,
Their hunger ne'er with brittle crusts were stayed,
Or onions that foul breath bestow alway.
Their buttermilk and other drinks, perfay,
Are in less worth than garlic held by me.
They boast of sleeping 'neath the woodland tree,
Doth not a chair-flanked bedstead better please?
What say you? Does it need a longer plea?
No treasure is like living at our ease.
They feed on coarse brown bread and grain decayed,
And all the year drink water, yea or nay.
From here to Babylon no serenade
Of birds would hold me for a single day,
No not one morn, for fare like this to May!
Franc-Gontier with Helen may agree
For joys beneath the eglantine to flee;
I need not frown, if such their hearts appease;
Whatever bliss in country life they see,
No treasure is like living at our ease.

Prince, judge between us all of each degree.
For me, let none be wrath at what he sees,
Still young in years I learnt to touch this key,
No treasure is like living at our ease.

J.H. Lepper

It is to be doubted that Couraud ever showed the poem to René.

Villon trudged dejectedly out of Angers, old memories of
Vausselles and the indignity reawakened in his depression. He
may have briefly returned to Paris with some poems to be
safeguarded, learning of Tabarie's blabbing tongue during the
stay. And as though that were not bad news enough he received
worse. Regnier de Montigny, one of his oldest, closest friends,
was dead. He had been hanged at Montfaucon on 15 September
on a new scaffold, 'Montigny's gibbet'. That young man, five
years older than the poet, with his pack of illicit but fictitious
hunting-dogs comically donated by Villon, had been a criminal
for years. Only the protection of his helpful clerical status had
kept him alive for so long. Fittingly, it was sacrilege that
doomed him.[13]

During 1456 he had broken into the church of St Jean-le-
Grève not far from the recaptured Pet-au-Deable of Mlle de
Bruyères. The church was famous for its valuable relics. With
Nicolas de Launay, most likely the Dom Nicolas of the Navarre
robbery, Montigny picked the locks of cupboards in the Sacristy,
ignored less costly articles and took a gold chalice to a jeweller,
Jacquet le Grand, for melting down. Discovered with the
remains of the chalice le Grand quickly informed his examiners
about Montigny who was apprehended and taken to the
Châtelet. His crimes were well known. He had experienced
prisons in Tours, Rouen, Bordeaux, four times in Paris, had
swindled a draper in Poitiers and had repeatedly been saved by
his bishop. This time, however, there was only the most
reluctant intervention.

On 24 August 1457 the bishop claimed that Montigny was a
clerk in Minor Orders, was unmarried, had a tonsure and was

therefore the property of the Church. The civic authorities replied that the man was a thief, a swindler and a recidivist having been forgiven so many times. The bishop did nothing and on 9 September Montigny was condemned to be hanged, 'pendu et etranglé'.

Abandoned by the Church he turned to his well-born family among whose uncles and cousins were highly placed government officials. Most were indifferent to the fate of a ne'er-do-well who had sullied their name. It was his pregnant younger sister, Jeanne, who implored the king to forgive her wretched brother. Louis XI consented but the conditions were harsh. The prisoner was to be incarcerated in the deepest cell of the Châtelet, fed on bread and water for twelve months, and then released to go on pilgrimage to St Jacques de Compostela, returning with a certificate of proof. The Letter of Remission listed Montigny's felonies, all of which were to be erased from the records.

Probably provided by Regnier himself, forgetting some of the many, diplomatically not admitting to some of the worst, the omissions were noticed by Council. He had not, they stated, confessed to forging some rings of imitation gold, nor to the killing of Thevenin Pensete, he had given conflicting accounts about the theft of the chalice and the 'pardon', therefore, was 'incivile', invalid. The original sentence was confirmed by Parliament. Regnier de Montigny was hanged. To the list of Dijon Coquillards executed in 1455 the prosecutor, Rabustel, laconically added:

Regnier de Montigny (mort et pendu)

and then 'ung nommé Rosay (pendu)', Montigny's companion in the 1452 brawl with sergeants outside the brothel of La Grosse Margot. It was one more loss in Villon's life.

His purse now even lighter if there had been repayment to an uncle in Angers, downhearted at his rebuffs in Blois and Angers, distressed at the death of Montigny, Villon set out on his third and last opportunity for patronage, the court of Jean, Duke of Moulins, south-west of Bourges and over two hundred miles east of Angers.

It was the autumn of his exile, a scarecrow existence in the year's weathers, sun-browned, rain-sodden, fog-lost, snow-trapped, a drudge of long, almost empty roads, encountering strangers, hand on the dagger at his belt, exchanging news, an exploratory change to an unintelligible language. Villon had come from Bourges, an acceptable place but 'enteruez a la floterie', but 'keep an eye out for the judges there', J, 5. The strangers looked at each other, 'spelicans', 'picklocks' they proclaimed, J, 3. Moulins was good too replied a reassured Villon, 'marque de plant dames et andinas', 'no shortage of tarts and trollops', J, 11. They nodded to each other. If Villon was going to Orléans, 'eschec, eschec, coquille si sen broue', 'watch out, take care, the Coquillards are finished', J, 10. They departed.

It is like watching a ghost pass through walls to follow Villon's steps but it could have been in the late autumn of 1457 that he decided to visit the village of St Généroux south of Thouars. Maybe one of his cronies confided that there were two very accommodating ladies there, 'deux dames . . . très belles et gentes'. Accommodating linguistically as well they taught him some of the Poitevin dialect.

Mais i ne dis proprement ou	Ah'm tellin' no one wheah
Yquelles passent tous les jours,	Those gals pass days so merrily,
M'arme! Ne suy moy si tres fou	Gawd! Ah aint no fool, so theah,
Car i vueil celer mes amours.	Ah'll keep those jig-a-jigs for me. [T, 104, 1066–9]

St Généroux, he added helpfully for subsequent seekers of accommodation, was close to St-Julien-de-Vouventes. It was Villonesque deception. In reality St Généroux was over seventy miles to the south-east. There may, however, be an elusive relevance in the fact that the hamlet was less than forty miles north of St Maixent l'École, a town that Rabelais was to associate with Villon.[14] From St Généroux it was a long road to Bourges. Once there, of all the mysteries in Villon's writing probably the most baffling is the mysterious affair of the city, flaming red tongues and the Perdrier brothers. They were contemporaries of Villon in Paris, Jehan to become the warden of a royal palace at Loges, François Perdrier one of ten privileged merchants of fish in the city. Both had money.

Yet these superficially unremarkable young men became the subjects of the most venomous of all Villon's angry ballades, every line filled with hatred and gall. The first stanza, translated by Lepper, reveals the rancorous hope that both the brothers' tongues be cooked in everything that was vile and loathsome:

> In arsenic, the white sort and the red,
> Saltpetre, quicklime, causing countless aches,
> To clean them better, adding boiling lead;
> In sulphur, pitch, and in those stinking lakes
> You may discover in a ghetto's jakes;
> In lotions that have cooled a leper's heat;
> In stuff scraped off from shabby shoes and feet:
> In blood of asp and drugs with death allied;
> In spleen of wolf and fox and pole-cat sweet
> May all such envious tongues as these be fried.
>
> [T,141+, 1422–31]

The succeeding, equally vitriolic stanzas added to the mixture: brains of a toothless cat, spittle, phlegm, navels cut from living snakes, cancers, sores, dishwater from dirty tubs, a concoction of the vilest ingredients for their tongues.

There have been half-hearted guesses about the cause of the rage. The least likely is that the Perdriers had refused to lend Villon money, or that they had criticised the poet in front of the archbishop when he had been expecting their recommendation. Another theory was that at the beginning of 1458 Villon had been part of a Coquillard church robbery that involved a pathetic goldsmith, Denis Marot, whose three children had just died of plague. Speculatively, the brothers had informed the authorities of Villon's rôle in the sacrilege. A fourth idea was that 'Bourges' had nothing to do with the brothers who had no known connections with the place and that Villon had simply played with words, really meaning 'bougres', or 'buggers'.[15]

None is convincing. Two stanzas earlier in T, 140, 1410–13 Villon, sarcastically calling François Perdrier his good friend, said the man had recommended the poet to some spiced, red tongues. This may wriggle behind the words. 'L'Inquisition contraignait de porter, cousues sur leurs vêtements, des langues de draps rouges.' 'Blasphemers condemned by the Inquisition had tongues of red cloth sewn to their robes like the flaming tongues of demons.'[16] Perdrier had 'me recommanda fort a Bourges'. Wyndham Lewis half-explained:

> From the significant *recommanda* it has been deduced that sacrilege or heresy was in the air; that Villon, either drunk and blaspheming in a tavern, or caught rifling an almsbox or prowling inexplicably in a church, was brought before the archbishop of Bourges, Jehan Coeur; that he discovered his old *compère* François Perdrier (and possibly his brother Jehan) and hailed François confidently, counting on his assistance; and that the snake François turned round and denounced him.[17]

A proven charge of heresy could result in the condemned person being burnt alive at the stake as Joan of Arc had been years before. It was a horrifying prospect. If that was what the ugly tongues of the Perdriers had been guilty of, stigmatising Villon as a heretic, then his relieved fury is understandable. His ballade ended:

> Prince, please strain these titbits of ordure.
> If you've no sieve or filter then be sure
> To use some filthy pants where shit has dried.
> But first of all, in stinking pig's manure
> May these lying, spiteful tongues be fried. [T, 141+, 1452–56]

It is compelling poetry but not for the squeamish.

It seems that Villon convinced the court of his innocence and was released just in time to avoid an epidemic that ravaged the

city in May. Innocent and free he went on his terrified, relieved
and resentful way to Moulins, making up rhymes and dam-
nations as he went. Whether the confrontation with the Perdriers
physically occurred in Bourges is uncertain. The poet may have
chosen the name as a convenient if imperfect rhyme for
'flambans et rouges'. But as Villon would have to pass through
Bourges on his way to Moulins and as it is known that he did go
to Moulins Bourges remains a geographical likelihood.

In the middle of the year a foolhardy Tabarie returned to Paris
and was arrested on 25 June, just over twelve months since his
confidant, the priest Pierre Marchand, had informed the
authorities of the braggart's revelations. Imprisoned in the
Châtelet, twice tortured on the rack, Tabarie admitted that everything he had said was true. He was released only when his
mother promised to pay the court fifty gold crowns, five times
the amount the fool had been given for his part in the Navarre
burglary. Through his confession the name of François Villon
was inscribed in the criminal records.[18]

The poet was in need of money. The coins were gone, mislaid,
filched, squandered, irretrievably vanished exactly as Panurge
regretted his own lost écus, saluts and crowns in *Gargantua and
Pantagruel*, 'They are far enough off by now if they are still
moving. "But where are the snows of yesteryear?" which was
the great preoccupation of the Parisian poet Villon',[19] and Villon
could only hope that Jean II, Duke of Moulins and his liege
lord, the aristocratic ruler of the lands from which the poet's
family came, would help with a purse if not with a stipend.

It was through pleasant but ordinary countryside that he
tramped to the attractive old town of Moulins. Today the
nineteenth-century Grand Café glitters like a gilded Hall of
Mirrors in the Place d'Alliers below the hill winding up to the
cathedral with its famous triptych by the Master of Moulins and
to the remains of the Vieux Château with its 'dishevelled' tower,
almost all that remains of the medieval castle. Here Jean, duke
and minor poet, held his court with its motto of 'Esperance',

The 'distorted' tower of the château at Moulins. (*Author photo*)

'Hope'. Villon stated that he had been there, despairing, penniless, when good fortune brought him to the beautiful city and gave him hope, 'et pourveut du don d'esperance', T, 13, 102. Jean was only three years older than Villon. He was a great patron of the arts, a friend of Charles d'Orléans, and himself a poet and moralist. His court was frequented by intellectuals from all over France, and this brilliant company spent its time in organising pageants, exchanging witty and learned conversation, and in the study of rare books and manuscripts. It was a younger, more easy-going court than that of King René, so that these recondite amusements were varied by hunting, hawking and music. Villon, hopeful as ever, immediately sent a petition to the Duke, commencing with a tactful reminder of their feudal relationship by addressing him as *le mien seigneur*.[20]

The castle that he saw was almost entirely destroyed by fire in 1755. Just one tower survived, the 'Mal Coiffée', so called because of the inelegance of its roof. Villon may have lodged there for a while, temporarily content with the money that the duke gave him. He must have been welcome for he had the confidence to beg for more.

> No prince to me has ever lent
> One sou except the loan you made.
> Those six écus have long been spent,
> The coins for food I had to trade.
> But further gifts will be repaid,
> My Lord, without an argument.
> To gather acorns, chestnuts I'm intent
> From the woods around Patay.
> Once sold their earnings will be sent.
> You'll only know a slight delay.
>
> [PD, 4 (L, 10)]

It was cheerful impertinence. There were no woods around Patay a few miles north-west of Orléans, the battlefield of a French victory in 1429, 'only gently rolling countryside with an occasional stand of trees' and the prospect of an industrious Villon scavenging there for two or three worthless nuts may have amused the light-hearted duke sufficiently for him to hand over a few more coins.[21]

Like all Villon's dreams of security the visit ended in a return to the friendless countryside, hopes of patronage lost in Blois, Angers, Moulins. There was nowhere else and bad luck stalked him like a hungry wolf. Leaving Moulins, fearfully avoiding Bourges, he came to Issoudun and to the magistrate's court, accused of some triviality, a brawl, drunken misbehaviour, nothing dangerous. Except for the magistrate. Macé d'Orléans was an opinionated, abusive bully. Pompously misusing long words, with malapropisms flowing from his gratingly high-pitched voice like a chattering termagant, he fined Villon an extortionate sum, perhaps almost all that the indigent poet possessed.

Villon did not forgive. He emasculated Macé, turning him into a scold. 'Mais qu'a la petite Macée . . .', as for the little woman, Macée of Orléans, who took his money-belt and purse, let justice give her a heavy fine as well, she's a whore who has cuckolded her husband, she's nothing but a rotten slut, T, 122. And having changed the magistrate's gender and vilified 'her' morals Villon went on his poorer way.[22]

Without sustenance 1459 was a year of aimless wandering in the Orléanaise, cursing Vausselles for having reduced him to this, chilled by the heavy, lurching winds, dirtied by the mud-toiling squelch of the roads, sponging on shopkeepers, complaining of poverty and hunger yet always steadfastly aware that his misfortunes came from himself. Such honesty was a constant virtue. He never deceived himself, regretting the thoughtlessness of his youth, T, 22, believing that had he studied more he would now be living in comfort, T, 26. He was not the one to judge anyone because he was the most imperfect of all, T, 33. In this he was remarkably like Rutebeuf, a thirteenth-century troubadour and satirist of Parisian life. He also had lacked patronage and income. No great lord supported him. Like Villon he knew privation.

Et froit au cul quant bise vente
Li vens me vient, li vens m'esvente
Et trop sovent
Plusors foïes sent le vent . . .

De la Griesche d'Yver

I am chilled to the bone when the east wind blows and
always it comes and blows through and through me. God so
tempers His seasons for me that black flies bite me in
summer, and white flies in winter. I am like the wild osier, or
like the bird in the tree. In summer I sing. In winter I weep
and lament . . . The dice from the dice-makers have robbed
me of all my garments; dice are my death . . . I lack food and
have lacked it for many years. No man offers it, no man
gives it to me. I cough with cold, I gape with hunger with
which I am eaten and maltreated. I lack a mattress, I lack a
bed. My ribs only too well know the taste of horse-litter. A
bed of straw is no bed, and I lie on nothing but straw.[23]

Villon also suffered. In his degradation no thought of Vausselles
remained, only survival. Mixing with untrustworthy Coquillards,
writing sardonically in jargon, eking out a semi-honest existence
as a pedlar with his pack, paper and poems, watchful for things
to steal, he retained his ironical sense of humour. 'What
happened to the money?', he asked in the ballade that inspired
Henley's 'booze and blowens cop the lot'.

Be ye carriers of bulls,
Cheats at dice – what'er ye be,
Coiners – they who risk like fools,
Boiling for their felony.
Traitors perverse – so be ye –
Thieves of gold, or virgin's pearls,
Where goes what ye get in fee?
All on taverns and on girls.

Song, jest, cymbals, lutes –
Don these signs of minstrelsy.
Farce, imbroglio, play of flutes,
Make in hamlet or in city.
Act in play or mystery,

Gain at cards, or ninepin hurls.
All your profits, where go they?
All on taverns and on girls.

Turn, before your spirit cools,
To more honest husbandry;
Grooms of horses be, or mules,
Plough the fields and plant the tree.
If you've no Latinity,
No more learning than the churls,
Work – nor cast your money free
All on taverns and on girls.

Stockings, pourpoint, drapery,
Every rag that round you furls,
Ere you've done, will go, you'll see,
All on taverns and on girls.   [T, 158+].

Henry de Vere Stacpoole

There was laughter in it but resignation as well. It was the work of a man whose life was in decay, all thought of the church long abandoned, patronage refused by those who could have offered it, Montigny hanged, Coquillards being harried in the ill-starred year of 1460 'for justice was making a clean sweep of "poor and indigent persons, thieves, cheats and lockpickers"'.[24] Villon was to join them. With no employment and no money crime, whether petty or desperately serious, was inevitable – and predictably it ended in disaster.

On 19 June he was in the prison of Orléans, arrested for some long-forgotten offence. He was tortured, confessed and was condemned to death. 'De Dieu, de vous, vie je tiens', 'through God, through you, I am alive', the words almost gasp at his unexpected escape. Harsh justice had doomed him, he had been thrown down by unlucky fate but now he was at liberty, PD, 1, 68–70 (L, 8).

Coincidence had rescued him. A fortnight after his capture Marie, the infant daughter of Charles, Duke of Orléans, made her first visit to Orléans accompanied by her mother, Mary, and her father. In her honour the city gave her a thousand livres with a further ten for her governess. There was a torchlit ball. The occasion was a lavish celebration of thanksgiving for her birth because Charles was almost seventy with no expectation of having more children. And amid the music and the wine and the public rejoicing there was near-hysterical rejoicing in the prisons at another medieval custom, an amnesty declared by the duke for all prisoners. They were given a *brevet*, a short-term warrant to safeguard them while they waited for the necessary Letter of Remission. Men with suspicious records did not wait. They took the *brevet* and left Orléans far behind.

Villon was released. Whether he blinked at the almost forgotten sunlight is unrecorded but his very long, rather forced double ballade to Marie, PD, 1 (L, 8), is almost a scream of exultation. 'O louee concepcion', it began, 'O praiseworthy conception's fruit', Marie was an indispensable child, a gift to earth from Heaven to whom he wished long life and every happiness. Then, at the end of sixteen strained verses, the ballade concluded with a completely sincere note. 'J'espoir de vous servir ainçoys . . . vostre provre escolier Françoys', 'I wish to serve you, your poor scholar, François'. As the young child almost certainly could not read it was a blatant request to the duke for Villon to be taken back into his favour. It may have happened. The ballade was copied into the duke's book of poems and Villon could have become a guest at Blois for a while.

On either side of the law there could be trouble. On 18 July it was not a convicted felon but the Criminal Lieutenant of Paris in charge of the Châtelet prison who was accused of frivolity, 'excesses committed by Monsieur Martin de Bellefaye and his sergeants, who insisted on playing a comedy in front of the Châtelet, in spite of the objections of the Parliament officials'.[25]

Eighty miles from this frolic Villon was free, perhaps temporarily living in some comfort, but 1460 was not done with him. On 26 September his other great friend, Colin de Cayeux, was executed. Villon wrote a ballade of lost children, 'enfants perdus', about it. 'Beaulx enfans, vous perdez la plus' [T, 156, 1675].

Heed, lovely youths, for you could lose
The fairest thing you'll ever know.
Pickpocket clerks, avoid the noose.
If you set out for Montpipeau
Or to Rueil, bad luck could grow.
When he was caught my friend was care-less
So sure his pleas would beat the foe.
Now Colin de Cayeux's throat is airless.

Nicknamed 'l'Escailler', 'the cat-burglar', de Cayeux was appre-hended by the Provost of Senlis 25 miles north of Paris in the church of St Leu d'Esserents where he was claiming sanctuary. The claim was ignored. He was taken to Senlis but before he had time to work the locks and bolts he was transferred to the secure cells of the Conciergerie in the Palais of Paris, a prison that Villon was to know two years later and which became notorious during the French Revolution when over two thousand prisoners were taken from it to be guillotined between 1793 and 1794.

Two bishops, Senlis and Beauvais, demanded that the clerk de Cayeux be passed to them but the royal Prosecutor's represent-ative, the attorney Barbin, refused. De Cayeux was 'an incorrigible thief, picklock, marauder and sacrilegious scoundrel'. He had already been in the Châtelet twice. The bishops themselves had failed to detain him in their insecure dungeons, 'les prisons duquel il a crochetées et s'en eschapé', he had picked the locks and escaped. On 23 September after an acrimonious debate about his clerical status he was indicted. Three days later he was hanged.[26]

In jargon Villon wrote a variant of his ballade to lost children, 'beaulx enfants', already quoted, T, 156–8. He warned Coquillards not to be slipshod. Two of their most accomplished associates had been over-confident.

Coquillars enaruans a ruel	Coquillards, on your way to sin,
Men ys vous chante que gardés	Take every care or I foretell
Que ny laissez et corps et pel	That you will lose your precious skin.
Quon fist de collin lescailler	Colin, nicknamed 'scallop-shell',
Devant le roe babiller	A court made tell all he could tell,
Il babigna pour son salut	He babbled on to dodge the noose,
Pas ne scavoit oignons peller	With onion-tears he pleaded well
Dont lamboureux luy rompt le suc.	But still the hangman sucked his juice.

The prison of the Conciergerie, Paris. Colin de Cayeux was taken there. (*Author photo*)

Changes andosses souvent
Et tires tout droit au temple
Et eschiques tost en brouant
Quen la iarte ne soiez emple
Montigny, y fut par example
Bien ataché au hulle grup
Et y iargonast: il le tremble
Dont lamboureux luy rompt le suc.

Disguise yourselves, change every day.
A church gives refuge in a town.
If danger threatens get away,
Don't end up in the hanged man's gown.
Montigny's capture let him down.
When married to a hempen noose.
He chattered, trembling like a clown,
But still the hangman sucked his juice.

Gailleurs faitz en piperie
Pour ruer les ninars an loing
A la sault tost sans suerie
Que les mignons ne soient au gaing
Farciz dun plumbis a coing
Qui griffe au gard le duc
Et de la dur si tresloing
Dont lamboureux luy rompt le suc.

Cheats who swindle clot and dud,
Dodge the archers and take care
To con fools quickly, don't spill blood.
Give your pals a proper share.
Don't feel the torture of the 'pear'
That fills the mouth in iron abuse
Before you're swinging in the air,
As the hangman sucks your juice.

Prince erriere du ruel
Et neussies vous denier le pluc
Quau giffle ne laissez lappel
Dont lamboureux luy rompt le suc.

Prince, stop fighting in the city
Even if your funds vamoose.
Don't choke on your cries for pity
Or else the hangman sucks your juice. [J, 2]

Villon's advice was excellent. He did not profit by it.

8

Meung-sur-Loire, 1461

The Perdrier brothers, the identity of Marthe, and the visit to Angers were not the only problems in Villon's uncharted life. Until recently there was another mystery. It was line 33 in his great ballade, 'Épître à ses Amis', PD, 12 (L, 9), written when he was imprisoned in Meung-sur-Loire. The poem began, 'Aiez pictié, aiez pictié', 'have pity, have pity on me' and the refrain at the end of each stanza was, 'Le lesserez la, le povre Villon?', 'will you leave him there, the poor Villon?'

Line 33 was enigmatic: 'Et me montez en quelque corbillon . . .' which was translated by Payne in 1892, 112, as 'draw me from this dungeon'; and by Atkinson in 1930, 229, as 'lift me out in some way or another'. In 1946, 224, McCaskie thought that 'let down some basket and so draw me clear' was a faithful rendering. Bonner, 1960, 153, offered, 'raise me up in some big basket'. Saklatvala, 1968, 170, was in agreement, 'high in a basket let me now be drawn'. Dale, 1979, 211, thought the same, 'to raise him back into the air inside a basket', and so did Kinnell, 1982, 193, 'haul me out of here in a basket'. In 1990, 74, Sargent-Baur gave, 'and in some basket or other hoist me out'.

Perplexingly only three of the seven translators made any attempt to explain the line. Of the three Atkinson, 277, indulged in a poetic fantasia whereby an amorous Villon attempted to reach the bedroom of a desirable lady by being hauled up to her in a basket much as Virgil had once done only for that Roman poet's nocturnal conveyance to jam, leaving him to spend the night in suspended frustration halfway between land and lust. Sargent-Baur, 79, thought that the 'basket' might have been little more than a literary device, implying that '"Corbillon" is there, in part, because of the rime', a mistakenly frosty thought. She also suggested that 'he is, in the strict sense of the expression, a "basket-case" ', surely a linguistic anachronism when applied to a medieval poet ignorant of modern slang. It was the earliest of Villon's translators into English, Payne, lxi–lxii, who came closest to the truth, believing that Villon was incarcerated in a cell to which there were no steps, into which he had to be let down by ropes and in which he was chained, gagged and half-starved. The full truth about the basket would not be known until 1973.

Meung-sur-Loire, a medieval town only marginally less attractive than its neighbour, Beaugency, had a long history. Near Villon's time it had been the birthplace of the thirteenth-century satirical poet, Jean de Meung, *c.* 1250–1305, whose full-length statue stands by the Loire on the quai Jeanne d'Arc. The bust of a later poet, Gaston Couté, 1880–1911, can be found on a plinth in the same road. There is no memorial to Villon, only the nondescript rue François Villon near the château.

People and places already mentioned in this book are associated with the town. It was from there on 15 May 1429 that Joan of Arc sent an army provided by Gilles de Rais to defeat the English at Patay 16 miles to the north. Thirty-two years later Villon was brought to Meung's prison. There is no legal record of what he had done. There is a vigorous local belief that he had been one of a band of wandering players caught stealing a chalice from the church of a nearby hamlet, 'un vol dans l'église de Baccon ou appartenance à un troupe de "théâtreux" malgré son état de clerc', an actor involved in 'a theft from Baccon church, dressed in theatrical clothing despite his clerical status'.[1]

It is plausible. A group or four of five increasingly harassed Coquillards could easily have been persuaded to masquerade as a semi-respectable troupe of strolling mummers and jesters with

The church at Baccon near Meung-sur-Loire which Villon is believed to have robbed. (*Author photo*)

a collection of playlets, mimes and simple stories to entertain unsophisticated countryfolk with slapstick humour and worthily pious sentiments. A few tawdry costumes would be enough to earn some money and deflect the suspicions of the law.

The time was right. By the mid-fifteenth century the religious Miracle Plays had gradually been replaced by the equally serious Mystery Plays such as Gilles de Rais' *Mystery of the Siege of Orléans* but these frequently included very realistic, sometimes funny displays of worldly life. 'Every mystery of the Christian story, and its central mystery of salvation through the birth and death of Christ, was made physical and concrete and presented in terms of everyday life – irreverent, bloody and bawdy. The shepherds who watched by night were portrayed as sheep-stealers', the Virgin Mary emigrated to Egypt on an ass 'and the turds dropped from a lifted tail evoked howls of delight' . . . 'Sex and sadism were relished in the rape of Dinah, in the exposure of Noah naked and drunk, the peeping of the Elders at Susanna' in her garden as she innocently undressed to bathe.[2] Audiences gaped, gasped and loved it.

Intermingled with much earnest moralising there was clowning and backchat, Noah arguing with his wife in the English *Towneley Plays*, a master whose apprentice answered back in another Cycle, and over the next century these farcical elements became complete comedies in themselves. In England there was *Ralph Roister Doister* with its rhyming doggerel, Meg Mumblecrust and Tib Talkapace the servant-girls, a boastful lover and a besieged widow, and there was the earlier *Gammer Gurton's Needle* (*c.* 1550) in which the loss of a darning-needle was blamed on a neighbour, turning the entire village into a squabbling match of accusation until Mrs Gurton's needle was found embedded in the trousers of her servant, Hodge. In France there were identical burlesques and buffooneries. It was just the kind of dramatic foolery that would appeal to the psychology and technical mastery of Villon. It does not have to be myth. There is, after all, a literary rumour that late in his afflicted life he did produce a Passion Play at St Maixent 'in the Poitevin manner and dialect'.[3]

That could be wishful thinking. What is fact is that yet another misfortune was to befall the poet because the Lord of Meung, bishop and occupant of the château and prison there was Thibault d'Aussigny, a person mentally and spiritually lacking any sympathy for the unclerically garbed and bedraggled prisoner in manacles before him, grubby, grovelling, pathetic, with his scarred lip and whining words. The bishop was unimpressed. He was stern, legalistic. To understand his character one has to know that he had been appointed by the Church to be Bishop of Orléans in 1447 only for Charles VII to reject him with the full support of the Pope. D'Aussigny not only defied both these dominant figures but refused to permit the enacting of any papal bull in his diocese. Finally, ignoring both king and Pope, he appealed to Parliament and won, taking his seat in 1552 after five embattled years. Certain of his rights, assured in his rectitude, he administered justice with impartial severity.

Each year in Orléans he commemorated the anniversary of the raising of the city's siege by Joan of Arc. It has been claimed that he also had officiated on one or other of the tribunals for Joan's rehabilitation but his name appears nowhere in Pernoud or in the five magisterial volumes of Duparc and the claim is probably a confusion with his annual honouring of the Maid.[4] He died in 1473 and was buried in St Lyphard church against the château. Neither tomb nor any plaque exists today.

None of this need have made things worse for Villon except that being the Bishop of Orléans the keen-minded d'Aussigny quite possibly had previously had the same wretch in front of him in 1460 only to have the condemned man freed by the amnesty of Charles, Duke of Orléans. Now, by providence, he had him again and nothing was in the prisoner's favour. The *brevet* from Orléans was long out of date. There was no Letter of Remission. He had been caught in an act of sacrilege and that, for a professed clerk, was beyond forgiveness. Typically it seems that Villon was the only one taken at Baccon. The law wanted the others. D'Aussigny's representative, Pierre Bourgoing, ordered the poet to reveal the names of his associates. The local story, perhaps a genuine relic of folk-memory, claims that he knew the others only by their Coquillard nicknames, fictitious titles that were useless for identification of the culprits. When he continued to insist upon his ignorance he was sent for questioning.

It is believed that he was imprisoned in the Tour de Manassés de Garlande, a tall twelfth-century tower a few steps north-east of the château at Meung, and it was from his cell, trembling, that he was taken for the Question. 'Question' was the cruellest of medieval euphemisms. It meant 'torture'. And torture could be anything from dislocation of the fingers to crushing of the feet, to branding, to the rack and, probably worst of all, the Ordeal by Water – which is what Villon received.

Wrists tied, half-walking, half-dragged he was taken across the yard to the château, down a darkening flight of stone steps, along a narrow underground passage to a room lit by burning torches. It was not large but it was ominous in the pain that it threatened. In the wavering light he could see the rack, the attendants of Étienne Plaisance and his assistant, Master Robert, and the clerk waiting to take down his confession and a list of the missing names.

There was no escapist thinking, no recollection of merry theatrical quips about the coat of many colours or about Salome's seventh veil or Lot's salty wife. There was no thought of witty repartee about Baal between Jezebel and Elijah with an unexpected Baalam's ass adding to the uproarious confusion. 'Make the greenhorns grin and the cash comes in', he had told the appreciative Coquillards. But now there was no hilarious 'business' like David killing Goliath with a cunning potshot over his shoulder, no guffawing yokels. There was only one truth. The rack was the reality.

In the chill air he was stripped. He was attached to the rack that sloped down from head to feet. His outstretched arms were strapped behind his head to iron rings in the wall. The middle of his naked back was arched on a raised, painfully wedge-shaped wooden block. His ankles were lashed to bolts in the floor. The rack was ratcheted, stretching his body. His penis was tightly laced, preventing urination. He was told to open his mouth. He would have been beaten had he refused. All this without haste. All this in numb terror. A pear-shaped metal object was pushed into his mouth, the *poire d'angoisse*, named after a bitter-tasting pear grown in the Dordogne village of Angoisse. The *poire* was hinged in upper and lower sections that could be levered apart with a key, widening them, forcing the jaws open. A strip of gauze was laid across the prisoner's mouth.

Then, slow dribble by dribble, pint by slow pint, pipkins of water were poured down the throat through a horn funnel, gradually poured but on and on, usually about four *coquemars*,

The tour Manassés, Meung, in which Villon is thought to have been imprisoned. (*Author photo*)

large kettlefuls, about two gallons, sixteen belly-swelling pints, water oozing from swollen eyes, ears, but always into the trapped bladder until the body was bursting, drowning, helpless, fainting. Then release, retching and spewing in the straw, the clerk asking for the names, getting no answer, the half-conscious victim roughly dressed and hauled in soaking clothes back to his cell.

Dieu, mercy – et Tacque Thibauld
Que toute d'eaue froide m'a fait boire
En us bas, non pas ung hault
Menger d'angoisse mainte poire
Enferré . . .

There was no chuckled rhyme. Thanks be to God, and to Tacque Thibauld, yes, Tacque, Thibault d'Aussigny, because you're no better than that cruel, dissolute bastard, the vile favourite of the old Duke of Berry, you sod, *you* had me taken down, not up, gave me cold water and a pear to eat while I was strapped. You're no better than the foul Tacque Thibauld, Thibault d'Aussigny.[5]

[T, 73, 737]

The torture was repeated until they believed that he was telling the truth. He did not know the names. Satisfied, d'Aussigny, ever the upright clergyman, then punished him even more severely. Because of his sacrilegious theft he told the agonised Villon that the poet had forfeited the right to be a clerk in Holy Orders. It was unfair. D'Aussigny of Orléans was not his bishop. That was the Bishop of Paris. 'Mon seigneur n'est ne mon evesque', T, 2, 9–16, 'he's not my lord or my bishop, I owe him no homage, I'm not his serf or timid doe'. Turned into English it is indignant. In the original it spits.

Je ne suis son serf – ne sa biche, T, 2, 12.

Even a non-reader of French can sense the poet's abhorrence of d'Aussigny in the hisses of vicious sibilants. It was not calculated assonance, not technique. It was as instinctive to Villon as the flowing waters of a hillside stream, an unconscious reproduction in sound of the hatred he felt in his mind: 'suis', 'son', serf', 'sa', sssss. It was in vain. His head was shaved of its hair, eyebrows, beard, tonsure, 'scraped and peeled like a turnip', T, 178+,

1896–7. It was the final abasement. The Council of Château-Gontier had decreed that disgraced clerics should be deprived of their status and every hair of their heads removed.[6]

Reduced to the insecure rank of a lay person Villon was condemned to life imprisonment and taken to the oubliette in which Nicolas d'Orgement had perished forty-five years earlier. The dungeon was unknown until 1973 when it was decided to demolish an ugly concrete water-tank just south-west of the château. Under it a small aperture was exposed. A plumb-line proved that it was at the top of a 40 foot deep bee-hive shaped cavity, stone-walled, the oubliette or 'forgotten' chamber, a 'cul de basse fosse', into which doomed men were lowered by windlass. Hence Villon's 'basket'. It was dreadful, gloomy, dripping, stinking, with a murderously deep (150 ft) rectangular well at its centre, the receptacle for urine and excrement.

Fettered to the walls, with no possibility of escape below the high, incurving walls, 'nourished' daily on one large round loaf, a *miche*, and one *pichet* of water, however many the prisoners, for Villon it was a living tomb. D'Aussigny knew it. A churchman was not permitted to draw blood nor to execute. Ordeal by water avoided the first. Death by disease, pneumonia and malnourishment avoided the second.

Peu m'a d'une petite miche	He fed me on one small loaf and cold water for
Et de froide eaue tout ung esté	a whole summer. Whether generous or mean
Large ou estroit, moult me chiche.	himself, he was a miser to me.

[T, 5, 13–15]

Prieure en feray de Picart.   But I'll still give him a prayer from the Picards. [T, 5, 37]

There was no generosity in this prayer for d'Aussigny's soul. The Picards of Douai and Lille, a long-exterminated but heretical sect, denied that there was any effectiveness in prayer. Offering one of theirs was offering nothing.

As he lay there in the almost darkness, cold, hungry, body in pain, Villon, who had been educated by the church, remembered

The torture of the ordeal by water. (*Trustees of the British Museum, London*)

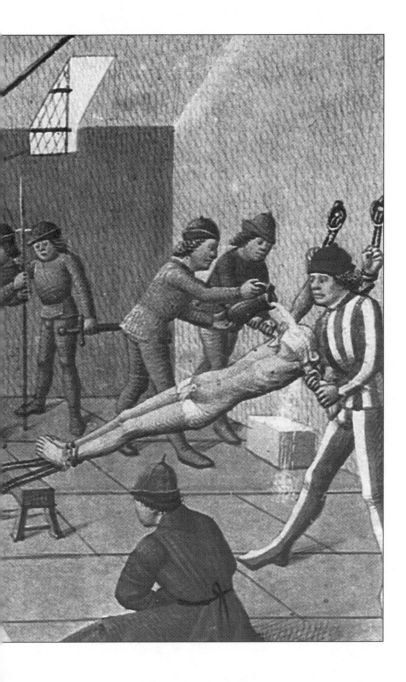

the story of Job and his afflictions, his endurance of them. There was a lesson for the poet 'that adversity, accepted as the divine will and borne with unflinching piety, is but a passing trial . . . A man who was undeservedly afflicted could see himself reflected in the Old-Testament patriarch. . . . And a man with a literary bent had an additional reason for appropriating a leaf out of Job's book, for Job had not only suffered but had (or so it was believed) recorded his experiences in immortal lines'.[7]

A great poem was born of Villon's belief that, like Job, he was being tested by God. It would surely be a mistake, however, to believe that this was the beginning of Villon's genius despite the statement that 'his most intense poetic creativity appears to have been largely confined to the period extending from then [mid-1461] until he disappearance into exile, roughly a year and a half later'.[8] This is unlikely. More convincingly, several of his finest ballades were probably composed two, perhaps three years earlier as individual pieces which were later discriminatingly integrated as centrepieces of the artistically planned stanzas of the *Testament*. Those poems that could not be assimilated appropriately into that Last Will and Testament became part of the independent *Poésies Diverses*.

There is, however, no doubt that his appeal to his friends. 'Aiez pictié, aiez pictié, de moy . . .', PD, 12 (L, 9), with its haunting refrain: 'Le lesserez la, le povre Villon?', 'Will you leave him here, the poor Villon?', did belong to the period of his imprisonment in Meung.

> Have pity on me, have pity I pray,
> My friends; may I pray you to grant this grace,
> For far from the hawthorn-trees of May
> I am flung in this dungeon in this far place
> Of exile, by God and by Fate's disgrace.
> New married and young; girls, lovers that kneel;
> Dancers and jugglers that turn the wheel,
> Needle-sharp, quick as a dart each one,
> Voiced like the bells 'midst the hills that peal:
> Will you leave him like this – the poor Villon?

Singers who sing without law your lay,
Laughing and jovial in words and ways;
Feather-brained folk, yet always gay,
Who run without coin, good or bad, your race,
You have left him too long who is dying apace;
Makers of ballads for tongues to reel,
Where lightning shows not nor breezes steal
Too late you will praise him when he is gone,
Around whom the walls are like bands of steel:
Will you leave him like this – the poor Villon?

Come hither and gaze on his disarray,
Nobles who know not the tax-man's face,
Who homage to kings nor emperors pay,
Only to God in his Paradise.
Behold him who, Sundays and holidays,
Fasts till like rakes his teeth reveal.
Who after crusts, but never a meal,
Water must suck till his belly's a tun.
With stool nor bed for his back's appeal:
Will you leave him like this – the poor Villon?

Princes, young, or whom years congeal,
A pardon I pray with the royal seal;
Then hoist me in a basket the earth upon.
So even will swine for each other feel,
And rush to help at the hurt one's squeal:
Will you leave him like this – the poor Villon?

H. de V. Stacpoole

The very first line, 'Aiez pictié . . .', would tell his readers that it
was the voice of Job from the Old Testament that spoke because
Job, 19, 21 pleaded, 'Have pity upon me, have pity upon me, O
ye my friends'. Villon transmuted the story into a statement of
his own personal adversities with his references to darkness, a
whirlwind and his own body's emaciation. He was, like Job, a
victim exiled by God's will.

The story of Job was a parable and Villon's use of it has been
well demonstrated.[9] When challenged by the Devil God chose to
try Job, 'a perfect and upright man' and caused him to lose his
family, property and health. His friends, 'Job's comforters',
attributed his misfortunes to his own sins of arrogance and

pride. Job protested his innocence. Despairingly, he cried, he could not understand the ways of God. Then God spoke to him from a whirlwind, convincing the stricken man of his ignorance. He rebuked him for questioning the ways of God. Job in 42, 2, 17, realised how little he did understand. 'I understood not, things too wonderful to me, which I knew not'. Through his humility he was restored to health and happiness and 'died, being old and full of days', a state of grace that Villon must have coveted in his present misery.

The entire book of Job was a criticism of the belief that sin and suffering were linked, the cause and the effect. This was to hearten Villon who used the book for comfort and hope. Temperamentally, he refused the company of Job's depressing 'comforters'. He preferred merry friends and young, laughing girls. In the medieval French the association between his ballade and Job is clear. The difficulty, already stated, is that it is impossible to make an accurate translation of a great poem into a different language. There are impassable barriers: the order of the words, their meaning, the scansion, the rhyme scheme and the rhymes themselves. The very simplest of examples demonstrates these problems.

There is an apparently straightforward line in Thomas Gray's famous *Elegy in a Country Churchyard*, 'The ploughman homeward plods his weary way'. On the surface it is an uncomplicated half-sentence but just changing it to 'The weary ploughman plods his homeward way' turns the emphasis from weariness to the return home. There is little any translator can do to overcome subtleties such as that. Other obstacles are less sensitive but just as important. Words matter. It would be ridiculous to substitute 'trots' for 'plods'. It would ruin the metre to use 'exhausted' instead of 'weary'; and it would wreck the rhyme to choose 'journey' rather than 'way'.

The translator of 'Aiez pictié . . .', Henry de Vere Stacpoole, Irish poet and novelist who also translated Sappho, had to face these challenges. Almost unavoidably he misled his readers in three vital lines in the second stanza, 17–19. The order of the lines was transposed, 18, 17, 19, a gentle pocket of air was chosen instead of a rough one (18) and the necessity of finding a rhyme (19) resulted in the Biblical context being obscured.

Where lightning shows not nor breezes steal	PD, 12 (L, 9), 18
Too late you will praise him when he is gone,	PD, 12, 17
Around whom the walls are like bands of steel:	PD, 12, 19

In his defence it should be added that a better poet, Swinburne, was little more helpful:

> Ye'll brew him broth too late when he is dead.
> Nor wind nor lightning, sunbeam nor fresh air
> May pierce the thick wall's bound where lies his bed.

For line 18 Villon had written, 'il n'entre escler [éclair] ne tourbillon', the poet was in a place where neither lightning nor a whirlwind could penetrate, an ironical reference to the 'protection' of his prison. His choice of 'whirlwind', however, was an obvious reference to God's admonitory words to Job, an allusion that Stacpoole's inexplicable selection of 'breezes' entirely missed.

His 'walls like bands of steel' is equally distorted. Line 19, 'De murs espoix ou lui a fair bandeaux' was translated by Bonner as 'thick walls are like a bandage for his eyes'; by Chaney as, 'thick walls shield his eyes'; and Kinnell, 'he's blindfolded by thick stone walls'. Sargent-Baur, anxious to stress the connection with Job wrote, 'of these thick walls they've made him swaddling bands', rather overstressing the connection with Job's 'when I made the cloud the garment thereof, and thick darkness a swaddlingband for it', Job, 38, 9. This is something of a quibble. The fact is that the consistent 'thick stone walls' and 'covered eyes' are more faithful to the original than the translation by Stacpoole with its steel walls and no mention of unseeing eyes.

The links with Job were reaffirmed in the third stanza, 26, 'dont les dens a plus longues que ratteaux', 'his teeth jut from his gums like rakes' a near paraphrase for, Job, 19, 20–2, 'My bone cleaveth to my skin and to my flesh, and I am escaped with the skin of my teeth. Have pity upon me, have pity upon me, O ye my friends, for the hand of God hath touched me. Why do you persecute me as God, and are not satisfied with my flesh?'.

'Have pity, my friends, help this helpless man'. Villon would endure his adversities but he desperately needed assistance. By another of his incredible coincidences, like a fairy-story, like a piece of Hollywood escapism for young children, it came.

On 22 July 1461, in agony from an infected jaw, the Dauphin's hated father, Charles VII, died. On hearing the news his son, Louis, went hunting. Mourning was forbidden. On 15 August the Dauphin, later known as the Spider King, was crowned Louis XI at Reims.[10] On his way from Genappe, he was appalled by the unrelieved, continuing desolation of the countryside. Then, by yet another coincidence, although more trivial, history repeated itself.

On 2 December 1431 the English child king, Henry VI, had entered Paris by the St Denis Gate. There the young pubescent boy stared for a long time at the naked girls splashing as mermaids in a fountain. Thirty years later on Monday 31 August 1461 the new French king, Louis XI, entered Paris by the same Porte St Denis seeing a fountain flowing with milk, wine and hippocras and an even more compelling sight, three pretty girls, completely unclothed, portraying themselves as Sirens in an artificial pond. In his *Journal Dite Chronique Scandaleuse* the chronicler, Jean de Roye, reported enthusiastically on 'three very handsome girls, representing quite naked sirens, and one saw their beautiful, turgid, separate round and hard breasts, which was a very pleasant sight, and they recited little motets and bergerettes; and near them several deep-toned instruments were playing fine melodies'. Such spectacles of unclothed females remained fashionable during the fifteenth and sixteenth centuries.

Philip le Beau saw one in Antwerp in 1494, the *Judgement of Paris*, the three goddesses represented in the nude by grown women. The displays were not always beautiful. At Lille in 1468 Charles the Bold was treated to the grotesque spectacle of a grossly obese Venus, an emaciated Juno and a hunchbacked Minerva. More aesthetically pleasing, as late as 1578 in Brussels, a tableau of a chained and nude Andromeda 'which one would have taken for a statue' was devised for William of Orange.[11]

In Paris there was pageantry, extravagance, self-satisfied indulgence which did not appeal to the austere Louis XI. As soon as he could he left the city on 23 September to go on a royal progress that would permit him to examine the state of his country, travelling through Touraine and the Orléanaise down to Bordeaux. It led him to Orléans on 19 October. Next day, the 20th, travelling towards Blois and Angers, his retinue passed through Meung 'freeing prisoners (according to the merciful custom) at all the stations on his journey'. A royal amnesty was announced. To the chagrin of Thibault d'Aussigny, Bishop of Orléans, the prisoners were released.[12]

Villon, astonished but elated at this second miracle, for surely that is what it had to be, did not linger in the vicinity of Meung-sur-Loire or Orléans. He limped and coughed his slow way towards Paris and safety. His relief and joy were affected by his awareness of the abuse his body had suffered, of how unwell he was. In this he was at one with his almost-contemporary, the Scottish poet, William Dunbar:

> I that in heill was and in gladness
> Am trublit now with great sickness
> And feblit with informitie.
> *Timor mortis conturbat me.*
>
> *Lament for the Makars*

'The fear of death disturbs my mind.' The poem was a lamentation that the pleasure of life was dominated by the inevitability of death. There is much of Villon in it.

Slowly he returned to Paris. Safety was not guaranteed. From his own words he lurked on the outskirts of the capital, possibly once more at Bourg-la-Reine, from November 1461 until January 1462. In hiding he began the arrangement of his *Testament*, starting with curses to d'Aussigny, then joyfully praising the king who had saved him from death, admitting his own faults, and almost two thousand lines later, after a glory of elegaically beautiful ballades, making his final bequests, jocularly arranging for his executors and for his funeral, when he would quit the world penniless but defiant.

A lot of the *Testament* was good poetry. Many of the ballades are part of the world's greatest poetry. There are clues that some of its flippant legacies were written while he remained outside Paris, ignorant of recent events there. In T, 138 he bequeathed a basket of cloves, the supposed safeguard against gaol fever, to three clerks of the Châtelet: Mautaint, Rosel, Ruel, telling them to serve and obey the 'lord devoted to Saint Christopher', namely Robert d'Estouteville, the Provost, a man devoted to the honouring of the saint and the husband of the beautiful Ambroise. Villon did not know that in the summer of 1461 his near-protector, Robert d'Estoutville was no longer Provost, having been deposed by Louis XI, and replaced by the unprotective Seigneur de l'Isle Adam.

In T, 102 a pompous pair of upstarts, the rich clothier, Pierre Merbeuf and the wealthy magistrate, Nicolas de Louviers, were lampooned. Intent on aping their betters they vaunted their skill at the chase although by their low birth they were permitted no falcons or hunting-dogs. Despite their ambitions they often returned with empty panniers. Villon advised them to conceal their failure, by buying partridges and plovers, spurious proof of their success, from the widow, Madame Jacqueline Machecoue, the poultress of a famous rôtisserie, the *Lion d'Or*, the Golden Lion in the Saunerie near the Châtelet. Unknown to the poet, by the end of 1461 she was dead and her shop was to let. Nor was he aware that the red-nosed Pierre Genevoys, Châtelet attorney and steadfast drinking companion of Jean de la Garde, T, 137, to whom he had appropriately bequeathed the Barrilet (Keg) tavern had died in 1461.[13]

Contentedly ignorant of such mortality Villon chortled that Robin Turgis, taverner of the Pomme de Pin, would not be able to find him in his hiding-place.

Item, viengne Robert Turgis
A moy, je lui paieray son vin;
Combien, s'il treuve mon logis
Plus fort fera que le devin . . .

If Robin Turgis turns up, then
I'll pay my debts from his wine-cellar;
However, if he finds my den
He's brighter than a fortune-teller.

[T, 103]

And so, through a bleak midwinter, he read, wrote, arranged his work. Slowly he regained some health. Always he wondered at his incredible good fortune.

Escrit l'an soixante et ung
Lors que le roy me delivra
De la dure prison de Mehun
Et que vie me recouvra . . .

Written in fourteen hundred and sixty-one
When the good king set me free
From the hard prison of Meung
And gave my life back to me.

[T, 11, 81–4]

For a while he was to know peace.

The Great Testament, 1462

Villon returned to Paris: unobtrusively, perhaps apprehensively. Early in 1462 he mixed with others as he walked through the Porte St Jacques, past the guards, down the street with the noise and the familiar stench of the city intensifying as he went down towards the river but not so far. Behind the great church of St Benoît was the house of the Porte Rouge and sanctuary.

His appearance must have startled the people in it, Guillaume de Villon, his housekeeper, servants. Five years earlier at the end of 1456 he had left the city a healthy young man, spruce, smilingly confident, going away to look for poetic patronage at Blois. He returned shabby, balding, stooped, coughing, almost broken. No word of his return occurs in his writings. He must have been welcomed for he stayed at the Porte Rouge. Whether his appearance stifled reproaches, limited questions is unknown. He would have forsworn crimes, asked forgiveness and it may be that Guillaume de Villon, his adoptive father, benefactor, priest, did forgive him. But he had returned and over the months he was to create the masterpiece of his *Testament*.

There was little outside the house for him. It was not the carefree Paris of five years before. The taverns were empty of his former light-hearted friends, most of them employed, married, some gone away, Montigny and de Cayeux dead. Now there were only casual acquaintances like Robin Dogis lodging at the Chariot in the rue de la Harpe or the clerk, Rogier Pichart, ruffians but not scoundrels. And five years was a long time to a man in the centuries when mortality came early and plague could kill almost half of those more than fifty years old. Death was a commoner. It is a fact often overlooked when discussing the Middle Ages. 'Unless it assumed truly catastrophic dimensions and caused terror and panic in the whole population, as in the case of plague, pestilence and famine, disease and death are rarely mentioned in extant [medieval] records. There is no mention of the common, if not almost universal presence of unrelieved pain from infected wounds suppurating for weeks, bad teeth and toothache, or gastric upsets following the eating of rotten foods. Expectation of life at birth for males was about thirty years, and after surviving the first and critical year it was still only thirty-four years'.[1] To many five years was a seventh of existence. Unsurprisingly, death was to be a recurrent theme in the Testament.

In the beginning it seems that Villon found little pleasure outside his room. His friends had gone, his own health was poor. Even the girls that once had laughed with him now laughed at him, worse perhaps, pitied him. And yet he was only in his thirty-first year, 'un jeune cocquart', 'just a cockerel'.

> Again my thirst returns. Again,
> I spit white phlegm. No sooner gone,
> More gobs like tennis-balls. More pain.
> What's there to say? Jehanneton
> No longer thinks me lots of fun,
> Just one more of Nature's wrecks,
> Croaking lips where dribbles run.
> Yet I'm still young enough for sex. [T, 72]

Had he died in Meung-sur-Loire there would have been little reason for the world to take an interest in François Villon, just three unmemorable poems in a duke's copybook. Nothing else. For if he had not preserved his poems, arranged them, copied them, nothing would have survived. Manuscripts would have been scrapped by gaolers, thrown away by tidying house-keepers. Preservation would have been accidental.

Although there is no authenticated knowledge of him after 1463 no manuscript of his complete works seems to be earlier than about 1470, one of them, the forerunner of others, perhaps being the Stockholm copy of Claude Fauchet [F]. The long silence of seven years can be explained.

In the Middle Ages minstrels going from court to court had been longed-for entertainers but once departed there were only the fallible memories of their audiences to recall the stories and ballades 'and men longed for a written record which would recreate the whole whenever they so desired. To meet such a demand manuscripts began to multiply, as more and more copies of poems or prose works were made, and each in its turn became the propagator of yet more copies. The survival of so many manuscripts of such things as *Piers Plowman*, the *Canterbury Tales*, the *Brut*, or the writings of Rolle, Hilton, Love or Lydgate is evidence of their great popularity, and of the fact that people liked them well enough to go to the trouble and expense of getting a copy for their own use'.[2]

Scribes and scriveners copied popular legends and poems on to their scraped, smoothed sheets of sheep, goat and calf skins, goose quill in one hand, sharpening knife in the other, inkwell on the writing-desk, copyists mis-spelling words, omitting others, but they copied and preserved the fragilities of literature until in 1469 the first printing-press in France was established in the Sorbonne. Thirteen years later a public press was set up, appropriately in the rue St Jacques near St Benoît. Seven years after that in 1489 Villon's first printed edition was issued by Pierre Levet. It was by such a worryingly haphazard sequence that the poems were preserved.[3]

At the end of chapter 2 it was noted that only four late fifteenth-century manuscripts exist of Villon's poetry where once there may have been scores.[4] The fullest and the most reliable is the Coislin (C), MS 20041, owned by Henri Cambout, Duke of Coislin and Bishop of Metz. Another, the property of Claude Fauchet (F), MS 53, later purchased by Queen Christina of Sweden, has the only copies of some poems in jargon. The oldest version of all, however, may be MS 1661 (B) of the

Ly comence le grant codicille ɛ te
stamēt maistre francois Billoŋ

Eŋ laŋ de moŋ trentiesme aage
Que toutes mes hontes ieuʒ Beues
Ne du tout fol encor ne saige
Nonoßstant maintes peines eues
Lesquelles iap toutes receues
Souʒ la maiŋ thißault danssigny
Seuesque il est seignant les rues
Quil soit le mieŋ ie le regny

Frontispiece of the first printed edition of the *Testament*, 1489.

Bibliothèque Nationale, arguably a transcript of an even earlier one because it consists only of the *Legacies* of 1456, nothing more. It omitted one of the forty stanzas, L, 23, in which Perrinet Marchand was presented with bales of straw to make the activities of his prostitutes less uncomfortable.

There is nothing of the *Testament* in MS [B], none of the *Poésies Diverses*, no ballades in jargon. It may have been copied as early as 1457 when its topical jests, teasing mockeries, occasional rudeness towards well-known, disliked characters in Paris were circulated from tavern to tavern, from fine house to mansion, even from church to court. It had been popular. Fifteen years later the *Testament* was to be given the same perpetuity.

Who the benefactor was that arranged its expensive transcription, all two thousand lines or more, who paid the scriveners for one or more copies, that person exists in anonymity. There is a hint. For obvious reasons Villon himself wrote the first draft, probably finishing it by the middle of the year. Most of the real poetry in it had already been written. Yet unless he was prepared to leave that one irreplaceable manuscript with someone else, unless that person were trustworthy beyond doubt there were very few candidates for the rôle. Guillaume de Villon was one.

As usual with Villon the hint is oblique, virtually untranslatable. But it exists. Of all the benefactors in the *Legacies* and the *Testament* Guillaume de Villon is the first in both. In the *Legacies* he was bequeathed the poet's reputation which, entirely fittingly, was immortalised in the priest's own name, L,9. In the *Testament* he was, significantly, given the poet's library and the *Romance of the Devil's Fart*, T, 87–8, which lay in some notebooks under a table. The 'romance' may never have been written. The bequest was either a deliberate insult, donating a crude piece of a students' riot to a clergyman, an unlikely slur as the next legatee was the poet's own mother, or, more feasibly, in his tortuous manner Villon was acknowledging the part his 'more than father' had in having his work, the *Testament* copied.

As the work was in the form of a legal and religious last Will and Testament the task would be acceptable to a churchman. He could also have afforded it. Sadly, dishearteningly, such an interpretation can be no more than speculation.

Whether a genuine Will of death-bed repentance or the parody of a mock Will of nonsensical gifts there was a preordained and strict order to such a document. In his *Testament* Villon accepted it. After an introductory preamble there had to be a statement of the testator's mental and physical health, an account of his sinful life and a solemn avowal of his religious faith. Following this, emanating from it, came admonitory advice to his friends before a commitment of his soul to God and his body to the earth. Only after such earnestness were there any bequests. The Will ended with the final arrangements for the dying man's funeral and burial.

It is profound evidence of the change in Villon's attitude towards life and death that his *Testament* should be so different from his *Legacies* of only five years before. In those forty stanzas the Preamble took a mere two before six angry verses about Catherine de Vausselles. The poem ended with six more in which the poet was awakened by the Sorbonne bell having given every one of his non-existent goods and chattels to his friends. The gifts to the companions, sometimes enemies or disagreeable citizens of Paris, occupied a full two-thirds of the poem.

Not so in the *Testament*. In that deeper work the one hundred and eighty-six stanzas were specially composed to be arranged fastidiously around magnificent ballades. Early in the *Testament*, in the first eight hundred of its two thousand lines there are recurring and detailed biblical references to Ecclesiastes, Ecclesiasticus, Ezekiel, Job, the Psalms and Luke. In contrast the bequests, ridiculous or unpleasant, plentiful though they are, come late in the poem and are of secondary importance to the serious thoughts that precede them.

By 1462 his mind was a scrapbook of memories of hardships, humiliations and horrors, rain drenching him along the muddy tracks of the plain of Beauce, dismissive rejections at Blois, Angers and Moulins, the sickening hysteria of the dungeons at Meung, corpses twisting in the winds at Montfaucon. Yet he was a craftsman and the emotions were controlled. It was within the unmalleable framework of a legal Testament that he chose to arrange an intimate statement of his thoughts, his realisation of the brevity of life, his images of Paris, his bitterness at the treachery of women so different from the care and affection that his mother had given him, his remorse for his weaknesses and the lessons learned that he could offer to his friends. All this came from poems already written, poems that he arranged appropriately within the *Testament*, smoothly introducing them by freshly composed linking stanzas, a hundred and eighty-six of them joining ballade to ballade, 2023 lines altogether.

He had perhaps a score of poems to choose from: ballades, songs, lays, rondeaux, charmingly light quatrains, sterner contemplations of his woebegone life. It is an enlightening glimpse of his mind to consider his choices and rejections. He used little of the Coquillard jargon, a snippet, no more. Omitted as irrelevant and so becoming members of the *Poésies Diverses* were the verses from Blois: the fountain, PD, 2 (L, 7); Marie, PD, 1 (L, 8), an exercise in old French, PD, 3 (L, –). The inappropriate plea for money at Moulins, PD, 4 (L, 10), was left out. 'Aiez pictié . . .', PD, 12 (L, 9), was history.

There were others that he wished to keep but which could not be integrated in the Testament's format: a ballade of proverbs, 'Tant grate chièvre . . .', 'so much a goat scratches . . .', PD, 5 (L, 2); 'Je congnois . . .', 'I know that flies like milk', PD, 6 (L, 3); a list of contradictions, ''Il n'est soing . . .', 'there is no care except when one starves', PD, 7 (L,4); the drum-beating decasyllables of the 'Enemies of France', 'Recontre soit . . .', 'may he encounter monsters', PD, 8 (L, 5). None of these was given a place.

He might have absorbed the ballade of good counsel somewhere, 'Hommes failliz . . .', 'feeble men, ill-provided with good sense', PD, 9 (L, 1), and his very good, self-critical ballade of fortune, 'Fortune fuz pas . . .', 'Long ago scholars called me Fortune, but you, François, say I am a murderess' with his repeated rebuke, 'Par mon conseil prens tout en gré, Villon', 'Just take things as they come, Villon', PD, 10 (L, 12). His judgement excluded them. The remaining five *Poésies Diverses*, PD, 11 (L, 4), the magnificent 'Frères humains . . .' and PD, 13 to 16, (L, 11, 13, 16, 15) were yet to be written.

These were lingering days, the lengthening days of spring, wandering unnoticed in the neighbourhood, down the rue de l'Hôpital opposite St Benoît, along the rue de la Harpe behind the church, past the Mouton inn, not seeing it as the mind changed a rhyme, deleted a phrase, constructed links between a new stanza and a year-old ballade, returning to the cramped room in the Porte Rouge as the light faded.

The *Testament* was an exquisite essay in craftsmanship. Almost without question the majority of its splendid ballades had been written as individual pieces of inspiration over the years yet here they became one great, indissoluble work.[5] It was art. Without obvious effort, itself a deception, the new stanzas and the existing ballades flowed together, unbroken, one moving naturally to the next. Stanzas 38 to 43, incorporating three ballades, are excellent examples of this.

Villon's ballade of *Dead Ladies*, T, 41+, with its famous refrain of 'But where are the snows of years gone by' had probably been composed some years before. Now stanzas had to be written that would lead imperceptibly up to that threnody of the dominance of death over all things. He achieved the effect by moving from the personal to the general.

In stanza 38 Villon told his readers that his father was dead and that his mother must also die as would, T, 39, rich and poor people, noble and peasant, just as Paris and Helen had died, T, 40, in the agonies of death, even the lovely Helen's body, T, 41. There would be death for her and for other famed ladies. 'Tell me where in what lost land is Flora the beautiful Roman?', T, 41+,

ballade 1, but 'where are the snows of years gone by?'*
Immediately this was followed and echoed by 'where are the lords
of years gone by?' [ballade 2], the brave Charlemagne, and 'the
good King Charles VII', a line, T, 41+, 363, that must have been
written by a poet unaware of the hostility of his contemptuous
son, Louis XI. After those dead lords [ballade 3], came the living,
the powerful men of the day, the Pope, the Emperor, the Prince.
All would die. 'Even so is everyone taken by the wind.'

Just as popes, kings, lords, T, 44, are dead, buried, so must he
perish, a poor pedlar from Rennes, but who had once lived
joyfully. The world was not everlasting, Death waited for all so
be comforted, aged man who once was famous for your jesting.
No one laughs today. Now you must beg, T, 43–6, like those
once-lovely hags who grieved at the sight of their pretty young
successors. But those too will die. Those were the miseries of
decaying age. It was the lament of the Belle Heaulmière, that
long-ago envy of Parisian women, the attractive armouress now
reduced to a withered crone. As normal as a cloud drifting
across the sky her long, mourning poem came next, T, 47.† The
entire scheme is artistic perfection.

Everywhere the stanzas were introductions. After the
armouress came the ballade of her advice to young prostitutes,
T, 56+, and that in turn led into a double ballade, T, 64+, in
which the poet told those daughters of pleasure and their men to
enjoy themselves, make love while they could, no point in being
circumspect, look what had happened to him through that
harlot, Catherine de Vausselles. It is a shrug of the shoulders
ballade with its refrain, 'Bien heureux est qui rien n'y a!',
'Happy the man who has nothing to lose'.

The arrangement was planned but it does not read like that. It
moves with no break, no hesitation. The gentle ballade of his
mother at prayer, T, 89+, came before the vilification of 'Rose'

---

* T, 41+: see Chapter 3, 54–5.
† Lament of the Belle Heaulmière: see Chapter 5, 93.

which instantly plunged into Catherine de Vausselles' ballade of betrayal, 'False beauty', T, 93+,* a descent from purity through derision to the foulness of deceit, from the best to the most corrupt. The construction was fluent as though the reader were listening to Villon's private conversation, hearing his quiet sadness at human frailties with their inevitable end. The theme pervaded the whole of the *Testament* from its angry beginning to the resignation of its ending.

The PREAMBLE was a diatribe against the tyrant Thibault d'Aussigny who so abused him in mind, body and rank. Yet his cruelty was as nothing to the clemency of that gracious king who had freed him from Meung and the merciless bishop. The encomium was brief but fulsome, wishing Louis XI long life, twelve sons and a place in Paradise.

After the Preamble came the STATEMENT of health, sins and life, T, 10–16. He would make his Will. He relived his early years. He had been a victim of circumstances just like Diomedes, a pirate who was forgiven and elevated by Alexander the Great because, like Villon, he had not been born into privilege. Villon knew no Alexander. Fortune had condemned him to wastefulness. Now his youth had passed, he had not studied, he had indulged himself without thought of the future.

ADVICE on life and inevitable death followed, T, 17–84. He was a sinner but God did not demand his death, only that he reform and live in goodness, T, 14, virtually a paraphrase of the Bible's 'Rejoice, O young man, in thy youth, and let thy heart cheer thee in the days of thy youth and walk in the ways of thy heart, and in the sight of thine eyes', but he had ignored the cautionary words that followed: 'As I live, saith the Lord God, I have no pleasure in the death of the wicked, but that the wicked turn from his way and live turn ye, turn ye from your evil ways; for why will ye die?', Ezekiel, 33, 11.

The poet's life had been no more than a burning thread. His

---

* T, 93+: see Chapter 6, 120–1.

friends were departed. Some had become great men and masters, others were beggars, more were monks and friars with good wines, rich food, comfortable self-satisfactions, but he was not the person to judge them. He had been born poor into a poor family. But it was better to be poor and alive than some mighty lord who now lay rotting under an ornate tomb. These meditations brought him to his central motet, that even the loveliest, richest, strongest have to die.

His father was dead. His mother would die. All died. And in this way Villon came to his trilogy for the beauty that had gone away, his sequence of three ballades beginning with the magnificent *Dead Ladies** and continuing with requiems for former lords and those who lived today. The second begins: 'Qui plus ou est ly tiers Calixte . . .'

> What more? Where is the third Calixt,
> Least of that name now dead and gone,
> Who held four years the Papalist?
> Alphonso king of Aragon,
> The gracious lord, duke of Bourbon,
> And Arthur, duke of old Britaine?
> And Charles the Seventh, that worthy one?
> Even with the good knight Charlemain.
>
> The Scot too, king of mount and mist,
> With half his face vermilion,
> Men tell us, like an amethyst
> From brow to chin that blazed and shone;
> The Cypriote king of old renown,
> Alas! and that good king of Spain,
> Whose name I cannot think upon?
> Even with the good knight Charlemain.
>
> No more to say of them I list;
> 'Tis all but vain, all dead and done:
> For death may no man born resist,
> Nor make appeal when death comes on.
> I make yet one more question;
> Where's Lancelot, king of far Bohain?

* *Dead Ladies*: see Chapter 3, 54–5.

Where's he whose grandson called him son?
Even with the good knight Charlemain.

Where is Guesclin, the good Breton?
The lord of the eastern mountain-chain,
And the good late duke of Alençon?
Even with the good knight Charlemain.

A.C. Swinburne

'The last two are usually looked upon are mere pale reflections of the first for, it is said, Villon's aim was to exploit this these to the utmost. Thus the *Ballade des Dames* is, according to Wyndham Lewis, "one of the towering poems of the world", whereas the *Ballade des Seigneurs* is "a piece of verse comparatively inferior", and the third ballade of the series sinks even further for it is "bald, dry and of little value". Gaston Paris was even more severe'. They were mistaken. Both had misunderstood 'the spirit of the *Testament* at this juncture, a spirit characterised by a continuously developing line of thought on death in which each ballade plays its part'.[6] Yet it is easy to understand their criticism. The magic of 'the snows of years gone by' gives a luminescence to the poem that superficially the two others do not have. But 'even so are all people taken by the wind', the refrain of the third ballade, is little less evocative and, 'I must say no more of this, it is all illusion, no one can resist death' is a bleak statement of reality in the second.

From the wealthy Villon's thoughts turned to the poor, the Danse Macabré and the charnel-houses with their muddled, nameless skulls. All die, young men, old women, fair, ugly, rich, poor, strong, weak, important, gutter-rubbish, all come to the fate of the 'Belle Heaulmière' and her dirge. In a ballade, T, 56+, with its modern title of 'The Fair Armouress to the Daughters of Joy', she spoke to those who were now what she had been then.

Or y penser, belle Gantière,
Qui escollière souliez estre . . . ,
....
Ne que monnoye qu'on descrye,

a refrain well translated by McCaskie as 'like a worn coin no man will take'.

> Now think of it, gay glover's maid,
> Who used to be my pupil fair,
> And you, Blanche of the slipper trade,
> Of changing times and loves beware.
> Take right and left, and do not spare,
> I prithee, any man you see:
> For age your value will impair,
> Like coin cried down you then will be.
>
> And you, sweet sausage-seller's aid,
> Whose dancing is so debonair;
> Costumier's Guillemette, you jade,
> To flout your master do not dare;
> To shut up shop you must prepare
> When old and loathsome like to me
> All service priests grown old forswear;
> Like coin cried down you then will be.
>
> Hood-setting Joan, be much afraid,
> Lest trouble catch you in a snare;
> Purse-bearing Catherine, get paid,
> Nor chase the lovers from your lair;
> An ugly woman ne'er can share
> Their boons, or from their jeers be free
> And hideous age of love is bare,
> Like coin cried down you then will be.
>
> Girls, why I weep and rend my hair,
> Just listen and you will agree:
> No cure is known of anywhere,
> Like coin cried down we all must be.

J.H. Lepper

Three of the chosen women deserve comment. 'Gantière', the glover's girl, has a printed variant, 'Gaultière', a word translated in Cotgrave's French–English dictionary as 'a whore, punke, drab, queane, gill, flirt, strumpet, cockatrice, mad wench, common hackney', leaving no uncertainty about her part-time profession. Similarly, Joan, 'Jehanneton' in the original and who no longer considered the poet attractive, was employed as a maker of the fashionable hoods that covered head and shoulders but as Michel observed, it was an 'occupation, at least by day'.[7]

'Purse-bearing Catherine, get paid', is the most tantalising. The reference to a purse, the instruction for her to be paid and not reject suitors, is very reminiscent of 'Une grante bourse de soye', a big purse made of silk, that Villon gave to Catherine de Vausselles in T, 90, 914. It would have been entirely in keeping with his wish for revenge that he should name and include her among the prostitutes.

It is noteworthy that the ballade of those ladies of delight came before a series of verses, T, 57–64, dictated by Villon to his non-existent secretary, Fremin. In them he warned his friends of the dangers of women, their deceit, their love of money. A man, he stated, should love only honourable women but were not Gaultière and Jehanneton honourable once, beginning by loving only one man before lapsing into promiscuity? It was simply female nature. They could not help it. For man, 'pour une joye cent douleurs', 'for one joy a hundred heartbreaks', T, 64, 624, and that outburst of amorous cynicism was the forerunner to a double ballade, T, 64+,

pour ce, aymez tout que vouldrez	as for that, love as you wish
....	....
Bien eureux est qui rien n'y a.	Happy the man who'll have none of it.

with its explicit hatred of Catherine de Vausselles.

> Now take your fill of love and glee,
> And after balls and banquets hie;
> In the end ye'll get no good for fee,
> But just heads broken by and by;
> Light loves make beasts of men that sigh;
> They changed the faith of Solomon,
> And left not Samson lights to spy;
> Good luck has he that deals with none!
>
> Sweet Orpheus, lord of minstrelsy,
> For this with flute and pipe came nigh
> The danger of the dog's heads three
> That ravening at hell's door doth lie;

Fain was Narcissus, fair and shy,
For love's love lightly lost and won,
In a deep well to drown and die;
Good luck has he that deals with none!

Sardana, flower of chivalry,
Who conquered Crete with horn and cry,
For this was fain a maid to be
And learn with girls the thread to ply;
King David, wise in prophecy,
Forgot the fear of God for one
Seen washing either shapely thigh;
Good luck has he that deals with none!

For this did Amnon, craftily
Feigning to eat of cakes of rye,
Deflower his sister fair to see,
Which was foul incest; and hereby
Was Herod moved, it is no lie,
To lop the head of Baptist John
For dance and jig and psaltery;
Good luck has he that deals with none!

Next of myself I tell, poor me,
How thrashed like clothes at wash was I
Stark naked, I must needs agree;
Who made me eat so sour a pie
But Catherine of Vausselles? thereby,
Noel took third part of that fun;
Such wedding-gloves are ill to buy;
Good luck has he that deals with none!

But for that young man fair and free
To pass those young maids lightly by,
Nay, would you burn him quick, not he;
Like broom-horsed witches though he fry,
They are sweet as civet in his eye;
But trust them, and you're fooled anon;
For white or brown, and low or high,
Good luck has he that deals with none!

A. C. Swinburne

Over the twenty ensuing stanzas, T, 65–84, he reviled her, castigated himself for being a fool, and then realising how ill he was after his dreadful mistreatment he decided to make his Will and give more presents before his death.

She, the despicable Catherine 'Rose' de Vausselles, had led him on, letting him speak as he wished but allowing him nothing more. He had been so besotted that he would have believed any idiocy that she chose to tell him, that white flour was ashes, that two aces were a pair of threes, that the sky was a brass pan, that clouds were cow-skins, morning was evening, stale beer fine wine, anything at all. No more. Now he renounced love. He had put away his fiddle. To the devil with it. 'A dying man is allowed to speak his mind':

> I spit white phlegm. No sooner gone,
> More gobs like tennis-balls. More pain. [T, 72, 730–1]

thanks to Tacque Thibaud and his cold water and his pear and his chains but I don't mind him or his officials, except for dainty Master Robert, I love them all as God loves Lombards – except that as the Lombards were the harshest, most hated money-lenders in Paris the 'affection' was not affectionate.

At this stage Villon remembered that he had made some legacies in 1456. Now he would generously dictate a new Will. Fremin take it down. But don't believe that all the dead are saints. Many of them fry in Hell. And if someone pointed out that he was not a Master of Theology he would tell him the parable of Lazarus about the rich man burning in damnation but let's get on with the Will. The dead are damned. He was in misery. In decay. He was as gaunt as a wraith and if he were not diseased then it was only by Heaven's mercy.

SOUL and BODY. He gave his soul to God, his body to the earth, T, 85–6.

Then came the LEGACIES and instantly there is something strange. Commented on by several critics is the fact that in both the *Legacies* and the *Testament* the first five gifts are presented to the same people: Guillaume de Villon; Catherine de Vausselles, who in the *Testament* is preceded by Villon's mother as though the poet were contrasting good with bad. There is no equivocation about the third legatee, Ythier Marchand, whose possible association with Catherine de Vausselles has already been debated. Then, perplexingly today because the context has no background, came Jean le Cornu, and Pierre de St Amant. Both the men were highly placed and rich. It is to be presumed that Villon knew all these people well.[8]

Legacies		*Testament*	
Guillaume de Villon	L, 9	Guillaume de Villon	T, 87–8
Vausselles	L,10	Mother and 'Rose'	T, 89, T, 90–3
Ythier Marchand	L, l1	Ythier Marchand	T, 94
le Cornu	L, 11	le Cornu	T, 95–6 ⎫ money?
St Amant	L, 12	St Amant	97 ⎭

Despite the scepticism of some critics who sensed that Villon was being sarcastic about his adopted father it is more likely that Guillaume de Villon was placed first because he had been so close and forbearing to the poet for so many years and had helped him in his predicaments. The second and third legatees, Catherine de Vausselles and Ythier Marchand need no explanation. Nor does Villon's mother whom, without prejudice, it may be assumed that Villon loved even though he did not care for his other, hardly mentioned relatives in Paris.

Jean le Cornu and Pierre de St Amant remain unsolved questions. Money, or their withdrawal of it, may have embarrassed and infuriated the poet at a time when cash was urgently needed for the continuing attentions of his teasing coquette, Catherine de Vausselles.

Jean le Cornu came from a family of well-to-do financiers. He was older than Villon, and an important officer in the Treasury, having been secretary to Charles VII in 1459. He died of plague in 1476. Predictably, his gift of Baubignon's garden was no gift at all. That avaricious man had not paid the rents of 'the ground and three little gardens' for nine years and the clerks of St Martin's had put them up for public auction. The Town Crier had already proclaimed the walls dangerous. For Villon to allow le Cornu to have the property as long as the door were mended and the roof fixed evoked little gratitude from the legatee.

Pierre de St Amant, whose wife was Jehanette Cochereau, was an influential administrator of the King's finances. It is surmised that he had helped Villon with 'loans' until his mean-minded wife interfered, calling the poet a sponging beggar. Her reward of a sexually 'red-hot ass' has been described in Chapter 5.[9]

The first bequests were given to Guillaume de Villon, asking his forgiveness for the poet's mishaps. It has already been suggested that the unlikely present of the *Romance of the Devil's Fart* was a concealed message of thanks for promising to have the Testament professionally copied.

Little in all Villon's works is more tender than the ballade he wrote in honour of his mother at prayer, T, 89+, *To Our Lady*, 'Dame du ciel, regente terrienne . . .'

> Lady of Heaven and earth, and therewithal
> Crowned Empress of the nether clefts of Hell –
> I, thy poor Christian, on thy name do call,
> Commending me to thee, with thee to dwell,
> Albeit in nought I be commendable.
> But all mine undeserving may not mar
> Such mercies as thy sovereign mercies are;
> Without the which (as true words testify)
> No soul can reach thy Heaven so fair and far.
> Even in this faith I choose to live and die.
>
> Unto thy Son say thou that I am His,
> And to me graceless make Him gracious.
> Sad Mary of Egypt lacked not of that bliss,
> Nor yet the sorrowful clerk Theophilus,
> Whose bitter sins were set aside even thus
> Though to the Fiend his bounden service was.
> Oh help me, lest in vain for me should pass
> (Sweet Virgin that shalt have no loss thereby)
> The blessed Host and sacring of the Mass.
> Even in this faith I choose to live and die.
>
> A pitiful poor woman, shrunk and old,
> I am, and nothing learn'd in letter-lore.
> Within my parish-cloister I behold
> A painted Heaven where harps and lutes adore,

And eke an Hell whose damned folk seethe full sore:
One bringeth fear, the other joy to me.
That joy, great Goddess, make thou mine to be,–
Thou of whom all must ask it even as I;
And that which faith desires, that let it see.
For in this faith I choose to live and die.

Excellent Virgin Princess thou didst bear
King Jesus, the most excellent comforter,
Who even of this our weakness craved a share
And for our sake stooped to us from on high,
Offering to death His young life sweet and fair.
Such as He is, Our Lord, I Him declare,
And in this faith I choose to live and die.

D.G. Rossetti

The church, famed for its beauty and its rich tombs like that of Anne, Duchess of Bedford, was probably the Celestins in the far east of Paris near the Bastille. A near-contemporary of Villon's, Guillebert de Metz, described it in 1434. 'In the Celestins there is a painting of Paradise and Hell, with other nobly executed pictures in a separate choir. Before the main choir there is an altar painted with the image of Our Lady and masterfully done.'[10] Villon's mother may have lived nearby to be closer to her relatives during one of her son's absences from the city.

Following that lovely poem of hers but juxtaposed to strengthen the contrast came the disparaging verses to 'Rose', presumed pseudonym for Catherine de Vausselles, whose own ballade, 'False beauty', T, 93+,* followed. Then came the bequests to the despised Ythier Marchand including the sadly beautiful rondeau to his *Dead Mistress*, T, 94+.†

The *Testament* changed. In imitation of the *Legacies* of 1456 the bequests that came after these personal attacks were almost frivolous afterthoughts when the genuine *Testament* was finished, a pot-pourri of presents to a cross-section of Paris

---

* T, 93+: see Chapter 6, 120–1.
† T, 94+: see Chapter 3, 61.

society. The legatees were a hotchpotch of occupations but analysis reveals the type of people with whom Villon was most, if not best, acquainted. Bequests to members of the police exceed all others. After them, in descending order, were demeaning gifts to successful merchants and sanctimonious friars, drolleries to honest craftsmen, legal and civic officials, ill-natured presents to usurers, with only a few, more gentle offerings to other people: noblemen, magistrates, rich men, inn-keepers, ordinary citizens, prostitutes, the clergy, servants and students. Men and women whose names, let alone their careers and personal foibles, would be no more than fading ink in disregarded histories are resurrected in the *Testament*, testimony itself to the assiduous dredging of details by the dedicated researchers of Villon's life.

Reading bequest after bequest it slowly becomes clear how much less gaiety, more realism there is in them. There are undertones of regret and sadness in the verses. Like the earlier section of the *Testament* the technique is the same. New stanzas were written to introduce old ballades. Among them was a preposterous lie that he could find no recipe for fricassees in the *Viandier Taillevent*, a well-known cookbook by the royal chef, Guillaume Tirel or Taillevent, a compilation of delicacies in which there is no mention of such a low-born dish for commoners. In consequence, Villon was forced to use one from Macquaire, the worst cook in Paris, to fry the lying tongues of the Perdrier brothers whose ballade came next, T,141+.* More amusingly, the sharp tongues of the pious Mlle Bruyères and her disciples were used as an introduction to the ballade of even sharper tongues, those of *The Women of Paris*, T, 144+.†

There are too many bequests, too many beneficiaries, too many jokes that have been forgotten in the fading whispers of the past to be repeated here. A few must suffice. There were the expected useless and unwanted donations of sour wine, a

---

* T, 141+: see Chapter 7, 146, 147.
† T, 144+: see Chapter 2, 39–40.

hundred sous to a millionaire, a liquidity of taverns, the entire contents of Villon's purse, a cheese soufflé, meaning a punch in the face, to a police sergeant, T, 105, loaded dice and marked cards to replace the bar sinister on the coat-of-arms of Perrinet Marchand, T, 108, cloves of Syrian ginger as a strong aphro-disiac for a sadistic torturer, T, 111, a noose, a third ruin to Philippe Brunel, quarrelsome Lord of Grigny, T, 136, as long as he would lavish his non-existent money for the repairs that were needed for the wreck. It was no benefit. The crumbling Billy tower had been legally sequestered in 1461 because of a lawsuit between its legal owners, the Carmelites, and a man with a lifelong lease on it!

There were affectionate bequests. Villon remembered Master Jean Cotart, clerical attorney, who, so the poet said, had successfully defended him in a slander brought against him by 'Denise', whoever she was. Nothing is known. She may have been generic, a general term for flighty women who cuckolded their husbands. She may have been Catherine de Vausselles and the affair of the libellous verses.[11] Whatever the outcome Cotart had protected him. Villon handed over the outstanding amount of his legal fee, a penny, T, 125, and, with apparent sincerity, the honour of a ballade of which a stanza is quoted here.

Comme homme beu qui chancelle et trepigne
L'ay veu souvent, quant il s'alloit couchier

Just an old drunk with tottering feet
Often seen lurching to his bed,
And once he stumbled in the street
Against a stall and bashed his head.
But of all the world it's truly said
No friendlier drinker at the bar.
Fling wide the gates when it is fled,
The soul of Master Jean Cotart.

[T, 125+]

He had died in January 1461.[12]

There were farcical bequests. Two flagrant courtesans, Big Jean, Jeanne de Bretagne, T, 151, who had been driven from her home by indignant neighbours, and Marion the Idol, Marion la

Dentue, whose associate, Colin de Thou, was accused of being her pimp, were granted the unscholarly right of opening a school in which the instructors would be taught by the pupils, an eye-opening inversion of the tricks of the trade. Orphans in the care of the city would be given nothing but waifs on the street would be welcome to partake of lessons in the establishment, T, 155.

There were crude bequests. A long-standing alderman of Paris, Michel Culdoe, T, 135, was told to go to the 'school' and greet the two ladies if he wished to receive his gift of sheepskin boots, a euphemism for intercourse. Villon then mangled the Christian name of that distinguished Provost of the Grand Brotherhood of Burghers by calling him, 'Michault' after the salacious womaniser of St Satur, T, 91, 922–3. Worse, the poet also corrupted the surname, changing Culdoe into 'cul d'oie', 'the arse of a goose', transforming the respectable dignitary into a half-man, half-fowl like the grotesque semi-creatures in the bizarre, nightmarish paintings of Hieronymus Bosch.

There were cruel bequests, T, 160. In the centuries when onlookers could giggle at the antics of lunatics and cheerfully pay to watch bear-baiting Villon gave his pair of spectacles to the *Quinze-Vingts*, the Fifteen-Score inmates of the hospital on the rue St Honoré so that on holidays they could go to the cemetery and charnel-houses of the Innocents where the glasses would help them distinguish between the good visitors and the bad. The gift may have entertained the poet's readers but not the Fifteen Score beneficiaries, all of whom were blind.

There were imaginative bequests such as T, 146, in which Villon had the considerate idea of donating a hermitage to a nunnery, two religious houses situated on the most conspicuous hills outside the walls of Paris, Montmartre, the mound of martyrs, and Mont Valerian, six miles to the west on the far side of the Seine. The nunnery on Montmartre was ancient, founded in the early twelfth century and once wealthy and active with sixty nuns in its sisterhood. By Villon's time, however, the house was in disrepair, buildings collapsing, the six remaining nuns so financially desperate that they had engaged in very un-nunlike ways of raising money, among the more socially acceptable being the opening of a public tavern, selling wine and, outrageously, permitting men to enter the premises. Professedly unaware of this the naive poet gave the nunnery the accolade of 'l'abbaye ou il n'entre homme', 'the abbey where no man has ever set foot'.

To help the sisters in their distress the poet offered them a three-month Pardon that he would bring from Rome, and to improve their lot he would unite them with the hermitage of anchorites on Mount Valerien. It has been cynically suggested that he had chosen the site simply because of a play of words upon its name, 'valente rien', 'worth nothing'. Unsurprisingly the imaginative gift achieved nothing. Less than fifty years later in 1503 'the abbess and some of the nuns had given birth, one to two, another to four, and that one nun was then in labour in the abbess' room and yet another pregnant'.[13] The Bishop of Paris proscribed the house. The legacy had been a failure. But Shakespeare would have perceived a triple coincidence.

> And, as imagination bodies forth
> The forms of things unknown, the poet's pen
> Turns them to shapes, and gives to airy nothing
> A local habitation and a name.
> Such tricks hath strong imagination . . .
>
> *Midsummer Night's Dream*, V, I, 7

'A local habitation and a name'. The like-minded Villon might happily have agreed. The nunnery did have a name, though a bad one. It also had a local of bad repute. And the nuns themselves had very bad habits. It was all amusement. It was all froth. Behind the light words, however, was a poet with laughing mockery in his mind towards the transience of the world. Beneath the laughing mockery was the serious knowledge that he, like everyone, would die.

With characteristic levity he made his Will, appointing Jean de Calais, T, 173, to ensure that it was properly drafted. As de

Calais was a notary at the Châtelet with the responsibility of verifying the contents of such testaments he was the ideal candidate, the only problem being that he had never met Villon in his life.

The poet was to be buried in the chapel of Ste Avoye on the rue du Temple on the far side of the Seine, a chapel chosen for its uniqueness among others in Paris. The hospital was run by widows who had become Augustinian nuns and their chapel was not on the ground as was customary but on the second floor which was far too weak to support the weight of a stone tomb.[14] Thoughtful as ever Villon stated that he needed no heavy sarcophagus, just a full-length portrait in pen-and-ink. For an epitaph it was to be recorded, in charcoal if necessary, that he had been killed by love, a light-headed clown and worthless scholar, François Villon, who had never owned anything but what he had never possessed he had liberally given away.

The first lines of the rondeau after this declaration, T, 178+, 1892–3, were

donne a cil	Rest eternal give him
Sire, et clarté perpetuelle	O Lord, and light everlasting . . .

almost exactly those of the Requiem Mass for the Dead. 'Requiem aeternam dona eis, Domine, et lux perpetua, luceat eis', reaffirming not only Villon's considerable theological knowledge but also his talent for merging the sincere with the satirical.[15]

Satire returned with his command, T, 179, that an enormous 'glass' bell be tolled in his respect. Church-bells were rung during thunderstorms and when the city was under threat of attack but Villon had demanded a very special one, the 1500 lb of Jacqueline that hung with another, Maria, in the great belfry of Notre-Dame, the Sorbonne bell that was rung at nine at night. Jacqueline was huge but fragile, cracking in 1429 and recast, its hammer repaired in 1434, the bell split and recast once more in 1451, yet again in 1479, it was a famous, or infamous, bell but it was not for an insignificant, impecunious poet.[16] Funeral bells rang only for the powerful and important. Villon did not qualify. Nor did the two men he chose as his bell-ringers.

Two less likely appointments it would be hard to envisage. Bell-ringing was hard work. In theory the paid task was performed by lay members of a congregation but many of them were too old and overweight to cope with the steep steps of a bell-tower, some of which were said to be 'as many as there were days in the year'. The work was farmed out for pittances to the poorest, most desperate men. These were quite certainly not Jean de la Garde and Guillaume Volant, Villon's preferred choices.

The first was a prosperous spice-merchant to the Queen, Valet de Chambre, trading also in the Levant and the east for cotton, wax, candles, sauces. In the *Legacies* he had given him a St Maur crutch to help him with his gout. No tower steps for him. Nor for Volant, obese and litigious, who had made a fortune in selling salt and as a speculator, an unscrupulous niggard who had sued the monks of Pommeraie over the weighing of some salt and who refused to pay tolls for his ships, claiming special privilege for the use of the Seine and Yonne.

Neither of these 'bell-ringers' would have appreciated what Villon had chosen to offer each of them as a traditional payment, two loaves. These were not bread but 'of St Stephen's kind', that is, stones of the kind used in the martyrdom of the saint. In medieval Paris stoning was the ordained punishment for condemned misers and money-lenders guilty of over-large rates of interest. The bequests brought chuckles from readers of the *Testament* but not a tintinnabulation of a bell from de la Garde or Volant.[17]

Ambitiously, Villon named three responsible men as executors, T, 181–2, Martin Bellefaye, Guillaume Colombel and Michel Jouvenal – but he can have had little expectation that Bellefaye, erstwhile Criminal-Lieutenant of the Châtelet and the Provost's right-hand man; or Colombel, rich financier, President of the Chamber of Judicial Enquiries and king's counsellor; or Jouvenal, cupbearer to Louis XI and Bailiff of Troyes, would accept the honour. Having understandable misgivings about their consent he named three deputies, T, 183–4, first, Philippe Brunel, the pennilessly disputatious Lord of Grigny; then Jacques Raguier, heavy drinker who had been given the horse-trough of Abreuvoir Popin to slake his thirst, the city's most disreputable lecher who had bought Regnier de Montigny's house. Third came the coarse, brawling Jacques James with his hot-bath brothel, l'Image de St Martin. These unreliable scoundrels were to safeguard his interests.

There was an instant of candour, T, 185, 1952. 'Des testamens qu'on dit le Maistre de mon fait n'orra *quy ne quot*', 'the Master of Wills won't hear my case'. No ecclesiastical judge would consider his Will, a grieving admission that d'Aussigny had defrocked the poet, removing all right to the protection of the church.

Finally, T, 186, Guillaume du Ru would be responsible for the funeral lamps. As du Ru was the biggest wholesale wine merchant in Paris his selection was entirely fitting because according to student lore wine was 'the holy oil which must be consumed lest the lamp of the spirit die out'.[18] Villon ended his last Will and Testament with two ballades, a plea for forgiveness, T,186+, from all people whether high or low, church or laity, his Ballade of Pardon, 'Je crie a toutes gens mercis'.* It was followed by the last ballade of the *Testament*, T, 186++.

Everything was over. At the funeral mourners were to attend in the brightest scarlet that they could find for that is what the clergy wore when attending Mass for martyrs. Villon was a martyr to love, he swore it on a holy relic, his one remaining testicle – or was it 'witness' that he meant? He was unsure. One or the other!

Love had expelled him. He had endured life in rags and tatters. Yet, predictably, the envoi to the ballade laughed at Villon's last intention.

* See Chapter 7, 135.

Prince, gent comme esmerillon
Sachiez qu'il fit au departire:
Ung traict but de vin morillon,
Quant de ce monde voult partir.

Prince, gentle as birds falconine,
Hear Villon's wish for his last breath:
He drank a deep flagon of red wine,
Smiled to the end and entered death.

[T, 186++, 2020–3]

Words were tools and toys to Villon, irresistible tools and toys. How irresistible is displayed by his subtle choice of wine, 'vin morillon'. This was a full-bodied red burgundy made from the black Pinot grape and widely sought although expensive. That Villon should prefer it for his last drink is understandable.

Knowing something of the poet's mind, however, it is not surprising that the word had other depths. It provided a rhyme for 'esmerillon', 'a merlin', unless 'esmerillon' provided a rhyme for 'morillon'. This is more probable because Villon with his love of puns could hear another, half-hidden rhyme, 'mor-riant', 'laughing at death', a sentiment entirely in accord with his graveyard mood. Lamination upon lamination. 'Morillon' also happened to be the surname of Hervé Morillon, late abbot of St Germain-des-Prés outside the city's western walls, a querulous man well-known for his repeated arguments and quarrels against the university and therefore against Villon. He had died on 25 February 1460 but by the metaphorical drinking of his name the poet had ended the man's existence.[19]

The layer over layer of meaning, from the obvious to the arcane, from epicurean discrimination, to the macabre jibe at death, to the casting into perdition of a soul, it is another insight into Villon's perceptions. It was the ghoulish, street-wise humour of a Parisian.

By the summer of 1462 there must have been contentment in him, the *Testament* done, his life of crime behind him, ease of living to come. Yet by the end of that year he was to be closer to violent death than ever before.

Interlude

The Debate between Villon and his Heart

This book has been much concerned with Villon's life and his attitude towards the way that he lived. For this reason it seems fitting at this stage to insert a brief interlude about one of his most unusual poems, PD, 13 (L, 11), because, more than any other, it illuminates his mind and personality. Perhaps written at the juncture of 1460 and 1461, some time between Orléans and Meung-sur-Loire, it was devised as a debate between the virtues of his heart and the inability of his body to withstand temptation. The ballade was translated by Swinburne in 1876.

'Qu'est ce qui j'oy?' 'Ce sui je.' 'Qui?' 'Ton cuer',
....
'Plus ne t'en dys'. 'Et je m'en passeray'.

Who is this I hear?

Lo, this is I, thine heart,
That holds on merely now by a slender string.
Strength fails me, shape and sense are rent apart,
The blood in me is turned to a bitter thing,
Seeing thee skulk here like a dog shivering.

Yea, and for what?

For that thy sense found sweet.

What irks it thee?

I feel the sting of it.

Leave me at peace.

Why?

Nay now, leave me at peace;
I will repent when I grow ripe in wit
I say no more. I care not though thou cease.
....

What art thou, trow?

A man worth praise perfay.

This is thy thirtieth year of wayfaring.
'Tis a mule's age.
Art thou a boy still?

Nay.

Is it hot lust that spurs thee with its sting,
Grasping thy throat? Know'st thou not anything?

Yea, black and white, when milk is specked with flies,
I can make out.

No more?

Nay, in no wise.

Shall I begin again the count of these?
Thou art undone.

I will make shift to rise.
I say no more. I care not though thou cease.

....

I have the sorrow of it, and thou the smart.
Wert thou a poor mad fool or weak of wit,
Then might'st thou plead this pretext with thine heart;
But if thou know not good from evil a wit,
Either thy head is hard as stone to hit.
Or shame, not honour, gives thee most content.
What canst thou answer to this argument?

When I am dead I shall be well at ease.

God! what good luck!
Thou art over eloquent.

I say no more. I care not though thou cease.

....

Whence is this ill?

From sorrow and not from sin.
When Saturn packed my wallet up for me
I well believe he put these ills therein.

Fool, wilt thou make thy servant lord of thee?
Hear now the wise king's counsel; thus saith he;
All power upon the stars a wise man hath;
There is no planet that shall do him scathe.

Nay, as they made me I grow and I decrease.

What say'st thou?

Truly this is all my faith.
I say no more.   I care not though thou cease.

....

Wouldst thou live still?

God help me that I may!

Then thou must

What? Turn penitent and pray?

Read always.

What?

Grave words and good to say;

Leave off the ways of fools, lest they displease.

Good; I will do it.

Wilt thou remember?

Yea.

Abide not till there come an evil day. I say no more.

I care not though thou cease.

A.C. Swinburne[1]

It is a poem written in hangover alley, head splitting, mouth a dirty bucket, mind crawling with the maggots of self-disgust and self-pity. But there are revelations. 'Skulking' suggests deprivation, far from comfort, hiding from the law, 'like a dog', penniless. 'Thirtieth year' suggests 1460 or 1461, the years when his ambitions were memories and when existence was at its lowest. 'Wayfaring' suggests lack of a home or safe refuge. 'Milk specked with flies' is likely to be a line abstracted from his less miserable ballade, 'Je congnois bien mouches en let', PD, 6 (L, 3). Indeed, the whole of the *Debate* is an enlargement of the refrain in that earlier ballade, 'I know everything except myself'.

The *Debate* is a defiant poem but it is not a cynical one that ignores good counsel. At first the body does deny the arguments of the heart, replying that they were not worth listening to. 'Leave me in peace.' It was repeated time after time, telling the heart that whatever it advises Villon could not care about. In any case, he'll be all right when he is dead.

Then there was a change as the mind cleared. 'Wouldst thou live still?' 'God help me that I may.' He would abandon his foolishness, he will remember this promise, he will reform. Nor will he leave it to the last minute.

The genius of Villon is revealed in the subtlety of this poem. It really is a debate, and does not remain static from beginning to end. The arguments intertwine and do not run parallel without ever meeting. The psychological interest is very real. It has been suggested that the *Débat* was written only to placate the authorities whose wrath had so often been roused by Villon's unruly conduct but this is pure conjecture, and if the theory contains any truth, it is clearly not the whole truth, for this would make of the poem a far more superficial work than it is in fact.[2]

This is true but it is unlikely to have been one of the eternal verities. Villon asserted, insisted that he would reform but his assurance has a feeling of early-in-the-morning-after sincerity that was more likely to be sustained by insufficient cash for pleasure than by any strength of will. Over the black-and-white years of his life Villon probably turned over so many new leaves that they would have filled a prayer-book.

The Third Exile, 1463.
Disappearance?

If all that remained of this stage in Villon's life were his own writings, three ballades and a quatrain, PD, 11, 15, 16 and 14 (L, 14, 16, 15 and 13), little would be known of the events in November and December of 1462. Fortunately, legal documents have been preserved, discovered and translated, not entire, not always explicit, but sufficient to reveal that the poet had been imprisoned twice, once unjustly, and that it had been to Parliament that he had appealed for clemency. The Bishop of Paris was no longer his lord and guardian.

At the very beginning of November he was in the prison of the Châtelet for some offence that must have been slight. Carco thought that money had been stolen from a prostitute but this is not notarised fact. Whatever it was the misdemeanour was so slight that the poet was about to be released when his black angel returned. By mischance the Procurator of the university's Faculty of Theology learned that a certain François Villon was being held by the authorities, a name grimly remembered in connection with the robbery of the College of Navarre.

Instantly Jean Colet sent his Grand Beadle, Laurens Poutrel, to the Châtelet with a request for *Ne Exeat*, no release before questioning. A payment of sixteen déniers was sent to implement it. The prison's registrar, Pierre Basanier, given 'presents' by Villon in both the *Legacies* and the *Testament* and a man suspected of favouring prisoners in return for monetary benefits, issued the writ.[1]

Poutrel, a canon of St Benoît, living in the rue des Noyers near the church, was personally concerned. He had lost sixty of his own crowns in the theft. For a further deposit of eleven sols Parisis Villon was brought from his cell for questioning; without waiting for torture he confessed that he had been one of those who had broken into the college, 'pro dupplo confessionis facte per dictum magistrum Franciscum Villon'. On 7 November he was set free with the sworn promise that one hundred and twenty crowns would be repaid to the Faculty in three annual instalments, the money coming, presumably, from Guillaume de Villon.

Two comments should be made. As late as March 1465 there is no record in the Register of the Faculty that any payment had been received but, as Wyndham Lewis observed, 'It must be remembered that this was, by God's mercy, before the age of Efficiency'. The other is that Tabarie had been fined fifty crowns for his peripheral involvement in the burglary. Villon as one of the four major offenders had to repay one hundred and twenty crowns. It suggests that the sum stolen had been five hundred and thirty crowns, the precise-minded church requiring precise compensation from the criminals in an age when rates of interest were considered against God's laws.[2]

Misfortune continued. Within a few weeks Villon was back in the Châtelet but this time on a charge that could lead to his execution. Had it been a year or so earlier he would have been little concerned. He had done nothing wrong and he could trust the Châtelet for justice. The Provost was Robert d'Estouteville, nobleman but long-standing acquaintance. The poet had even written a ballade to him that contained the acrostic of the name of his beautiful wife, Ambroise, T, 139+. The Provost would grant him no special favours but he would be fair. So would his Criminal-Lieutenant, Martin de Bellefaye, a man of Villon's age, a man not noted for his severity. He would be tolerant.

But that was in the summer of 1461, not December 1462. By then d'Estouteville had been deposed and Bellefaye had become a lay counsellor to Parliament. Their places and their power had been transferred to men who would not have a flicker of mercy to a vagabond who also was a writer of scurrilous verses. Villon was confronted with certain torture by the bestial Jean Mahé and probable hanging under the authority of the new Provost, the severe Jacques Villier, seigneur de l'Isle Adam. His like-minded Criminal-Lieutenant was Pierre de la Dehors, a violent man nicknamed the 'Butcher', partly because of his shop and largely because of his cruelty and hatred of all clerics. Villon faced agony and death and yet, for once, he was blameless.

It had begun with a visit to an acquaintance, Robin Dogis, who lived at the Chariot in the rue des Parcheminières close to the corner of the rue de la Harpe. A Letter of Remission dated November 1463 stated that late in 1462 the two had supper together and were joined by Hutin du Moustier, a sergeant at the Châtelet but a man of variable honesty, and Rogier Pichart, truculent, troublesome clerk. After the meal and too much wine the quartet left the Chariot between 7 and 8 o'clock on that winter's evening on their unsteady way for more drinks with Villon at the nearby Porte Rouge. They never reached it.

From Dogis' lodgings they turned into the rue St Jacques, went reluctantly past the Mule tavern opposite the convent of the Mathurins and were just a few yards from St Benoît when the aggressive Pichart noticed copyists working in the office of the scrivener, François Ferrebouc, a craftsman so highly regarded for his handiwork that he had been entrusted with making copies of the documents for the rehabilitation of Joan of Arc and the responsibility for producing the six volumes of her trial.[3]

Pichart was drunkenly unimpressed. He spat at a clerk through the open window, probably ruining the man's work. In the shouting and the threats another clerk dragged du Moustier into the building, Ferrebouc rushed out and shoved Dogis over. Dogis pulled out his dagger and wounded the scrivener. There is no mention anywhere of the apprehensive Villon taking part in the affray. In the darkness the instigator, Pichart, slunk off only to be discovered outside St Benoît by Dogis who called him 'a wicked bastard' before going home. Pichart ran off, through the alleyways, down the rue de la Harpe to the sanctuary of the convent of the Cordeliers. Du Moustier vanished. Villon slipped back to the Porte Rouge. He had never been a coward but as a child of the slums he had always been discreet. Unluckily, being a man well-known in Paris he was recognised by Ferrebouc. By the morning he, Dogis and du Moustier were in the Châtelet.[4]

Despite his innocence and despite the matter being no more than a civic disturbance in which nothing had been damaged or stolen, in which no one had been badly hurt, let alone killed, Villon was doomed. After some perfunctory questioning he was dragged, struggling, to the rack and the choked-off screaming of the ordeal by water. He would have confessed to anything to avoid it, the sodden cloth across the mouth, the pouring and flooding of water, the body swollen to an impossible bursting. It could not be borne. He agreed to everything.

He was taken before the Provost. The sentence was announced. There was no pity in de l'Isle Adam for the shivering, notorious rascal in front of him. No Bishop of Paris came to save him. 'Pour avoir été le témoin d'une rixe où Ferrebouc reçut une blessure légère, François Villon fut condamné à mort, à être "étranglé et pendu au gibet de Paris", for having been a [mere] witness to the scuffle in which Ferrebouc received a scratch François Villon was condemned to death, to be hanged and strangled on the gallows in Paris'.[5] So were Dogis and du Moustier.

Only days were left. First it had been Regnier de Montigny. Then Colin de Cayeux. Now it was him. Even five hundred years later it is unjust. All three men appealed. Du Moustier was refused and was hanged. Dogis was reprieved when the Duke of Savoy visited the king in November 1463, and an amnesty was declared. Pichart came out of sanctuary and was sent to the scaffold some years later. Villon slumped in his straw-stinking cell waiting for the hangman. And his spirit triumphed.

Death was nudging his shoulder. Life was to be reckoned in hours, no more than days. There can have been few minds that would have made a joke of it. There have been even fewer poets of genius that could have written one of the world's most piteous, most poignant ballades about it. Villon did both. He snarled at his tormentors, laughed at the world in four brief lines. It was the time when both sides of his contrasting nature appeared, ironical jest and complete sincerity. First there was the quatrain.

> I am François and I'm glum.
> Born near Pontoise in the Paris slum.
> Now, through a noose, my neck will come
> To know the weight of my hanging bum.

PD, 14 (L, 13)

If it was bravado it was courageous bravado for a man awaiting death.

Then there was the ballade:

> Brothers among men who after us shall live,
> Let not your hearts' disdain against us rise,
> For if some pity for our woe ye have,
> The sooner God your pardon shall devise.
> Behold, here five or six of us we peise.
> As to our flesh, which we fed wantonly,
> Rotten, devoured, it hangeth mournfully;
> And we, the bones, to dust and ash are riven,
> Let none make scorn of our infirmity,
> But pray to God that all we be forgiven.
>
> If, brothers, we cry out, ye should not give
> Disdain for answer, even if justice 'tis
> That murders us. This thing ye should believe,
> That always all men are not wholly wise;
> Pray often for us then, not once or twice,
> Before the fair son of the Virgin Mary,
> Lest that – for us – his grace prove injury
> And we beneath the lord of Hell be driven.
> Now we are dead, cease importunity
> And pray to God that all we be forgiven.
>
> The rain doth weaken all our strength and lave
> Us, the sun blackens us again and dries;

Our eyes the ravens hollow like a grave.
Our beards and eyebrows are plucked off by pies.
Never rest comes to us in any wise;
Now here, now there, as the wind sways, sway we,
Swung at the wind's high pleasure ceaselessly,
More pecked by birds than hazel-nuts that ripen.
Be ye not then of our fraternity,
But pray to God that all we be forgiven.

Prince Jesus, above all hast mastery,
Let not high Hell become our Seigneury;
There we have nought to do nor order even.
Brothers, keep here no thought of mockery,
And pray to God that all we be forgiven.

PD, 11 (L, 14)
A.C. *Swinburne*

Wherever it has been translated by other good poets it always affects by its simple clarity and truths. The thoughts transcend the language.

Brothers that live when we are dead
don't set yourselves against us too.
If you could pity us instead,
then God may sooner pity you.   *Peter Dale*, 219

We five or six here swinging from the tree,
Behold and all our flesh that once was fair
Rotted, and eaten by the beaks that tear,
Whilst we the bones to dust and ash dissolve.   *H. de Vere Stacpoole*, 17

Let none make fun of our adversity,
But pray God that he forgive us all.   *Norman Cameron*, 111

If brothers, we cry out, ye should not give
Disdain for answer, even if justice 'tis
That murders us . . .   *Richard Aldington*, 73
                      From: eds. A. Deutsch and M. Savill

We are whiles scoured and soddened of the rain
And whiles burnt up and blackened of the sun:
Corbies and pyets have our eyes out-ta'en
And plucked our beard and hair out one by one.   *John Payne*, 115

At the wind's changing pleasure buffeted
This way and that; and where the birds have fed
Our cheeks are pocked like thimbles . . .   *H. B. McCaskie*, 236

Prince Jesus, you have mastery far and wide;
Against Hell's Lordship be our guard and guide.
We would not pay Hell's due, nor be its thrall.
Men – here's no place to mock us in your pride,
But pray to God that He'll absolve us all.   *Beram Saklatvala*, 181

In the dregs of the gaol Villon waited for the inevitable. Cells in the Châtelet could be pleasant, roomy, with windows and light, offering privileges to those that could afford them. Others, and they were many, 'a marvellous number of cells', mused Guillaume de Metz, were gloomy pits, sour and filthy in the depths of the prison. Villon knew. In the *Legacies*, L, 29, he had given his polished looking-glass to the caged 'pigeons' in their dungeons, an unreflecting gift in the blackness. As for the promise of good graces from the jailer's wife, there was none without money. For Villon there was bread and water.

He endured the darkness waiting for the never-arriving answer to his appeal. Forget about hope, Étienne Garnier, Châtelet gatekeeper and Job's comforter, told him, forget about a pardon. No point in appealing. Parliament always confirmed sentences passed by the Provost. Always. Villon lay there like a cornered animal. Waiting after Orléans and Meung-sur-Loire for another miracle.

In its commitment to the banal Hollywood overlooked the incredible. A third miracle occurred. Like a time-warped Houdini flung centuries back into history Villon lost his chains. He was reprieved. It was not a Pardon. But it was freedom. Even today, after all the research and the speculation, it is not clear why he was released. Three judges sat for his appeal, Boulenger, Nanterre and Thiboust. The answer may rest with the last. Henri Thiboust, President of Parliament, was also a canon of St Benoît, and would have known his fellow-canon, Guillaume de Villon, for years. It may have been his wish to soften the pain that led to the Court's decision. Villon was not to be hanged. He was to be exiled. Wyndham Lewis read the precious document 'in thin faded ink in vile crabbed characters, devilishly cramped and run together, as much like colloquial Urdu as French: in the left-hand margin a laconic signpost, the one word *Villon*'.[6]

'Ladicte appellacion et ce dont a esté appellé mis au neant, et eu regard a la mauvaise vie dudict Villon, le bannist jusques a dix ans de la ville, provosté et vicomté de Paris'. The sentence of hanging was annulled, the appeal was allowed, but because of his bad life Villon was to be immediately banished for ten years from Paris and its surrounding territories. On 5 January 1463 he was freed.

It was a third exile but it was life.

The whoop still echoes. 'Que vous semble de mon appel, Garnier . . . ?' What about my appeal, now, Garnier? If I'd listened to you I'd have had more water, more racking, and then the rope. 'Estoit il lors temps de moy taire', was that the time to hold my tongue?, PD, 15 (L, 16). And Parliament. 'Tous mes cinq sens . . .', PD, 16 (L, 15), all my five senses, eyes, ears, taste, smell and touch . . . praise this gracious Court that has saved me, let every thanks be spoken to extol the Court . . . And then a supplication in the Envoi.

> Prince, troys jours ne vueillez m'escondire . . .

> Prince, do not forbid me three more days
> For farewells and some cash to raise,
> I've not a sou in wallet or in chest.
> Triumphant court, grant what this poor man prays,
> Sister of angels, mother of the blest.

It was granted. Three days were allowed him. He said goodbye to his mother, to Guillaume de Villon, his 'more than father'. They gave him some money. Nothing came from his other kinsmen in the city. 'Des miens le mendre, je dy voire . . .', 'my other relatives have disowned me for no reason than that my purse is full of air', T, 23. At every crossroads town-criers proclaimed his banishment.

On 8 January he left the Porte Rouge, cloaked against the winter, trudged muffled up the rue St Jacques, St Benoît-le-

Bientourné behind him, through the gate of the city, on to the road to Orléans, into the wide, weary countryside, down the long mile after mile of track, slowly dwindling under an overcast sky into nothingness. And disappeared.

There is a consensus of pessimism about Villon's fate, a morose agreement among critics that he died shortly after leaving Paris. Thuasne thought that the silence was sad proof that the poet did not live long.[7] Others concurred. It was accepted that Villon died in obscurity, declining into fatal illness in a hovel, coughing and choking in a filthy cell, collapsed and unnoticed in a ditch, stabbed with a dagger in a tavern over an unpaid reckoning, hanged on some small-town gallows.

The foundations for this cheerless prognosis are surprisingly weak, formed as they are on two facts, one strong, one negative, and a syllogistic supposition.

1. The first fact, undisputed, is that in 1467, because the population of Paris was in serious decline, Louis XI promised that 'any one in danger of his life for the crimes of theft or murder could find a safe asylum in Paris'.[8]
2. The second fact is entirely negative. There is no record of Villon taking advantage of the amnesty.
3. From those facts the syllogism was born that (a) because there is no record (b) he did not return, and (c) because he would have returned had he been alive (d) it follows that he was dead.

Consensus is comfortable but it does not have to be correct. Near-contemporaries of Villon did not believe in his early death. 'Most of the early commentators believe that he died about the year 1484, at which date he would have been fifty-three years old. Nothing is known of his end.' Before Mackworth's words Wyndham Lewis had quoted Guillaume Colletet, an early biographer of about 1650. 'As for me, I conjecture that he departed this life at the end of that of the king, Louis XI, that is to say around the year 1482.' La Monnoye, another seventeenth-century writer about the poet, agreed.[9]

These were opinions, not proofs, but later critics could be mistaken in their unsound argument. There have been early reports elsewhere in history that have been unjustifiably rejected on the grounds of negative revisionism. Two anecdotes, unrelated to Villon and unrelated to each other, prove this.

In the seventeenth century John Aubrey, author of *Brief Lives*, was informed by a reasonably reliable source, the son of one of Shakespeare's fellow-actors, that the dramatist 'had been in his younger days a schoolmaster in the country'. It has been disbelieved because of the poet's lack of academic qualifications. Simply because the story was recorded within a couple of generations of Shakespeare's death does not make it true. Nor does that chronological fact invalidate it. To the contrary, in 1985 Honigmann made a very strong case in favour of the bard-cum-schoolmaster, supporting Aubrey's casual note.

An even more extreme example of biased rejection of the seemingly ridiculous came with the sixteenth-century claim of that 'father of lies', the Scottish historian, Hector Boece, that prehistoric stone circles in Aberdeenshire had been used for moonlit ceremonies. As the pre-literate rings were erected, used and abandoned three thousand wordless years before Boece his words had to be preposterous. Over four hundred years later he was proved correct.[10] The same could be true of those statements, written within a generation or two of his disappearance, that Villon did not perish in 1463 or shortly afterwards. They could be genuine folk-memories rather than fanciful whimsies.

With this in mind an alternative interpretation can be constructed for the silence of 1467. In Book Four of his *Gargantua and Pantagruel* Rabelais wrote that Villon in his old age, 'sur ses vieux jours', had settled in St Maixent l'École, a town in Deux-Sèvres near Niort. Rabelais could have been mistaken but there are reasons for disbelieving this and here it is argued that he was correct. From that several probabilities emerge.

The amnesty of 1467 was proclaimed in Paris and was to be broadcast throughout the cities and towns of France. But 'broadcast' misleads today. News was not instant. It was transmitted through the medium of human bodies travelling by horse across the land. It was slow. And imperfect. Even the most shocking information could be misconstrued, misreported or never heard.

St Maixent is two hundred miles south-south-west of Paris. Nantes is the same distance south-west. There in 1440 Gilles de Rais was executed for his appallingly sadistic murders of children but far away in Paris the Bourgeois was unaware of the affair and did not mention it.* A similar remoteness may have affected St Maixent. It was an ancient town with a magnificent abbey but it was a small town and announcement of the amnesty may not have reached it until late in 1467. Only then would a hopeful Villon leave for the capital.

He would be disappointed. Paris was suffering one of its periodic outbreaks of plague. On 6 January 1468 the seventy-year-old Guillaume de Villon died, probably during the same epidemic that killed the still-lovely Ambroise de Loré.[11] With no guardian, with no home now that the Porte Rouge was locked against him, unwelcomed by offhand relatives and with mortal sickness all around there was no reason for Villon to stay. He left, perhaps returning to St Maixent. It is hypothesis. Yet there are arguments in its favour. The theatre is the clue. Rabelais said that Villon produced a Passion Play in St Maixent. Such histrionic participation by the poet is given credence by some little-considered items.

A folk-memory survives at Meung-sur-Loire of the poet being one of a makeshift theatrical troupe. Early chroniclers like Colletet stated that Villon had survived into the 1480s. They could be wrong but there was no cause for them to lie.

Longnon was convinced that Villon perished quickly in 1463. 'In the case of so eminent a poet, there is no stronger proof of his death than his cessation to produce verse'.[12] This is yet another example

* See Chapter 1, 17.

of supposition becoming fact. To upturn the argument there is no evidence that further poems were not written. There is no diary, no log-book. Absence of evidence is not evidence of absence. It is simply not known whether anything was written by Villon after early 1463. Wyndham Lewis thought that there might have been.

He drew attention to a Villon-like piece of stage buffoonery entitled *The Monologue of the Free Archer of Baignollet*, a popular farce about a member of the hated Free Archers, a poltroon full of braggadocio until converted into quivering cowardice by a scarecrow. It was funny, it was witty and it was accepted as part of the Villon canon and was printed in three early editions until rejected by Marot and every editor since.

Lewis also quoted a cynical ballade once attributed to the poet about love with its refrain, 'Riche amoureux à tousjours l'advantage', 'the rich will always have the upper hand'. The words echo with pain. The poet would have clambered into the sky for the woman he loved, brought her the moon but,

> Et nonobstant, son corps tant vicieux
> Au service de ce vieillard expose . . .

yet notwithstanding, she opens her vicious body to this old man.

The caustic Envoi is reminiscent of Villon. Early editors included it. Later ones expunged it.

Prince, tout bel, trop mieulx parlant qu'Orose,	Most handsome prince, more fluent than Orose,
Si vous n'avez tousjours bourse desclose,	Unless the money from your wallet flows
Vous abusez: car Meung, docteur tressage,	You'll fool yourself. Best understand Life-hardened Meung. To pluck a rose
Nous a descrit que, pour cueillir la rose,	The rich will always have the upper
Riche amoureux à tousjours l'advantage.	hand.

Puns on 'rose', a double-entendre on Meung the poet and Meung the town of torment, the jeers at a rapaciously open purse like that of Catherine de Vausselles, the sex-purchasing coins of rich Ythier Marchand, the poem could well be by Villon, written some time after 1463.[13]

His survival beyone that date was theoretically confirmed by two anecdotes written ninety years later by the arch-jester, François Rabelais. The first, that Villon had gone to England and the court of Edward IV, can be discounted. Rabelais merely used Villon's reputation as a prankster to make a coarse joke about the English king's defective bodily functions. The 'report' was fiction. The second story is more persuasive.

In his old age Master François Villon retired to Saint-Maixent in Poitou, under the protection of a worthy churchman who was abbot of that place. There, for the people's amusement, he undertook the production of a Passion Play in the Poitevin manner and dialect; and when the parts were distributed, the actors rehearsed, and the theatre ready, he told the Mayor and aldermen that the Mystery could be acted at the end of the Niort fair. It only remained to find dresses to suit the characters.[14]

Straight away there was Rabelaisian uproar with a sacristan refusing to lend the players any costumes. Days later the miserly man was waylaid and his horse frightened by a mob of Villon's followers with cow-bells, horns, squibs and fireworks so that the mare 'broke into a gallop, reared and plunged, and broke away, all the time dealing her rider double kicks, and farting with terror'. It is typical Rabelais but his Villon is a cartoon from a comic-book, a parody rather than a portrait. It is as fictitious as the conversion of the monstrous fifteenth-century Gilles de Rais into the seventeenth-century pantomime Bluebeard who murdered six wives for entering a forbidden room and was only prevented from killing a curious seventh by the arrival of her brothers. It is entertaining but it is not history. Neither is the Rabelaisian caricature of Villon. The history of the poet was not distorted but it was certainly camouflaged. For the truth behind the nonsense the history of Rabelais himself has to be known.

Because of the crude slapstick, the bawdiness, the repetitious bellows of delight at lavatorial mishaps Rabelais is widely admired for his coarse humour but disregarded as a chronicler. Yet this erudite Franciscan friar turned Benedictine accompanied his energetic Bishop of Maillezais for several years around 1525 on ecclesiastical journey after journey, criss-crossing Poitou. He itemised itineraries.[15] He noted local terms, the rural Poitevin dialect. He admired the lively market fairs and the spectacular Mystery Plays. 'Theatrical performances were then numerous in Poitou, those of Montmorillon, of Saint-Maixent and Poitiers were famous'.[16] Through his constant travelling and with his inquisitive, receptive mind Rabelais acquired an intimate knowledge of Poitou, its inhabitants and its gossip.

Of the three towns with their renowned plays Montmorillon, a charming little town, is of interest today for Villon's allusion to the splendid wine of Morillon. More interesting still is the realisation that it is quite possible that within sixty years of Villon's 'disappearance', maybe only a short decade or two after the poet's death, the ever-enquiring Rabelais was listening to trustworthy reminiscences about the poet.

There was no reason for Rabelais to connect Villon with a Passion Play. Although tales of Villon's tricks were widespread there were no rumours of his involvement with any form of theatrical work, only one very localised memory at Meung-sur-Loire nearly 150 wordless miles to the north-east. The story was either an inexplicable invention on the part of Rabelais or, more probably, came from genuine memories in St Maixent of Villon and the plays that he had produced.

It will never be proved. The biographer of Rabelais, joining the consensus and accepting the unverified belief in an early death for the poet, wrote that 'This picturesque story is founded upon a tradition of doubtful authenticity. Villon being dead at thirty-three could not have retired *in his old age* to Saint-Maixent', disregarding both the demographic reality of 'old age' in the fifteenth century and the fact that had Villon lived for some time in St Maixent he would have been older than thirty-three when he died.[17] Given the little that is known of those vague years St Maixent does have a name and a location unlike the anonymous ditches, cells and gallows favoured by biographical Jeremiahs. That so much of the town survives is almost unique among the places that Villon knew.

It is as though France were determined to eradicate all physical associations with the poet. The Porte Rouge, St Benoît, the old dwellings around the rue St Jacques, all of them vanished during the brutal mid-nineteenth-century restructuring of Paris by Baron Georges-Eugène Haussmann when twenty thousand buildings were demolished. The convent and church of the Celestins, founded in 1352 and where Villon's mother had prayed, was levelled in the early sixteenth century to make room for a royal cannon foundry which exploded in 1563. The medieval castles of Blois, Angers, Moulins and Meung-sur-Loire were remodelled into Renaissance châteaux. The ancient abbey of St Maixent whose 'worthy churchman' is said to have befriended Villon was destroyed by Huguenots in the seventeenth century. Even the Châtelet in Paris has gone. Architecturally the world of Villon has been annihilated.

The place where he was buried has been forgotten. If it had been in the cemetery of St Maixent's abbey it is ironical. Of all the First World War memorials to the dead in France the longest roll of honour is at St Maixent. But the name of the poet who may have died in the town five centuries ago is mentioned nowhere.

Villon is dead. No one knows when or where he died. His grave, if there were one, is lost. Only his words remain.

> Proud as a falcon, this Villon,
> No tears from him but only mirth.
> He drank one draught of Morillon
> And drifted gently from this earth.

It would be pleasant, although entirely wishful, to believe that he did.

Notes

Chapter 1

1 Henry VI: McCall, 196; Shirley (Bourgeois), 269; Thompson, 200–1.

2 Countryside: Boutruche, 28, in: Lewis, P. R., 1971. Abbeville: Tuchman, 587. Wolves: Shirley, 161, 162, 188.

3 Fleas and flies: Power (Goodman), 173.

4 Whooping-cough: Shirley, 85–6.

5 For the extravagance and crimes of de Rais, see: Benedetti; Hyatte; Wolf.

6 Rape: Shirley, 339.

7 Paris mud: *The Diary of John Evelyn*, I, London, 1906, 71, Note 2.

8 Starvation rations: Shirley, 323.

9 Guillaume de Villon and St Benoît: Mackworth, 28–31.

10 Bodies at Champtocé: Benedetti, 143; Hyatte, 83.

11 Courtaut: Shirley, 332.

12 Accusations against de Rais: Benedetti, 170.

13 Crows, rain: Shirley, 348, 349.

14 Cost of a pint of good wine: Pernoud, 114.

15 Margaret of Scotland: Kendall, 63–4, 68.

16 Prostitutes, dress and streets: McColl, 191n.

17 Death of the Provost of Paris: Shirley, 363.

18 Agnes Sorel: Kendall, 67–8; A. de Wismes, *Les Grandes Favorites Royales*, Arnaud Frères, Nantes, n.d., 6–9.

19 Agnes Sorel in Paris: Shirley, 366.

20 Thunderstorm: Shirley, 371. Bell dissipating the storm: John Aubrey, *Miscellanies*, 1696, 'Magick'; Bonner, 1960, 215.

21 Tomb of Agnes Sorel: Hansmann, W. (trans. Stockman, R). *The Webb & Bower Dumont Guide. Loire Valley*, Exeter, 1976, 139. Cost of the tomb and a man's wages: Shirley, 34, 356.

22 Jean Fouquet: P. Weschler, *Jean Fouquet and His Times*, Basle, 1947, 16.

Chapter 2

1 Montfaucon. Bodies from all over France: McCall, 75. Details of the scaffold: Champion, 246–8.

2 Filles-Dieu: Sargent-Baur, 1994, 48, n.250. Villon made them an insulting bequest, T, 116.

3 Rabelais, 1955, II, 16, 222.

4 There are many accounts of the famous affair of the Pet-au-Deable. The best are: Champion, 58–63; Favier, 145–8; Wyndham Lewis, 83–90. In most editions the stone is called the Pet-au-Diable. Sargent-Baur preferred the Rychner/Henry reading of Pet au Deable: Sargent-Baur, 1994, 112, T, 88, 858; 208, note 858.

5 Stone circle: *Antiquity* 47, 1973, 292–3; *ibid* 48, 1974, 134–6.

6 Master of Arts: Champion, 46–7.

7 Hopkins: R. B. Martin, *Gerard Manley Hopkins. A Very Private Life*, Harper-Collins, London, 1991, 242–83. Donne: J. Carey, *John Donne. Life, Mind and Art*, Faber & Faber, London, 1990, 153–216.

8 Police destruction: Favier, 148–50.

9 Wyndham Lewis, 89.

10 Champion, 63.

11 Catullus. Measuring vessel: *The Poems of Catullus*, F. Raphael and K. McLeish, Jonathan Cape, London, 1978, 11. The poems and their copies: G. Lee, *The Poems of Catullus*, Clarendon, Oxford, 1990, ix–xi.

12 Early manuscripts of Villon's poems: Dufournet, 39–44.

13 Clément Marot: Favier, 11. 'Entre tous les bons livres imprimés . . .'

14 Lawsuits in 1454. Details of these can be found scattered through Champion. They are more accessible in Pierre Giraud, 1970: Bruyères, on pp. 10–20; Colombel, 22–3; Fournier, 27–8; de la Garde, 29; Merbeuf, 39–40.

Chapter 3

1 Villon and taverns: Wyndham Lewis, 1928, 38.

2 Joan of Arc. The second enquiry: Pernoud, 27–37.

3 Realism in plays: Tuchman, 587.

4 Danse Macabré: Chaney, 1945; Huizinga, 145–51; Villon and the Danse: Varty, 1989.

5 The Pope: Chaney, 1945, 17, 47.

6 Introductions to Villon: Fox, 1962, v.

7 Courtly love: Payne, 1892, xi–xii.

8 Chandler, *The Big Sleep*, Hamish Hamilton, London, 1953, 3.

9 Quotations from Jean de Meung: *The Penguin Book of French Verse*, I. *To the Fifteenth Century*, ed. B. Woledge, Harmondsworth, 1966, 187.

10 Thomas Campion: M. M. Kastendieck, *England's Musical Poet: Thomas Campion*, Russell & Russell, New York, 1963, 86, 97–102.

11 For a discussion in English of the structure and complexity of medieval French poetry the most accessible is Fox, 1969, 91–2. For the caesura, see: Fox, 1962, 48–55.

12 Ythier Marchand: Demarolle, 41, 123–4; Kuhn, 402, 425.

13 'Branc d'acier': Dufournet, 393, n.83; Favier, 456; Kuhn, 258. For a discussion of the cryptic sexual allusions, see: Kinnell, 1982, xiii–xv.

14 The anagram: Demarolle, 1232, n.7; Dufournet, 403, n.199; Favier, 445; Kuhn, 140. For a discussion of the anagrams and the work of the surrealist poet, Tristan Tzara, and of Edith Seaton, see: Fox, 1984, 99–102; Siciliano, 1973, 58–61; Seaton, 1957. See also: T. Tzara, *Oeuvres Complètes*, VI. *Le Secret de Villon*, Flammarion, Paris, 1911.

15 Marchand: Demarolle, 123; Dufournet, 392–3, n.81; Kendall, 261–2; Champion, *Louis XI*, II. *Le Roi*, Honoré Champion, Paris, 1927, 176, 184, n. 4.

16 Villon and women: Mackworth, 56.

17 Girls from Poitou and their dialect: Sargent-Baur, 1994, 127.

18 Battle of Castillon: Seward, 240–3.

19 'Le Jardin Plaisance' and the

rondeau: Lanly, in Longnon, 1982, xiii, 131.

20 'Jenin', a henpecked husband: Dufournet, 436, n.1354–5.

21 Étuves and brothels: Michel, 198.

22 Le Mardi's interference: Cameron, 123, no. 46; Michel, 30, n. 10.

23 The Sermoise affair: Champion, 260; Favier, 195–8. Wyndham Lewis, 97–101, *Chancellery of France*, JJ, 187, 149, fol. 76v; 343–4.

Chapter 4

1 Barber-surgeons: Basing, 114–19.

2 The countryside: Boutruche, in Lewis, P. S.,1971, 27, 29.

3 Villon and the countryside: Lepper, 17.

4 Écorcheurs in Switzerland: Kendall, 56–7.

5 John de Roghton: McCall, 76.

6 The Coquillard way of life: Wyndham Lewis, 105–10. The same passage, slightly different in interpretation, appears in Mackworth, 65. 'Highwaymen and murders': Chaney, 1946, 76.

7 For a glossary of what words in jargon might mean, see: Lanly, 149–84.

8 Reference to the jargon: Wyndham Lewis, 108. The stanza quoted, J, 7 in the canon is J, 10 in the Stockholm MS.

9 Jehan des Loges: Thuasne, I, 33–7. The question was slightly misreported in Wyndham Lewis, 110–11.

10 Tabarie and Villon's uncle in Angers: Wyndham Lewis, 131n.

11 Rehabilitation of Joan of Arc: Pernoud, 45–61.

12 Sex rather than religion: Dale, 236, note 47.

13 Sergeants of the Verge and the abbess Driete: Giraud, 34.

14 Alison: Champion, 261–3; Favier, 199–200 [Alipson].

15 Letters of Remission. These are given in detail with translations in Chaney, 1946, who quotes the originals: *Arch nat.* JJ, 180, piece 67, fol. 49f. There are also versions in Saklatvala, xi–xiii.

Chapter 5

1 The Dauphin and Charles VII: Kendall, 80–3.

2 Eviction from the Queue de Renard: Favier, 311; Michel, 82.

3 D'Orgement: Bonner, 196, n.53; Shirley, 99–100.

4 Long-winded and succinct: Siciliano, 1934, 1934, 106, n.3.

5 'Chenevotes': Fox, 1962, 114.

6 First and third person writing: Fox, 1962, 137, 140.

7 Burgon and Petra: Ian Browning, *Petra*, Chatto & Windus, London, 1977, 117–18.

8 'Copa Surisca': in the Appendix Vergiliana quoted in *Songs of the Wandering Scholars*, Helen Waddell, Folio Society, 1982, 46–9.

9 Food: Hammond, P. W., *Food and Feast in Medieval England*, Sutton, Thrupp, 40–62. Recipe for stuffed sausage: *Daily Telegraph*, 12 May, 1999, 9. Variety of dishes: Power, 149. Hippocras: Power, 196–7.

10 Descriptions of Villon: Rabelais, 1532–51: II, 14, 214, II, 16, 222. Huysmans, in: Wyndham Lewis, 1928, 342–3, It was translated in the New York edition, 1928, 171–2.

11 The unnamed woman: Sargent-Baur, 1994, 18–21.

12 Sexual allusions: Dale, 228, 3; Dufournet, 391, notes 29, 31–2.

13 Affected rhyme scheme: McCaskie, 35, n.5.

14 Marot and the forgotten allusions: McCaskie, 12.

15 William Langland: 'Piers Plowman', Prologue, 58–61. *Piers the Plowman*, trans. J.F. Goodridge, Harmondsworth, 1960, 64–5.

16 Conflict between the Church and the friars: Guiraud, 42.

17 Jean de Meung, Villon and the friars: Dufournet, 397, nn. 249–55.

18 The Rehabilitation of Joan of Arc: Pernoud, 173, 244–60. Verdict of the court: F. Grayeff, *Joan of Arc. Legends and Truth*, Goodall, London, 1978, 115.

19 L, 39, 311. The Longnon rendering of this line, 'Si m'endormis, tout enmouflé', 'I fell asleep with mittens on', is to be preferred to the Henry-Rychner version, 'C'estoit assés tartevelé', 'I'd rattled on quite long enough'. That two such different texts exist reveals the problems that editors of Villon are confronted with.

Chapter 6

1 Confession of Tabarie: Chaney, 1946, 120–5, where the complete text is given. Also see: Wyndham Lewis, 120–32: *Arch nat*, M. 180, n.9.

2 Acrostics. There are no fewer than six of these: T, 89+, Envoi, Villon; T, 93+, Françoys, Marthe, Viilvon; T, 139+, Ambroise de Loré; T, 150+, Envoi, Villon; PD, 7 (L, 4), Envoi, Villon; PD, 13 (L, 11), Envoi, Villon.

3 'Grosse Margot' as a biographical poem: Rychner and Henry in: Fox, 1984, 88–9; Bonner, 212; Favier, 313–19; McCaskie, 163; R. L. Stevenson, 'François Villon, student, poet and housebreaker', in: *Familiar Studies of Men and Books*, Chatto & Windus, London, 1924, 198.

4 For a discussion of the *sotte chanson*, see: Siciliano, 1934, 397–406. Its intentions are described in: Chaney, 1941, 165–6.

5 The mistress of Ben Jonson: 'Notes by William Drummond of conversations with Ben Jonson at Hawthornden, in January, 1619', *Archaeologia Scotica* IV, 1857, 256. Sargent-Baur, 1994, 204, 657ff.

6 Shuttle: Dale, 17. Spindle, Kinnell, 1982, 5. *Twelfth Night*, 1, III, 99–100.

7 Possible address of Catherine de Vausselles: Champion, 476–7.

8 Erotic meaning of Vausselles: Dufournet, 414, n. 661; Michel, 5.

9 Ythier Marchand as the rival: Favier, 456–7; Michel, 12, 2; 62, 3; 126, 6.

10 'Rose' not a Christian name: Michel, 4; Dufournet, 421, n.910; Chaney, 1941, 140.

11 Marthe: Bonner, 73, 199; McCaskie, 108. Blois: Chaney, 1941, 140–1, a theory of Foulet's.

12 'Frappa au cul la pelle': Dufournet, 453, n.1900.

13 Noel Jolis: Champion, 477.

14 The biography of Villon: Kinnell, 1965, 8; ibid, 1982, xi–xii.

15 The Sorbonne bell and other bells in Paris: Bonner, 154–5; 190, 33; 214–15. Wyndham Lewis, 1928, 3.

16 F. Bengtsson, *A Walk to an Ant Hill*, Chatto & Windus, London, 1950, 46–7.

17 The search: Champion, 285–6.

18 Counterfeiters: Champion, II, 1933, 81n; Favier, 344, 400; Thuasne, I, 37.

Chapter 7

1 Marc Bloch, *The Historian's Craft*. Manchester, 1954, 60.

2 The court at Blois: McLeod, 298–301.

3 S. Purcell, *The Poetry of Charles of Orléans*, Carcarnet Press, Cheadle Hulme, 1973, 98. This anonymous but good translation of Charles d'Orléans' rondeau was published in the *London Magazine* in September 1823.

4 Bullrich: Purcell, 11.

5 Burns and the Riddells: *The Life and Works of Robert Burns*, ed. A. Smith, Macmillan, London, 1891, xxxii.

6 'My shamed disgrace': Fox, 1962, 81n.; Fox, 1984, 12.

7 Tabarie and Pierre Marchand: Champion, 283–91; Lewis, 1928, 125–31.

8 Colin de Cayeux?: Wyndham Lewis, 128, n.2.

9 Tabarie's testimony. The original Latin and French depositions are quoted in full in Chaney, 1946, 120–5.

10 Rabelais, Book V, 35, 685.

11 Couraud, Villon and René: Thuasne, I, 240; III, 389–97.

12 'Ah got plenty of nuttin': Bonner, 210, n. 125.

13 Regnier de Montigny: Champion, 306–8.

14 St Maixent and Villon: Rabelais, IV, 13, 478; Plattard, 41.

15 Bourges and the Perdrier brothers: no help, McCaskie, 148; the goldsmith, Thuasne, I, 47, n.3; 'bougres', Dufournet, 438, n.1413, Kinnell, 1982, 237.

16 Red tongues and the Inquisition: Thuasne, III, 373; Dufournet, 438, 1410–13.

17 Heresy: Wyndham Lewis, 145.

18 Tabarie and the Navarre robbery: Wyndham Lewis, 120–32.

19 Panurge: Rabelais, II, 14, 216.

20 The court of Jean, Duke of Moulins: Mackworth, 88.

21 Patay: J. H. Smith, *Joan of Arc*, Sidgwick & Jackson, London, 1973, 73.

22 Macé d'Orléans: Champion, 204–5; Dufournet, 431, n.1210.

23 Rutebeuf: H. S. Bennett, *Chaucer and the Fifteenth Century*, Oxford University Press, 1961, 107; Arié Serpier, *Rutebeuf. Poète Satirique*, Éditions Klincksieck, Paris, 1969.

24 1460 and justice: Stevenson, R. L., Chapter 6, Note 2, 213.

25 de Bellefaye: Mackworth, 114.

26 The indictment of Colin de Cayeux: Chaney, 1946, 116–17, *Arch nat*, X, 28.

Chapter 8

1 Villon in actor's clothing: *Meung-sur-Loire. La Belle Histoire*, Anon, Maury, Manchecourt, 1996, 205.

2 Realistic plays: Tuchman, 312.

3 France: Axton, R. and Stevens, J., *French Medieval Plays*, Blackwell, London, 1971. St Maixent Passion Play: Rabelais: IV, 13.

4 D'Aussigny. the disputed bishopric, Guiraud, 15–16. The Rehabilitation: Pernoud; Duparc. Commemoration of Joan of Arc: Fox, 1984, 13.

5 Favier, 417–18: Villon insulted Thibault d'Aussigny was using his name to compare the upright

bishop with the loathed Tacque Thibauld, the hated lowborn, favourite of Jean, Duke of Berry, who was licentious and avaricious. He was had been given 200,000 crowns of public money.

6 Sibilants: Fox, 1962, 61. Clerical debasement: Sargent-Baur, 1990, 138, n.80.

7 Job, Villon, patience and immortal lines: Sargent-Baur, 1990, 61–2.

8 Period of poetic creativity: Sargent-Baur, 1990, 70.

9 Villon's use of the Book of Job: Sargent-Baur, 1990, 70–82.

10 Coronation of Louis XI: Kendall, 107–13.

11 Nude displays: Huizinga, 314–15; McCall, 196.

12 Royal progress: Kendall, 113. Release of Villon: Wyndham Lewis, *King Spider*, Heinemann, London, 1930, 428–32. The amnesty: Wyndham Lewis, 1928, 159.

13 Mme Machecoue: Champion, 492. Pierre Genevoys: Michel, 160, n.8.

Chapter 9

1 Rates of mortality: P. Ziegler, *The Black Death*, Pelican, Harmondsworth, 1970, 109. Average age of death for men: G. M. Howe, *Men, Environment and Disease in Britain: a Medical History through the Ages*, David & Charles, Newton Abbot, 1972, 105–6.

2 The copying of poems: H. S. Bennett, *Chaucer and the Fifteenth Century*, Oxford University Press, Oxford, 1961, 118–19.

3 Scribes: P. Baring, *Trades and Crafts in Medieval Manuscripts*,

British Museum, London, 1990, 110, 114. Printing presses; Wyndham Lewis, 1928, 206, n. 3.

4 The early manuscripts: Sargent-Baur, 12; Chaney, 1943, v–vi.

5 Three ballades of death: Fox, 1964, 148. Varty, 1989, suggested that their background was the sequence of mortality in the Danse Macabré.

6 Lines 1–832 of the *Testament*, 1–832, have been considered written later than the remainder: A. Campaux, *François Villon, sa Vie et ses Oeuvres*, 1859, 247; I. Siciliano, 1934, 447. The present writer disbelieves that.

7 'Gaultière': Fox, 1962, 65, n.1. 'Joan': Michel, 90, n.11.

8 The first legatees: Chaney, 1946, 88–9.

9 Le Cornu: Champion, 481–2; Dufournet, 393, n.84; Michel, 128, n.6. Baubignon's garden: Guiraud, 17–18; Michel, 128, n.8. St Amant: Dufournet, 424, n.1007–13; Favier, 456; Michel, 14, n.8.

10 The Celestins church and its art: Mary, 243; Bonner, 198, n.76.

11 'Denise': Dufournet, 432, n.1234.

12 Jean Cotart: Champion, 503–4; Dufournet, 400, n.34.

13 The Montmartre nunnery: Bonner, 211, n.129.

14 The chapel of Ste Avoye: Lepper, 145.

15 Requiem Mass: Bonner, 214, n. 153; Kinnell, 1982, 239, n.1892.

16 Jacqueline: McCaskie, 184–5.

17 De la Garde and Volant: Guiraud, 29; 50.

18 Guillaume du Ru: McCaskie, 190.

19 Hervé Morillon: Thuasne, III, 548.

Interlude

1 Swinburne, 1970, *The Dispute of the Heart and Body of François Villon*, Mouette Press, Oxford.
2 Fox, 1962, 28–32.

Chapter 10

1 Colet and Poutrel: Champion, 431–2; Favier, 487–9. Basanier: Guiraud, 16.
2 Villon and the repayment of money: Chaney, 1946, 44–5; Mackworth, 112; Wyndham Lewis, 173–5. MS Lat 5657 C, fol. 79.
3 Ferrebouc: Chaney, 1946, 45.
4 The Ferrebouc affair: Champion, 432–5; Demarolle, 47–8; Wyndham Lewis, 176–85. *Arch. Parlt.* X, 30, fol. 294.
5 Sentence of death: Champion, 435.
6 The sentence of exile: Wyndham Lewis, 188, MS Dupuy 250, fol. 59. Demarolle, 48.
7 Belief in Villon's early death: Thuasne, I, 71–2.
8 The amnesty of 1467: A.C.P. Haggard, *Louis XI and Charles the Bold*, London, 1913, 291.
9 Belief in Villon living into the 1480s: Mackworth, 123; Wyndham Lewis, 198. 'Vie de Villon' by Colletet: P. Lacroix, *Oeuvres de François Villon*, Paris, 1877, xxii, xxxii. La Monnoye:

10 Thuasne, I, 130. The *Life* was not published until 1867.
Shakespeare as a schoolmaster: O.L. Dick, *Aubrey's 'Brief Lives'*, Secker & Warburg, London, 1949, 276. Shakespeare no schoolmaster: M. Chute, *Shakespeare of London*, Souvenir Press, London, 1977, 349. More uncertainty was expressed by P. Honan, *Shakespeare, a Life*, Oxford University Press, Oxford, 1998, 60–2. For its likelihood, see: E.A.J. Honigmann, *Shakespeare: the 'Lost Years',* Manchester University Press, 1985. Boece, Scottish stone circles and the moon: A. Burl, 'Science or symbolism: problems of archaeo-astronomy?', *Antiquity* 54, 1980, 191–200.
11 Death of Guillaume de Villon: Champion, 446; Thuasne, III, 698. Ambroise de Loré: ibid, III, 690.
12 Longnon, quoted in Payne, lxxviii.
13 The farce and the ballade: Wyndham Lewis, 288–94.
14 England and Edward IV: Rabelais, *Gargantua and Pantagruel*, Book IV, Chapter 67, 595. Villon at St Maixent: ibid and *Pantagruel*, Book IV, Chapter 13, 478.
15 Places in Poitou: Rabelais, II, 5, 181–3.
16 Mystery Plays: Plattard, 40.
17 Doubts about Villon and St Maixent: Plattard, 42; Payne, lxxiv.

Select Bibliography

Atkinson, G. trans. (1930), *The Works of François Villon*, Eric Partridge, London.

Basing, P. (1990), *Trades and Crafts in Medieval Manuscripts*, British Library, London.

Benedetti, J. (1972), *Gilles de Rais*, Stein & Day, New York.

Bonner, A. trans. (1960), *The Complete Works of François Villon*, Bantam, New York.

Burger, A. (1957), *Lexique de la Langue de Villon. Notes Critiques*, Minard, Paris.

Cameron, N. trans. (1952), *François Villon. Poems*, Jonathan Cape, London.

Champion, H. (1933), *François Villon. Sa Vie et Son Temps*, I, II, Honoré Champion, Paris. Updated edition, 1967.

—— (1984), *Ibid*, Preface by J. Favier, Honoré Champion, Paris.

Chaney, E. F. trans. (1940), *The Poems of François Villon*, Blackwell, Oxford. [English prose translation.]

—— (1941), *Ibid*, Blackwell, Oxford. [French text with Notes.]

—— (1943), *François Villon according to the Stockholm MS*, Blackwell, London.

—— (1945), *La Danse Macabré des Charniers des Saints Innocents à Paris*, Manchester University Press, Manchester.

—— (1946), *François Villon in his Environment*, Blackwell, London.

Dale, P. trans. (1971), *François Villon. 'The Legacy and Other Poems'*, Agenda Press, London.

—— (1973), *Selected Poems. François Villon*, Macmillan, London.

Demarolle, P. (1973), *Villon. Un Testament Ambigu*, Larousse, Paris.

Deutsch, A. and Savill, M. eds. (1946), *Villon. Ballades French and English*, Alan Wingate, London.

Dufournet, J. (1984) *François Villon. Poésies*, Flammarion, Paris.

Duparc, P. (1977–88), *Procès en Nullité de la Condemnation de Jeanne d'Arc*, I–V, C. Klincksieck, Lille.

Evans, J. (1925), *Life in Medieval France*, Oxford University Press, Oxford.

Favier, J. (1982), *François Villon*, Fayard, Paris.

Foulet, L. (1982), see: Longnon.

Fox, C. (1962), *The Poetry of Villon*, Nelson, London.

—— (1969), *The Lyric Poetry of Charles d'Orléans*, Oxford University Press, Oxford.

—— (1971), *La Poésie Lyrique de Charles d'Orléans*, Nizet, Paris.

—— trans. (1984), *Villon. Poems*, Grant & Cutler, London.

Guiette, R. (1964), *Villon. Poésies Complètes*, Gallimard, Paris.

Guiraud, P. (1970), *Le Testament de Villon. Ou le Gai Scaveur de la Basoche*, Gallimard, Paris.

Huizinga, J. (1955), *The Waning of the*

Middle Ages, Pelican, Harmonds-worth.

Hyatte, R. (1984), *Laughter for the Devil. The Trials of Gilles de Rais, Companion-in-Arms of Joan of Arc (1440)*, Fairleigh Dickinson, Cranbury.

Kendall, P. M. (1971), *Louis XI. 'The Universal Spider . . .'*, Allen & Unwin, London.

Kinnell, G. trans. (1965), *The Poems of François Villon*, Signet Classics, New York.

—— trans. (1982), *The Poems of François Villon*, University Press of New England, Hanover and London.

Kuhn, D. (1967), *La Poétique de François Villon*, Armand Colin, Paris.

Ladurie, E. le Roy (1987), *The French Peasantry, 1450–1660*, Scolar, Aldershot.

Lanly, A. (1971), *François Villon. Ballades en Jargon*, Honoré Champion, Paris.

—— (1982), *François Villon. Oeuvres*, Honoré Champion, Paris.

Lepper, J. H. trans. (1924), *The 'Testaments' of François Villon*, Casanova Society, London [also New York edition, 1924].

Lewis, D. B. Wyndham. (1928), *François Villon. A Documented Survey*, Peter Davies, London.

—— (1930), *King Spider. Some Aspects of Louis XI of France and his Companions*, Heinemann, London.

—— (1952), *The Soul of Marshal Gilles de Raiz. With Some Account of his Life and Times, his Abominable Crimes, and His Expiation*, Eyre & Spottiswood, London.

Lewis, P. R. ed. (1971), *The Recovery of France in the Fifteenth Century*, Macmillan, London.

Longnon, A. (1892), *Oeuvres Complètes de François Villon*, Lemerre, Paris.

—— (1982), *François Villon. Oeuvres*, eds: Foulet, L. and Lanly, A., Honoré Champion, Paris.

Mackworth, C. (1947), *François Villon*, Westhouse, London.

McCall, A. (1979), *The Medieval Underworld*, Dorset Press, New York.

McCaskie, H. B. trans. (1946), *The Poems of François Villon*, Cresset Press, London.

McLeod, E. (1969), *Charles of Orleans. Prince and Poet*, Chatto & Windus, London.

Michel, P. (1972), *Villon. Poésies Complètes*, Générale Française, Paris.

Payne, J. trans. (1892), *The Poems of Master François Villon of Paris*, Villon Society, London.

Pernoud, R. (1955), *The Retrial of Joan of Arc. The Evidence at the Trial for Her Rehabilitation, 1450–1455*, trans. Cohen, J. M., Harcourt, Brace, New York.

Plattard. J. (1930), *The Life of Rabelais.* Trans. Roche, L.P., Routledge, London.

Power, E. trans. (1992), *The Goodman of Paris (Le Ménagier de Paris). A Treatise on Moral and Domestic Economy by a Citizen of Paris*, c. 1393. Folio Society, London.

Rabelais, F. (1532–51), *The Histories of Gargantua and Pantagruel*, trans. Cohen, J. M., London, 1955.

Rossetti, D. G. (1913), *Poems and Translations, 1850–1870*, London.

Saklatvala, B. trans. (1968), *Complete Poems of François Villon*, Introduction, J. Fox, Everyman, Dent, London.

Sargent-Baur, B. N. (1990), *Brothers of Dragons. Job Dolens and François Villon*, Garland, New York & London.

—— trans. (1994), *François Villon. Complete Poems*, University of Toronto Press, Toronto.

Seaton, E. (1957), *Studies in Villon, Vaillant and Charles d'Orléans*, Blackwell, Oxford.

Shirley, J. trans. (1968), *A Parisian Journal, 1405–49. Translated from the Anonymous Journal d'un Bourgeois de Paris*, Oxford U.P., Oxford.

Siciliano, I. (1934), *François Villon et les Thèmes Poétiques du Moyen Age*, Armand Colin, Paris.

—— (1973), *Mésaventures Posthumes de Maître Françoys Villon*, A. and J. Picard, Paris.

Stacpoole, H. de V. trans. (1914), *The Poems of François Villon*, John Lane, New York.

Swinburne, A. C. (1905), *The Poems of Algernon Charles Swinburne*. Vol. III. *Poems and Ballads. Second and Third Series*, Chatto & Windus, London.

—— trans. (1970), *The Dispute of the Heart and Body of François Villon*, Mouette Press, Oxford.

Thompson, G. L. (1991), *Paris and its People under English Rule. The Anglo-Burgundian Régime, 1420–1436*, Clarendon Press, Oxford.

Thuasne, L. (1923), *François Villon. Oeuvres. Édition Critique avec Notices et Glossaire*, 3 vols, Picard, Paris.

Tuchman, B. (1979), *A Distant Trumpet. The Calamitous Fourteenth Century*, Macmillan, London.

Varty, K. (1989), '*Villon's three* Ballades du Temps Jadis *and the Danse Macabre*', in: Trotter, D.A., ed. *Littera et Sensu. Essays in Form and Meaning in Medieval French Literature Presented to John Fox*, University of Exeter, Exeter, 73–93.

Vertone, T. (1983), *Rythme, Dualité et Création Poétique dans l'Oeuvre de François Villon*, Rome.

Wharton, L. trans. (1935), *The Poems of François Villon*, Dent, London.

Wolf, L. (1980), *Bluebeard. The Life and Crimes of Gilles de Rais*, Clarkson A. Potter, New York.

Further Reading

There are biographies in English by Wyndham Lewis, 1928, and Cecily Mackworth, 1947. A critical background study of Villon's life and times can be found in Edward Chaney, 1946, and a meticulous analysis of Villon's poetical techniques was published by John Fox in 1962. A complete text in English with critical notes was published by Barbara Sargent-Baur in 1994. Another good translation, again with helpful notes, is that by Anthony Bonner, 1960.

In French the reader is recommended to: Auguste Longnon, edited by Lucien Foulet and with notes by André Lanly, 1982; Jean Favier, 1982; and Jean Dufournet, 1984. The most detailed biography is by Pierre Champion, 1984, with its extensive bibliography. In the book-lists can be found numerous references to other studies of Villon.

References to the many articles and papers in learned journals such as *Romania* are itemised in Sargent-Baur, 1994, 330–7.

Index

Ballades and other poems are indexed under their English titles followed by their first words in French. Sargent-Baur's numbering and that of (Longnon) are appended, e.g. *Proverbs, a ballade of,* 'Tant grate . . .' [PD5 (L, 2)]. **Bold** indicates a major entry. Illustrations are *italicised*.